# HANDLE IT

### by JOYCE HARRIET, MPA

*I must take a stand, so step back stay on track. Let's take back what the devil has stolen, recognize that we were chosen. Anita, enjoy the read..*

**FriesenPress**

Suite 300 - 990 Fort St
Victoria, BC, Canada, V8V 3K2
www.friesenpress.com

**Copyright © 2016 by Joyce Harriet**
First Edition — 2016

All rights reserved.

No part of this publication may be reproduced in any form, or by any means, electronic or mechanical, including photocopying, recording, or any information browsing, storage, or retrieval system, without permission in writing from FriesenPress.

**ISBN**
978-1-4602-6354-9 (Hardcover)
978-1-4602-6355-6 (Paperback)
978-1-4602-6356-3 (eBook)

1. Biography & Autobiography, Women

Distributed to the trade by The Ingram Book Company

# TABLE OF CONTENTS

| | |
|---|---|
| DEDICATION | VII |
| ACKNOWLEDGEMENTS | IX |
| THE BEGINNING | 1 |
| FATE | 3 |
| SHAPING | 7 |
| MR. ROGERS | 9 |
| WHITE SUITS | 13 |
| NEXT | 15 |
| HYMEN | 17 |
| STEPPING UP | 21 |
| BYE FRIEND, HI FOES | 25 |
| GANJA | 33 |
| RICHIE RICH | 37 |
| LISA CHINA WHO | 43 |
| MY FIRST LOVE | 49 |
| SURPRISE | 53 |

| | |
|---|---|
| UNBELIEVABLE | 61 |
| PASS IT LISA | 69 |
| LOVE PREVAILS | 73 |
| THE SYSTEM | 77 |
| SOMETHING'S GOT TO GIVE | 83 |
| $27.00 | 87 |
| FAVOR | 95 |
| HERE WE GO AGAIN | 97 |
| R U KIDDEN ME? | 103 |
| TEARS THAT NEVER DRIED | 115 |
| NEW BEGINNINGS | 119 |
| DANG | 131 |
| SWITCH OFF | 137 |
| MOMMA BECK | 139 |
| CRAZY IS AS CRAZY DOES | 149 |
| A LITTLE BIT OF THIS, A LITTLE BIT OF THAT | 157 |
| R U KIDDIN ME | 165 |
| NJ KIND OF LOVE | 173 |
| CONGRATULATIONS | 179 |
| WALK AWAY | 181 |
| SHYNESE | 183 |
| GOOD 4 U GOOD 4 ME | 203 |
| THANK GOD FOR JESUS | 207 |
| TRUST | 213 |
| BABE AND WOOKA | 221 |
| OPEN AND OUT | 229 |

| | |
|---|---|
| UNSPOKEN | 247 |
| I CAN DO THIS | 259 |
| MOTHER LOVE | 265 |
| CONFESSION | 267 |
| IN ACTION | 273 |
| HELP! | 277 |
| BREATHE, JOY | 293 |
| MY FRIEND | 297 |
| RESEARCH | 305 |
| HUGGIE | 307 |
| MOMMA B | 311 |
| SURGERY | 315 |
| THAT'S WHAT'S UP / CHURCH LADY | 319 |
| SNAKES | 323 |
| HIT THE ROAD JACK! | 325 |
| ENUFF | 327 |
| STEPPING IT UP | 341 |
| INSIDE OUT | 359 |
| A DIFFERENT PLACE | 371 |
| FREE | 373 |
| ABOUT THE AUTHOR | 379 |

# DEDICATION

To: God The Father

Jesus Christ My Lord and Savior

The Holy Spirit

My Personal Assigned Angel

Anthony Boyd Jr.

Kentaya Wilson

To: Every Individual that can identify with "HANDLE IT"

Most importantly, I dedicate "HANDLE IT" to YOU!!!

# ACKNOWLEDGEMENTS

To: God The Father I would not and could not have written "HANDLE IT" If you had not instructed me.

To: Jesus Christ my Lord and Savior I would not be here if you would not have sacrificed yourself for me. And I wouldn't be free from my guilt or shame.

To: The Holy Spirit you instructed and guided me as I typed every word, allowing me to be transparent all though my tears flowed.

To: My one and only son T.J. I Thank you for always being selfless always offering yourself to me no matter what! I thank you for being the kind of son that makes my heart smile.

To: Vivian Manderville for being selfless in your giving, in your time, with your encouragements, and your love for me that has helped me grow. You showed me myself in ways that I needed to understand. You helped me understand the true purpose of "HANDLE IT" as you were learning me. Thank you for allowing me to cry when I needed to get out of my own way.

To: Anthony Boyd Sr. (Tony) for being selfless in everything that you do. You have always given me the support I needed from the beginning and I know that it will never end. I thank you for being my true friend.

To: Anthony Brown my brother. Thank you for being the kind of big brother that a sister can appreciate. I thank you for your selfless ways, your encouragement and your many praises over the years, and for helping me during times that I needed help. I couldn't ask for a better brother.

To: Pastor Anthony V. Brown. I thank you for being a true Man of God. I honestly don't know how I could have gotten this far in my Spiritual walk without you. You taught me and you loved me. You stood by me, and encouraged me. Most importantly, I thank you for always keeping T.J. and I in constant prayer.

To: Ecclesia Deliverance Church of God members. Thank you for every prayer while praying for my son and I, and thank you for your love.

To: V. Butler. Thank you for sending out daily Bible quotes over the years and still. I have read everyone, and often times it was what you sent me that got me through. For that I am very grateful.

To: My Publisher, FriesenPress, and my Account Manager, Scott Barber.

To: Everyone who will read "HANDLE IT" and tell someone about it, I thank you in advance!

# THE BEGINNING

This is my beginning as I recall it. Her name was Rebecca however, people called her Becky or Beck and during her earlier years people called her Chink. It must have been what she preferred because that was the only tattoo that she had on her body. It was scripted on her right ankle very nicely. It actually looked cute on her almond colored skin. It wasn't colored in or anything it was just neatly written. However, the only name that I ever called my mother was Becky.

On July 7, 1966, at Brookdale Hospital on the Emergency Room floor, I was born. In my opinion it is considered one of the worse hospitals in Brooklyn. My mother said that I was considered a "Dirty" baby because she wasn't shaved before giving birth. That itself might explain some of my behavior, being told I was a "Dirty" baby. She was my mother, and I was the youngest of four children. I had many names but for now my name is Joyce, which is part of my birth name Joyce Harriet. Honestly, I'm not sure if it's Joyce Harriet, or Harriet Joyce. Over the years, I have heard conflicting stories. But, what I do know is the time I saw a birth certificate, it read *Female*. And since everybody called me Joyce, and Becky said my name was also Harriet, I told the woman down at the Clerk's Office that my name was Joyce Harriet. The name Harriet was my grandmother's name. Her friends would all call her Hattie for short. It seems like I am the only one named after her, at least from what I know. You can't quote me on it, because there are many things within my family that I am not aware of. However, today it is no longer important.

My last name came from Becky marrying my sister Sherlene's father. I personally have no recollection of him ever being in my life nor was I mentioned at the funeral when he passed as a surviving child. Although I didn't attend the funeral, I had read his Obituary to see if I was mentioned. It was fine that I wasn't, because like I said I didn't recall him ever being in my life. The good thing was, at least Sherlene did know her father and he remained in her life until his death. However, having no sense of belonging, I only use Joyce Harriet. FYI, I hold no bad feelings, this is just for me as I come into my new identity.

My mother told me that when I was a toddler, I was admitted into the hospital because I had crawled out of my bed and somehow I had gotten ahold of some Lye that either she or my Aunt Brenda hid under the bed. She said that I put some of the Lye inside of my mouth and that was when she and my Aunt Brenda heard this horrific cry. My brother Anthony reminded me that I was between 16 and 18 months old. Nevertheless, I had gotten ahold of a poisonous dangerous chemical that could have killed, damaged, or permanently scarred me. Instead, I came out of it without injury. I think!

I was told by Becky when I was admitted into the hospital that my sister Abby would not stop crying. My mother said that Abby wouldn't eat or sleep. She just cried. Becky said that the only way she could get Abby to stop crying was to bring her to visit me in the hospital. Abby was only 12 years old, and they didn't allow children that age to visit anyone in the hospital. My mother dressed Abby up like a little woman, and walked her right into the hospital and into my room.

I asked if there were any pictures taken so I could see how my sister looked, but along with many other photos Becky said that they all burned in a fire. I always felt that that was one of the chunks that had been missing in my life. Sometimes photos tell stories and fill in the gaps; and I had a lot of gaps that needed to be filled. I was told that once Abby saw me, and was able to play with me, she had stopped crying. Whenever I would hear that story years later, it would always make my heart smile knowing that my sister was that close to me. But after the good thoughts there would be a real sadness that came over me. Why in the hell was I able to get to this Lye in the first place?

# FATE

Shortly after the Lye incident I was told that my mother had passed out in the Welfare Center, and then she was taken to prison. My siblings and I were taken to the Children's Aid Society in Manhattan. My grandmother had taken my oldest sister Abby who was twelve years old, home with her. My brother Anthony who was nine years old and my sister Sherlene who was seven years old were both taken home by Sherlene's father. I hung around for a bit waiting for someone special to come and get me. Sherlene says that she was left behind, but in either situation we were there and we waited in that place for somebody to come and take us home.

I am not too certain of all of the particulars regarding who left first or last but I was taken home by my Aunt Beverly and her husband Jay who I would come to think of as my parents (from here I will refer to them as my parents). Mommy and Daddy both had city jobs. Daddy was a New York City Transit Cop, and Mommy was a New York City Token Booth Clerk. In addition to me they had two girls named Diane and Dana. Diane was five year old and she was the oldest. Dana was four and then there was me, just about two years old (from here I will refer to them as my sisters). We lived in the projects on Park Avenue in Manhattan at the time. And often times, we would have to spend the night over at our relatives because of our parents' work schedule.

Living with my "parents" wasn't bad at all. Yeah, outside of them there were some family issues but my temporary parents were the best. I cannot remember a single moment that either one of them mistreated me. My sisters and I did what siblings did, like arguing and fighting. I can admit that there were times when I initiated some of the fights and arguments because I was told that I had a fresh mouth being sarcastic, and all. *Nothing major*! It would be something like if Dana and I were playing a game and I won, I would sing my winning in a song "that's why I beat you, that's why I beat you, that's why I won." Boy, Dana would get so upset at me and punch me so hard and tell me to "Shut up!" Then of course I would tell, and she would get a beating for hitting me. I know, I could have just shouted "I won!" and left it that way. But that would have been boring for a kid like me. But truly, they were as close to me as real sisters can be.

Living in the projects wasn't nothing like how they portrayed the TV sitcom "**Good Times**." It seemed to me that we were doing extremely well. We always dressed decent, our Christmases were wonderful, and we traveled often. I remember shopping at the major stores like A & S and Macy's. My favorite times were when we would go to Carvel on Fridays and we would all get our favorite ice cream, and our parents would also buy the Flying Saucers and put them in the freezer for a treat throughout the week.

I especially enjoyed playing with my best friend Eric who starred in the movie "**Claudine.**" Eric and I would play skelly together. Skelly was a game that was on the ground. I say was because I haven't seen anyone play it since I was a child. To play this game you had to pluck a top to get from one point to the next. You would have to go from box to box before winning the game. The top had to have been filled with tar to give it weight. I mean that top had to be filled right. Depending on how much effort you put into that top it could have been the reason behind you winning. Skelly was an all-time favorite growing up, and children back then loved it.

During those days the games we played as children didn't require money, they just required another person. But of course, it would be even more fun when everybody got involved to play games like: *Co Co Leave 123, Simon Says, Red Light Green Light, Mother May I, Steal the Bacon* and so many others. And I guess if your parents had some money you had the bike with the basket in front, or the bike with two seats. I think Dana's was yellow, and Diane's was red, and I would ride on the back or in front. Whatever and however it was, we had bikes and skates with the key. The skates were one-size fits all. All you had to do was place your feet inside the metal skate for measurement then lock it with your key when you felt that it was a good fit. This way your entire family could share one pair of skates.

My memories of my family then was what I wished family could have continued to be for me. Two parents working together to reach a common goal. It appeared to me that their goal was to live in the projects for a period of time while working two decent salaried jobs so that they can save up to move out of the projects into their family home of which they eventually did.

We had gotten beatings for what we did wrong, and it taught us what not to do any more. However, we preferred to have gotten beaten by Dad because his beatings were simple. First we had to hold our hands out in front of us. Then Dad would take his belt and whack us one side. Then we would turn our hands over. Then he would whack us on the other side. And that was it! That was our beating from Daddy. My Dad was as cool as cool could get. I remember the first time watching "***The Cosby Show***" when I had gotten older and was no longer living with them. I would say that Bill Cosby "before the scandal" reminded me of my Uncle Jay so much. Even till this day he reminds me of him whenever I see him working on the grill, or just by listening to him speak. My Uncle Jay is such a cool guy. He's smart and filled with so much wisdom, and if you listen you might learn something.

On the other hand Mommy's beatings were brutal. Whenever it was my turn to get one, she would be sitting in the living room polishing her nails. She would call me into the living room and calmly tell me to take off my clothes. I'm talking bone naked! Meanwhile, Mom would be blowing or flagging her nails to dry. Then after I had already anticipated the pain, standing there anywhere from five to fifteen minutes, she would call me over so she could start whaling on my skin. Man I tell you, I hated to get beatings from Mommy. The beatings weren't often, but they were enough.

The cool thing about parents sharing responsibilities is having Mom ask us girls who we preferred to get whipped by. Of course we all would shout out "Daddy!" Then when Daddy had "whipped" us a few times, we would pretend to cry so Mommy would think that Daddy did his thing. But then we would go into our bedroom that us girls shared and laugh. I'll tell you this though, even though Mom's beatings were crucial, had I known my future, I would have settled for more beatings from her instead of taking door number two.

My "parents" are the epitome of what I think parents should be. As husband and wife, they did the right thing in raising their family. Whatever ups and downs if they had any, us children were not subjected to them. And at the end of the day they were both there.

# SHAPING

I remember when I was about four years old, it was a Friday and we had just come from Carvel. We were all enjoying our ice cream when Daddy asked us girls whose house we wanted to spend the night at. Diane shouted out Aunt Erline's house, Dana calmly said Aunt Winnie's. For some reason Aunt Erline wasn't going to be home that weekend so Daddy said that we would go to Aunt Winnie's house instead.

I started crying immediately. Mommy asked why was I crying but I wouldn't say anything. But I knew that before she asked me a second time I'd better tell her what I was crying about. I said "Every time we would stay at Aunt Winnie's house, cousin Reecie would come home in the middle of the night and wake me up. Then she would drag me into the bathroom by my ear, punch me, and then say that I am not wanted by you and Daddy and she would say how much a drug addict my real mother is. And she makes me pull down my panties touch me down there and hit me some more, calling me nasty because I had stained my underwear. And her son Ray always touched me down there too." In a loud voice my Mom said, "Jay, take me there right now!"

I'm not sure what Mommy did or said, but I had never seen or heard about Reecie again until thirty five years later when I was told that she had passed. Nevertheless, my parents decided that we would stay home and be babysat by Moms' youngest sister.

Why can't I play is what I asked my aunt and my sisters who were playing a game inside the closet. They all shouted that I was too young, and that I could hurt myself. But I insisted that I play and said, if I don't play I'm gonna tell because we all supposed to be in bed anyway. Since they had all taken me serious, they had stopped playing and went into the kitchen to get a snack. So I decided to play the game on my own. Within the first minute of me trying to do what they were doing I had busted my mouth, cracked my tooth and started crying out loud.

They all came running into the room. My aunt took me into the bathroom to wash my mouth out noticing that I had chipped my front tooth. My sisters started getting scared, saying that I always get them in trouble. That was the reason they didn't want me to play with them in the first place. I rolled my eyes, moved my head side to side and said "I'm telling Mommy and Daddy that y'all wouldn't let me play wid y'all. And Mommy gonna listen to me like she listened when I told on Reecie. That's why we don't go dere no more, and now she can't bother me no more eva!"

We finally went to bed and during the stillness of the night when we all should have been sleeping my aunt had decided to introduce me to something new. The *"House"* game without a mommy, without a daddy and without children, and I had better not say a word. She touched me in my private area and got on top of me and guided me to move with her. I did just what she asked me to do busted mouth and chipped tooth and we were at it until she was where she needed to be.

Actually it felt better than when my male cousins over at Aunt Erline's house would make me feel. Every time we stayed at their house we would play House. I mean, what was up with this House game? Anyway, the difference with these guys was that it stunk, and that smell would take me through the rest of my life. A few years later I came across that scent again, and many years to follow I would be reminded while doing a search in a male prison. I had finally put a distinction to the scent. It smelled like sweaty men's balls. And I hated it! The blankets smelled and they smelled. However, out of the choices regarding whose house we were going to for the weekend, I'd rather had smelled the sweaty balls. But, if I had a choice as to who I preferred to play house with, I would have always chosen my aunt who babysat us. And without me realizing it, I would always be in need of that feeling as I grew.

# MR. ROGERS

After a period of time Mom and Dad were no longer working overnights, and I was five years old still too young to go to school. So often times they would make accommodations for me to spend the day over at Aunt Burt's house. Aunt Burt was my grandmother's oldest sister. Aunt Burt was an elderly woman who also lived in the projects in Manhattan. She didn't have any children so it would be just us two in her apartment. She didn't talk to me at all. She mostly stayed inside her room watching the Soap Operas. "*As the World Turns,*" "*The Guiding Light,*" and "*The Young and The Restless.*" I remember her apartment being like a railroad. Her room was at one end of the apartment where she stayed watching her Soaps. And the living room was at the other end of the apartment where I was told to stay and watch TV.

Although I was only five years old, I knew that I was only allowed to watch certain TV shows, and those shows came only on Channel Thirteen. I knew that with or without supervision I had better not change that channel. Therefore, during the hours that I was there, I would be excited to watch a show called ***"ZOOM."*** *"ZOOM"* was my favorite day time show. I would sing and dance along with the kids in the show, and it was lots of fun. Then I would watch "***Magic Mirror.***" When the show would start, a woman would hold up a mirror and say all the names of the children that she would see in this magic mirror. What I could never figure out was why didn't she see me? Every day she would call out names like "I see Mary. I see Joshua. I see Carol. I see Thomas. I see Jacqueline. I see Sara. I see Pete. I see Rebecca." 'What about me?" I would shout out at the TV, "Say my name! Here I am! Here I am! Say my name. Say Joyce. Don't you see me?"

9

After weeks of the woman on the television not seeing me, I would just sit in envy of the names she would announce, and I began to accept the fact that she would not be calling out my name. I had made up my mind that my name wasn't popular, nor was I special, and that I was probably invisible.

Then depression would hit when "**Mr. Rogers**" came on. He bored the hell out of me. He would walk into the house, and say, "Hello boys & girls." and while moving and talking in slow motion. He would take off his hat and hang it on the coat rack. Then he would take off his coat and hang it on the coat rack. Then Mr. Rogers would walk to the chair and sit down and untie one shoe. Then he would untie the other shoe. Then he would take off one shoe place it under the bed. Then he would take off the other shoe and place it under his bed neatly next to his other shoe. Meanwhile he would be talking very slowly about something that never stood out to me. I guess I didn't get it. Was he showing us what to do first when we came in the house? I would just stare at the TV, because I couldn't turn it. I had to figure something out. Something had to make my stay here a little more enjoyable.

The next day I came, I decided to see what was inside the refrigerator. I thought maybe I can snack on something while I watch my shows. To my surprise, there was nothing that looked appetizing or available for me to snack on. Hell the only thing to drink was some milk, and I didn't want that. But ah, cough syrup was lined up on the door of the refrigerator. There was a purple color, a red color, and orange. I decided to pick a flavor that had the most cough syrup, and sit in front of the TV. Before I knew it, I didn't give a damn if that woman from "**Magic Mirror**" called my name or not. I said to the TV, "I don't care if you don't see me, cuz you blind is why." Then I would crack up at myself. Then by the time "**Mr. Rogers**" would come on I was drunk. Finally I would find his show to be hilarious and I couldn't stop laughing. I had found a new way to entertain myself at five years old. By the time my Mom and Dad would come and get me I would be passed out.

After I drank all of the cough medicine at Aunt Burt's house, I started drinking the cough medicine at home. However, at home there was only one flavor for whenever any of us caught a cold. I was still excited to see it. But it didn't take long for Mom to find out. You couldn't get anything past her. I remember this day, she went into the refrigerator and one second later she called out my name in a loud shout, "JOYCE!" Maybe I was acting strange or something that made her curious. Because how else would she have known that it was me who drank the cough syrup. It's like she went to investigate or something. When I came into the kitchen I said, "Yes Mommy?" She said, "Joyce, I'm going to ask you one time, did you drink …?" I started crying before she could finish because I'd already knew it was going to be clothes off and a whipping to remember. I was right, and I never did it again. I'm kind of glad she was paying attention because what I know today, I could have died behind drinking the medicine the way that I did. As a matter of fact while Mommy was whipping me she was letting me know how dangerous it was.

# WHITE SUITS

"Maybe Aunt Burt noticed her medicine gone and told on me. And maybe that was why my parents didn't ever bring me back. Why are they bringing me to my grandmother's house today instead? I don't like coming over here because I don't like how my grandmother treats me. I don't like the things that come out of her mouth and I don't like the way she looks at me. She always reminds me that my Mom and Dad are not my parents in a very evil spirited way. She constantly reminds me that my biological mother is a drug addict. And she is just down right mean." That day I decided to do my best and stay clear of my grandmother so I stayed in the living room playing with the plastic fruit that everybody in those days had on their kitchen, dining or living room table. Some would look greasy as hell while other people like my grandmother kept it clean enough to trick you into thinking it was real. A song was playing by The Edwin Hawkins Singers "**Old Happy Day**." The adults were in the kitchen. I heard the doorbell ring and I looked to see who it was. To my surprise I saw this beautiful woman wearing a white pant suit with a white brim hat cocked to the side, and with her comes this handsome tall dark skinned man who was also wearing a white pant suit and they walked in. I didn't remember the last time that I had seen her, but I had known that she was my biological mother.

My mother gave her greeting to everyone who was inside the house knowing that she looked good when she said, "Hey y'all!" Then she walked towards me while I was standing there staring at her. Although knowing, my mother asked me who was I. When I told her my name she gave me a hug that was so tight it felt like I had become her. She had such an alluring scent that I can remember it as if it were yesterday. She introduced me to the man who was with her as Lem. Lem happened to be the second best man in my life next to my Dad that I had known. I knew who she was just like she knew who I was. And at that moment, I knew I was ready to come and live with her. I don't know if it was because she was fly as hell or because I was sick of the bullshit from family members outside of my Mommy and Daddy.

Later on that night while we were back at home, my Mom had called me into the living room, and said that she needed to talk to me. She asked me how I felt when I saw my birth mother. When I told her that I had felt fine, she continued the conversation by letting me know the agreement that she and my biological mother had made. She said to me that it was understood that when and if my biological mother were to get back on her feet that she would come for me. And that my mother had contacted her, letting her know that she was ready for me to return.

Then she asked me the big question. Was I ready to go and live with my mother? It was like asking me did I want chocolate candy or a complete meal with desert. I loved my Mom and Dad but at five years old, I didn't know which was better for me. My fate was totally up to me, a five year old girl. Or maybe it wasn't! Maybe if I would have said no, I could have stayed with them. They did just purchase a big house in Long Island with room for me. Maybe when I said yes, I really hurt their feelings. Or maybe this was just how it was supposed to go down. In any case, that was the beginning of me making choices. Good, bad or indifferent!

When I had answered yes, I had asked would I still be able to visit and spend the night. I also asked would I continue going to The Fresh Air Fund as I was leaving to go for the very first time in a few weeks after my sixth birthday. My Dad said, "Yes, yes, and yes." He said that my biological mother had agreed to allow me to continue going to camp, and would allow me to come over and spend the night whenever I chose to. They had told me how much they had loved me, and said that they would always be there for me. Although I heard every word they were saying, I didn't comprehend everything because again, I was only five years old. It seemed like my life was speeding up even faster than it already had been going. And now it seemed as if I had become old enough to make major decisions on my own. If I could turn back the hands of time!

# NEXT

I had gotten off the bus at the Port Authority returning from camp. I was standing on line waiting for Becky to pick me up and take me to my new home. Sure enough Becky and Lem showed up. They didn't have on a white suit, but they had looked great! We all seemed excited. My mother didn't have any shame walking with her thumb in her mouth. As a child I didn't see anything wrong with Becky sucking her thumb in public or in private. On the other hand my Mommy must have seen it as a problem. When I was about four years old, I had put my thumb in my mouth. When she saw that I was sucking my thumb, she put a stop to it immediately. I don't know whose mess was inside the toilet, but she made me put my thumb in it. After that, I would never suck my thumb again. Anyway, Lem picked up my suitcase, and I was on my way to my new home.

We arrived at a six story walk up in Manhattan on the Lower East side, and we were on the top. The building smelled like it was reaping rats. If I were to spread my arms and legs out I would have been in every part of the apartment. I had gone through a shocking moment regarding my transition. All I can remember about that apartment was that I loved sitting on the Fire Escape while enjoying my favorite candy. That entire living arrangement seemed strange to me. But I was just a kid and I had to adjust. My only thought was that I'd wished I had never seen the new house that Mommy and Daddy had just bought in Long Island. Maybe if I had left with only a memory of the Projects, it would not have been so bad.

I didn't understand it then why we walked from Manhattan to Brooklyn almost every day. But the Williamsburg Bridge was no stranger to us. It would be Becky, Lem, me and my nephew Jamel walking over that bridge faithfully. Becky and Lem would have Jamel almost all the time. Then when my seventh birthday had come Mommy and Daddy bought me a blue bike with red, white and blue tassels on it. Lem had promised me the next time that we walk across the bridge that he would show me how to ride my bike. He showed me, and when Jamel's little legs would get tired, Lem would carry him on his shoulders.

Lem was a great guy and I had loved him dearly. His mother Ms. Hattie, as I remember, had become what a grandmother was meant to be. She did grandmotherly things like love you, bake cookies, and cupcakes, give you birthday gifts, talk to you, and most of all she hugged me often. It was ironic that both Becky and Lem's mother name was Hattie. However, very very different in nature.

# HYMEN

I am about eight years old, and have been living with my mother for about two years. We have already moved two times since I came to live with her, and now we live in Bedford Stuyvesant on Dekalb Avenue. We are living with my Aunt Brenda, her two teenage boys who were both five and six years older than I was. I'm not certain as to what my aunt and Becky's choice of high was, but I do know that they were on a narcotic and they drank. Either way they were always high off of something.

Lem and Becky were still together however he didn't live with us at my Aunt Brenda's house. Supposedly, he went back to live with his mother Ms. Hattie. Becky was more out of the home than she was at home. All I could think about was why did she lie and say that she was ready to take care of me. Why didn't she leave me where I was at? I didn't think she was rushed to get me. I could have been raised by two parents, and I would have had a hot meal to look forward to. In addition, I could have been raised with two sisters who love me, and whom I also love. I couldn't figure out this way of life, but I had to adapt fast.

Waking up every day was like a mystery for me. I would go into the bathroom, and wonder why all of a sudden I would wake up feeling like somebody smeared a whole jar of Vaseline between my legs. For several weeks, I couldn't figure it out. I wasn't hurting or anything, I was just greasy. To my surprise, I opened my eyes in the middle of the night and there he was. My Cousin Thomas who was fourteen or fifteen years old inside of me lying on top of me humping very slowly. He didn't know that I had opened my eyes because I was too scared to let him know that I had woken up. So I just pretended to be asleep. When he was finished, he pulled out and let his sperm fall on me. Then he got up and semi-wipe me off. That's when I realized I was greasy for a purpose.

At that moment I didn't know if I should cry, continue to pretend to be asleep, or keep my mouth shut. My decision was to tell Becky whenever I would see her. The next day it was obvious to me that Timothy, Thomas's brother was very much aware of what his brother was doing to me. That day I asked Timothy can I wear his sneakers. Although his foot size was slightly larger than mine, I would stuff tissue inside the front to fit me perfectly. During this time my cousins and I weren't doing too good. We did some borrowing, and washing out on our own to have something clean to wear.

When I asked Timothy can I wear his sneakers, he had the nerve to say "I'll let you wear them if you suck my dick." I looked at him and said "Okay, okay, I'll do it." Timothy went to put his stink penis inside my mouth, and I took a bite. I had bit the hell out of it. He screamed, he continued screaming, and I got up, snatched the sneakers while he laid there in the bed in pain.

That night I didn't go to sleep. I sat up by the door waiting for Becky to come home. When she walked through the door I let her know when she didn't come home at night Thomas puts his thing inside of me. And I told her that he had been doing it for a while. I even explained to her why I didn't know it was being done until I had opened my eyes. I was rambling. I went further and told her what I had did to Timothy, and why I had done it.

Surprisingly, I didn't get a reaction or a response. If I did it must have been a pittance of a response because I can't remember. My cousin had taken my virginity. Years later I would understand what a Hymen was. And Thomas had broken it. I wished that I had had the experience for my husband if I were to have one, to have been the one to break it. The sad thing is, is that I don't even know when it was broken. All I know is based on how I know a Hymen is broken and that this cousin had to have broken it.

On the contrary, when I had told Mom what Reecie had been doing to me, she went ballistic, and I had never seen her again. Yet for this, my biological mother had no reaction. I was being raped repeatedly by her first nephew and she did nothing. I had become an eight year old confused little girl as to what was right and what was wrong. Because the highlight of what would follow had definitely changed the way I had viewed life all together.

## HANDLE IT

We had moved and they, my cousins, had moved right along with us. Now at nine years old I didn't know what to think. What I did know was that my body had changed from within, and I had to please my flesh.

# STEPPING UP

I have been living with my mother for four years now, and we have moved three times. My mother had decided to cut my hair because I would always come home with it looking messy. She told me one day when I came home from school, "Joyce, if you come home with your hair messed up again, I am going to sit you right here and cut your hair. I send you to school looking like a little girl, and you come home looking as if your hair was never combed." I was like really! She wanted me to go to school to look like a little girl with crazy ribbons and funny looking barrettes in my hair, yet I was no longer a little girl. I was almost ten, and at age ten having experiences of an adult. Last time I checked, I didn't see any adults with ribbons in their hair. So I intentionally came home with my hair messed up. And she kept her word. She cut my hair. And now I would rock a little afro. I had a new style with a new name. "Baldy!" Kids can be very cruel.

*Song*

"Hey…….. A….. Hey…… A……, what's… the matter with your afro… won't grow into a natural. Go and get your comb ome…go and get your comb!"

I would say, "Yo momma needs a comb!" Then I would run because everyone would start chasing me. My sister Sherlene who was fifteen years old had now come to live with us. She had been living with her father up until now. Now it was official for my mother to have gotten back all of her children. However, my oldest sister Abby had her own apartment in Brooklyn. When I did run home Sherlene would always be around, and would put an end to them chasing me for the day.

All of my siblings knew how to fight very well, and didn't hesitate to do so. I knew that because back then they would have family fights. It would be Becky, Lem, Sherlene, my Uncle Roy and their friends. Everybody would be fighting while my nephew Jamel and I would be looking through the window ducking as if we were also in the fight. Actually, the neighborhood was terrified of my family.

Still, I would have my run-ins with the kids that were my age. Some would say that it was my mouth that would get me in trouble. I say, it would be what I say out of my mouth after they would say something not so nice to me. Like calling me names like Baldy. I think I had momma issues because I would always say, "Ya momma!" And haul ass running up the block.

My best friend's name was Donna, She was a year older than I was, and she was also cute, petite and she dressed really nice. She lived a few doors down from us with both of her parents along with cousins, uncles and aunts. Donna and I were the best of friends. We were so close that the both of us together would engage in sexual acts. Yeah, it was quite obvious that Donna had a story of her own regarding sexual encounters.

One day while Donna and I were sitting on my stoop, my cousin Thomas had come out of the house and passed us. Donna said "Joyce your cousin is so fine." I sucked my teeth and said I couldn't believe that my mother let him come and live with us after he did what he had done to me. Donna said that it must have been okay because nothing happened to him. After talking about it for a while, Donna asked me was anybody else home because all that talk about what Thomas had done to me made her feel horny, and she wanted us to go upstairs and have some fun.

While Donna and I were in the bedroom under the covers kissing, touching, and humping, Thomas had peeped in. The way I figured, three was better than two so I had summoned Thomas to come and join Donna and me between the blankets. He was happy to do so. The three of us did what Thomas had been doing to me in the past. This type of behavior went on for quite some time. I was ten years old and I had already experienced what some adults had never experienced and some never will. Besides, who was home to stop us? But honestly, I am not bragging. I'm embarrassed and ashamed of the things that I was doing at such a young age.

Perversion entered me partially at four years old, but then at ten years old perversion had entered me completely. Therefore, what you are about to read was very difficult for me to write. I tried to write this book without sharing this particular story. But, I wasn't allowed to. So near the end of writing *Handle It*, I had to return to this section to complete what I am supposed to share. My tears continue to fall while writing this part of my life. It hurts to share this side of me because this along with everything else that I have shared would have exposed me completely. Although it is my Autobiography it's not about me at all. So don't judge me, this is transparency in its entirety.

The place where we were living during this time was a two family house on Herkimer Street in Brooklyn. On the ground floor lived a mother with two kids ranging from ages six and seven. I'm not sure if back then parents made it a habit of leaving their kids home alone but it seemed like the norm growing up. This particular day I don't know if I was babysitting or just in the house with these two kids. Whatever the reason was, Donna and I were home with them. We were playing and then we decided to play House. That old faithful House game that I was taught at an early age, how to play very well. Only this time I didn't have to be a parent.

The brother and sister decided to be mommy and daddy since they too obviously played the game among themselves quite often. Since that was the role that they chose Donna and I allowed them to do whatever they wanted to do. Then the unthinkable happened. The sister asked did we want to see how she suck her brother's penis and Donna and I encouraged her to do so. We stood there and watched the sister do that to her brother and didn't say a word although I knew it was wrong. Or did I? Besides, in our minds we were just playing "House," and we were all kids. We were children without supervision.

Over the years the thought of what I had done haunted me. It haunted me so much that when I had a child I had become overprotective. I was overprotective of my child because of all of the things that had happened to me as a child. I was even overprotective over my nieces, nephews, and my godchild. I often wondered would I ever be able to apologize but I don't even know their names. I forever will continue to pray that I didn't mess their lives up by allowing such a perverted act. Unfortunately, I can never undo what I have done. But instead, I will never stop praying for the sister and brother whose lives that I may have possibly ruined. I was ten years old and we were children without supervision and apparently we were all perverted.

# BYE FRIEND, HI FOES

We moved to another location. This time it was Becky, my sister Sherlene, Anthony, me and Becky's new man Pete. Oh, how I was frightened of him. He used to scare me just by the look of him. He wasn't attractive at all! Later, he and my mother would break up. The break-up may have been due to him going to jail. Pete was a Jostler, another name for picking people pockets.

Often times I was home alone which was no surprise to me. But I would enjoy the few times that my brother was with me. I remember this particular day that he and I were home alone and we were hungry, having no food in the house. The good thing was it was summertime, and summertime also meant it's free lunch time. I thanked God for free lunch, because I had gotten so creative with it that I would look forward to the weekdays. I would always take the shopping cart up the street and go where free lunch was given out. I would tell the person who was giving out the food that I had six siblings, so they would fill the cart. I believe they knew I was lying.

After I would bring the food home, my brother and I would put the juices inside the freezer to eat later, pretending that they were store-bought ices. I would tell Anthony that some of the food had to be saved just in case we needed to eat it for dinner. I would then fry up the bologna and make grilled cheese sandwiches. Anthony would always tell me to turn the fire down. But I would tell him that I was hungry and that if the fire was high the food would cook faster. Then being frustrated he would say, "Then you gonna burn up the damn food!" He used to get so upset with the way I cooked until he would finally say, "Just make the Kool-Aide!" The "Kool-aide" was simply water and sugar, but when I put it in the refrigerator it became cool.

We lived at 1319 St. Johns Place in Crown Heights. It was a private house and we lived on the third floor. The apartment was decent, and I had my own space. However, sometimes I hated coming outside because of this tall girl who lived right next door in the attached house. She had to have been way older than me. Why else was she so tall I thought. Every day this girl would pick on me. I still didn't like to fight so therefore I wouldn't. I was terrified of this girl. Her arms looked long like an octopus. Her legs were like stilts, and she wasn't very nice at all. I would tell her that it wasn't nice to bully me around, but she didn't care, she enjoyed it.

That would all change the day she tried to stop me from entering into my gate. She must have waited for me to return from the store because all I seen was these long arms come from nowhere holding the gate closed. She had the nerve to say to me, "If you want to get in the gate you gotta fight me first." I asked her, "What, are you bored or something? You don't have homework or nothing else to do?" I wanted to know what was the damn girl's problem; maybe she was mad at me because she was so tall, and I was short and chubby. Did she want to switch? Heck I would have if I could. Then she started poking me in my face saying, "Umma beat your ass, umma beat your ass." I told that girl to go ahead because I'm not gonna fight. To my surprise Becky and Sherlene were looking out of the window and saw the entire thing. I felt relieved because I thought for sure they were going to stop this nonsense.

"Kick her ass right now!" is what Becky shouted. "You better whip her ass!" is what my sister Sherlene shouted. I looked at both of them as if they were crazy. Didn't they just hear what I just said to the girl that I wasn't going to fight her? I yelled up at the window to my mother and to my sister so that if they had missed what I had said previously they can catch it this time. "I don't want to fight her!" My sister shouted, "If you don't whip ha ass I'm gon' whip yours!" This went on for quite a while.

But then the girl's mother looked out of her window and shouted to her daughter, "Kick ha ass!" That was all Becky and Sherlene needed to hear. They came outside and summoned the mother to come outside. Becky started shouting, "If you don't bring your ass down then I'll come up there and drag your ass down the steps my damn self!" It was getting crazy. Sherlene tossed the girl who was bullying me to the side and said, "Fuck with my sister again

# HANDLE IT

and see what will happen to you!" Then she was yelling at the mother to come outside. I was like, why does everybody want to fight but me? At that moment I thought to myself, and said I'm going to move myself out of this equation because these people were all crazy.

Not one person asked the girl why she'd wanted to fight me. Not one person! There was nobody around who was rational. Well the girl's mother never came outside. As a matter of fact she must have gotten scared because she closed her window, and turned off her lights. And me, I never was bullied by that girl again. At least something good came out of it.

Come to find out our family wasn't the only family who enjoyed family fights. My mother had gotten me a pair of rust pants with the patches on them and a pair of Earth shoes for Christmas. Boy didn't I love those shoes, and pants. I was finally in some kind of style. I had put my clothes on and walked down the block to my supposedly best friend Kimie's house and was showing off what I had gotten for Christmas. Hell, Kimie's family was just as poor as we were. She had sisters younger than her and a big chubby brother. Kimie's younger sister Brit said, "So what you got the new Earth shoes. Why you come over here showing off anyways for?" Now I'm only eleven years old and I guess I did what eleven year olds did when they got something new and not being used to it. I started teasing her saying, "You just jealous cuz you ain't got nothing for Christmas." Why in the hell did I say that?

Next thing I knew, Kimie's younger sister had tossed her Grape Kool Aid on my pants, and Brit had kicked me in the leg. Then it seemed like kids were coming from everywhere and we were all fighting in the middle of the street on the corner of St. Johns and Schenectady. At that moment I just started swinging and swinging. I was crying out loud because I had already new that my pants were messed up. That must have been a hurtful feeling when I said what I said, knowing that they didn't get any gifts. Who was I to show off, anyway? Hell, they were already mad because they didn't get anything. They sure as hell didn't need me to add to their sadness. Besides, I should have known better. But I was also happy about getting something, and getting something that I liked. Either way, I had learned my lesson that day.

When the fight was over, I was standing in the street alone with one Earth shoe on. I yelled out, "Gimmie my shoe! Gimmie my shoe! Stop playing y'all, gimmie my shoe back!" Then Brit shouted, "Go home wid out it!" And they all started laughing at me. I walked home feeling so bad. I was still crying while I was limping from side to side walking with only one shoe on. I couldn't believe what had just happened to me. I had left home feeling happy and fresh, and returned home feeling like a mess and I was depressed. I didn't seem to have any bruises nor was I in any physical pain. I was just sad. I had lost my shoe and my friend.

As you already know, we never stayed at a location for more than two years. But this new location was insane. 598 A, Marcy Avenue still in Brooklyn. It's me, Sherlene, Becky, and a male friend of hers. Sherlene was never home. What made this apartment crazy was that there were rats the size of cats living with us that ate Ivory soap and Junior's Cheese Cake that Becky's friend would bring home every night. And in our bathroom overlooking the toilet was a hole in the ceiling big enough for a body to fit through it. So when you sat on the toilet, the rats would literally be above your head watching you. I would make sure that urinating or any other kind of business was not being done in there. Usually at school or at someone else's house. Yeah, it was that kind of crazy.

I was lying across the top of our sofa. That's right, on top of the sofa where you lean back when sitting down on the sofa. I was across the top of it watching the television series **"Roots."** I had been counting down the days waiting for it to come on. I thought the only safe spot in the house was on higher ground. If I could have gotten on top of the dresser I would have but instead I opt for the top of the sofa. I had to sit up there because if I just sat on the sofa, I would have been to close to the rats that were shooting back and forth. I used to think that they knew when I was home alone because it seemed that they would torment me. But **"Roots"** had just come out and I knew everybody was glued to their television sets. And I'm sure they sat on the couch or on the floor without worries. All except my neighbors; however, it didn't seem to bother them because they had lived there for 14 years. Maybe they had figured out something that we didn't.

"Oh no! oh no!" I shouted out. "Run Kunta, run! Oh my God! Run, run, run faster!" For a minute it looked like the rats had stopped to watch the show with me because two of them just sat there facing the TV. Kunta was captured, and I had got so mad that I grabbed one of the pillows from off the sofa and threw it directly at the rats. The rats jumped up and ran back in the other direction. Hell, I couldn't take my frustration out on no one or nothing else. Afterwards, I thought to myself if I had killed a rat, who was going to pick it up because I wouldn't have.

When ***Roots*** went off, I was too afraid to go to sleep. I waited for the moment to jump off the sofa to run out of the house. It was like I had flown, because of my quickness. I didn't go any further than the stoop because it was late and I was supposed to be in the house. Instead, out of fear of being home alone, I decided to wait outside until somebody would come home to be with me. When Becky walked up she yelled at me for being outside, and told me to get in the house. To our surprise, our apartment was burglarized. Our 32" inch Television was stolen along with furniture items and some clothing. Becky was upset with me because I had left the house. Then once she applied some of her street knowledge she had solved the case. She said, "Umma get the nigga who did this!" Then she walked upstairs to the family who lived on the top floor. There were two brothers ranging from the ages of thirty four to forty five years old. They may have been younger but their lifestyle made them look older. They lived upstairs with their mother that everybody called Ms. Jozy. They wanted to call her Ms. Nosy but that would have been a dead giveaway. She was always in everybody's business, but never took care of her own.

I heard some banging on the door. Then I heard my mother say, "When I come back home in an hour, every mother fuckin' item of mine better be back in my house!" When she returned downstairs, she said to me that she will be back, and then she left. Next thing I know, the oldest son was bringing all of our things downstairs. I stood there on the stoop with the door opened and watched it all. I just knew my mother was a bad somebody! My mother had more street knowledge than anyone I've ever known. She was fearless and no matter where she went, everybody knew it.

-----------------

Darlene had to be about seventeen or eighteen years old. She and I had about the same dark brown complexion. I think we were close to the same height, 5'7" or she might have been about 5'8". Darlene wasn't an attractive female at all. She looked sort of masculine in her face. She actually looked just like her father. I wasn't sure back then what Darlene's major malfunction was. I didn't even know if she was diagnosed with having a mental illness. What I did know was that every day I was this girl's target. Darlene would have me running for my life. I could be in the middle of playing Handball, somebody would shout out, "Joyce run, she's coming!" And I would run for my life. It amazed me how I would be running, she would be walking and somehow Darlene would still catch up to me. She was like the female Jason from "***Friday The 13***th*"or* something. This chick would come after me smiling and sometimes laughing to herself. She even had the nerve to call me to come to her. Can you believe that? Who did she think she was, my Aunty Beverly? Only Aunty Beverly was allowed to call me over to get my ass whipped. Yeah, she had to be mental.

I never mentioned to Beck nor Sharlene what Darlene was doing to me. I'm not even sure why I didn't mention it. I think because they both were always on the go and I simply had to "*handle it*!" This girl would sneak behind me and intentionally scare the hell out of me. Then I would take off like a bat out of hell. I ran so much from Darlene that I wanted to run away from my life. Instead, I had joined Colgate at Pratt Institute where girls and boys ran for championships. When I was on that track, I would run as if I was running for my freedom. I think running from Darlene had trained me. When I would run, I would think about that big house in Long Island with Aunty Beverly and Uncle Jay. I would think about my cousins who were like my true sisters. I would think about what family was to me and what I wish that it could be. I would think about Carvel Ice Cream, and playing games with Dana. I would run, and I would win. But that would all come to an end, because I wasn't able to go to the Championships. It required a parent's signature along with money to purchase running gear, which I didn't have.

I wish the drama would have ended with Darlene as well, but it didn't. I was returning home from Pratt Institute about to walk into the building when Darlene was exiting. She was coming towards me with this look as if she was waiting all day to fight me. I was not in a good mood. I was feeling sad, and discouraged when I saw her, but then another feeling came over me. I felt like I can take her on because I wanted somebody to feel what I was feeling. So before she could take another step, I grabbed her and beat her as if she had stolen everything that I had. She was screaming and yelling for me to stop and I wouldn't. Darlene's oldest sister who was about twenty one years old had come out of the house and was about to jump in when, to my surprise, Sherlene was coming home. And might I say that I was never bothered nor affected by Darlene or anyone else again. Sherlene whipped her sister's ass, and I whipped Darlene's. End of story!

Well, that was the beginning of who I had stepped up to being. I was no longer that scared and timid person. I started taking on all of the bullies, boys or girls. Whenever I noticed that somebody was being bullied I took up for them and would fight their battles. I would say to the bullies, "I see that you like to pick on people, but obviously she/he is afraid of you. So I tell you what I'm gonna do. I'm gonna fight you instead. And if you beat me then you continue on bullying him/her. But if I win, you better not ever bully them again." I felt that my speech was important because I needed them to understand that they had to stop what they were doing. It worked. People had stopped being bullied around me. Bullying is a horrible thing. It causes people to commit suicide, it causes depression, separation, feelings of inadequacy, drug and alcohol addiction, and it's just simply horrible. So if that's something that you do, or know someone that does, please stop it! You're so much better than that! Ask yourself this question, if it were you would you like it?

# GANJA

Of course we moved again and again, but now I'm thirteen years old in junior high school. We live in a one bedroom apartment. It's Becky, Anthony, Sherlene and her newborn baby my first niece. Next door to our apartment Marijuana "Weed" was being sold. My brother would work there from time to time calling it his hustle. During this time he started buying some gear that I wanted to wear. I often asked my brother can I wear his sneakers although they were slightly too big for me. However, putting some tissue in the toe area would always solve the problem. I wanted to wear them because his sneakers were fashionable and I wanted to wear something that other children were wearing, and Adidas was being rocked in every color by girls and boys.

I hated coming home from school during this time because our apartment would always smell like a liquor store. I would go immediately for the spray and start spraying! It would often be the same people in the house with my mother drinking. Sometimes the spray would go in some faces because I really didn't like Becky's friends. I know, I was a child and I should have had more respect. But, I didn't ask for this life, I was put into it! Therefore, I had adopted attitudes and frustrations that required spray in some faces.

"You are so evil!" Becky would say. "And the house smells like a liquor store, and it's making me nauseous." Was what I said. Then I walked into the living room and began my homework. I liked doing homework. It gave me a purpose. I looked forward to getting great grades in school, and being smart. When I was in the fifth grade, they wanted to skip me a grade but Becky was against it. Ask me why, I couldn't tell you.

Soon after we had moved there my sister Sherlene had moved out into her own apartment. Immediately after, Becky had gotten a close friend of hers to live with us, and she had the same name as I did. I think that was why I liked her because she was definitely part of the drinking crew. And I hardly liked any of my mother's friends. Joyce, my mother's friend, had two children a girl and a boy. Her daughter Loanne was my age, and we went to the same school. Joyce, however, didn't have custody of neither one of her children during this time. Based on that alone, I can see why her and my mother and had a lot in common. Joyce would appear to me to be sad often times when she would share the story of wanting to see her children. I didn't know what the truth was but I was asked to do what I thought was a simple task.

On this day I thought I was too cute. I wore Joyce's green blouse, with a black fitting skirt, and a black belt around my blouse with black low heeled shoes. They may have been her shoes as well, but I was rocking the outfit. Ms. Joyce asked me can I please tell her daughter Loanne that she would like to see her and her brother tomorrow. She said for me to say that she lives with my mother and me, and that she misses them very much. I didn't think that that was a problem so I responded by saying, "Sure, I'll let her know." When I reached school, I was walking up the stairs when Loanne walked up and we started talking. I told her exactly what her mother had asked of me, and that was that. Sometimes Loanne and I would have lunch together but this day, she said that she had to go home for lunch.

Later on that afternoon while sitting in class, people kept walking past my class room pointing their fingers towards me and boiling up their fist. I would turn around and look behind myself to see who they were directing their anger towards. But to my surprise there was never anyone behind me. It took a while, but then after several people going past doing the same thing looking at me, I realized that those people were threatening me. Man, I had gotten so scared I think I almost wet myself. I asked to be excused and I went to my Dean and told him what was happening and asked can I please leave school fifteen minutes earlier, and he said yes. I was thinking that if I left fifteen minutes early and came out through the side entrance I might be able to slip past them.

I get outside and look toward the direction I am to walk home and I see a crowd of people coming towards me slowly. I turned around and looked in the other direction and notice a crowd of people coming in that direction walking faster and faster. There was nowhere for me to go. I just stood there. I dropped my book bag, and as the people got closer to me I notice people of all ages coming towards me to fight. Out of fear, I blacked out and started swinging, tossing people around, kicking, fighting, and when it was all over I was the only one standing. I fixed my clothes, picked up my book bag noticing that people who were "supposedly" my friends stood around and didn't help me, I nodded my head, and I walked home.

When I reached home, I was furious. As soon as I walked into our apartment I saw Ms. Joyce and I said, "This morning I did what you asked me to do Ms. Joyce. I told your daughter that you wanted to see her and her brother. Why was that a bad thing? Why did your entire family come up to the school to fight me? Why? What did I do so wrong that over fifty people of all ages came to fight me? Did you forget to tell me something? Or you just didn't give a damn what consequences you thought I would have suffered?" Immediately Becky became mad as hell and said, "They did what? And what did you do?" I told her that I beat them all is what I did! Becky shouted out, "I'm gonna wring some necks if they wanna fight my baby. I'm kicking some ass today jack!"

At that moment, I had gotten a little confused. I didn't understand why my mother had gotten so upset about people jumping me compared to someone raping me. Because she didn't get upset at all when I told her about what my Cousin Thomas had done to me. I was confused as hell. I didn't know at that moment if I was more upset with Loanne for telling her family and getting me jumped, or Becky being angry at something that I actually had already taken care of. I wanted to see that anger when I told her about her nephew. Suddenly the world became different to me. Different in a way a mother cares for her child. Different in a way that we react to what we can relate to, opposed to what is right and wrong.

I went next door to the Weed Spot where my brother used to work, and knocked on the door. A new younger guy was now working there and he had quite the crush on me, and I played right into his hands on purpose. I told him to let me in and he did. I immediately took the joint out of his mouth and started puffing when I asked him to let me help him out sometimes so that I can earn a little bit of money now that my brother wasn't around to help me. Rasta said, "Joi, ya not gon sell na Weed, ya mudda kill I. Ya too young. Go skoo al." I said, "Juma, I'm invisible. And you're the only one who sees me." Juma said, "Ya lie, cum here na!" I then told him how I have been watching and I already know what to do. Then I convinced him that he could use my help.

As time went on, selling Weed had become like a full time job to me. I would come from school, and go directly next door. Whenever somebody would knock on the door all I had to do was open the peep hole and they would put their money through and say either tre, nickel or dime. A tre bag was $3. A nickel bag was $5. And a dime bag was $10. When I wasn't selling I was bagging up Weed in these small yellow envelopes that I would fill then fold it down before sealing it with tape. When I wasn't selling or bagging I was eating some serious Rastafarian food and making time to do homework. Actually, I had mastered doing my homework in school. I had a good gig going on. My hustle was helping me have money for lunch like my friends, and buy me whatever simple things I may have needed for the few weeks I was in business. I was where I needed to be. I had become my Junior High School Drug Dealer with straight A's.

After the fight I had become somewhat popular. I had become the girl who knew how to fight. I started hanging out with some popular girls at school. Often times I had felt out of place because my new friends always dressed nice. And me, I was trying to do my best. In all honesty, I knew the only reason that I was allowed in their circle was because I was the "Weed" supplier and I knew how to fight and had somewhat become a Bodyguard to one of them. However, as the years went on and still till this day we remain friends wright wrong or indifferent.

# RICHIE RICH

Nothing good lasts for long. I was coming home from school and my building was on fire. I overheard Becky talking, saying she had fallen asleep with a cigarette in her hand and before she knew it she was running out the house. I was angry as hell. I had just started making a little bit of money from selling Weed. I had a few new pieces of clothes, and just like that it was gone! The building was in flames. No more Weed, no more money. And no more style because that too was gone.

This time the journey was with Becky and her new man Bobby. We were transported by the American Red Cross to live on Amboy Street in Brownsville at a shelter. It wasn't set up like a shelter. They were huge apartments inside apartment buildings that were converted for shelter purposes. There were four full blocks with these buildings that housed nothing but displaced families. I continued going to Halsey Junior School that was a thirty five minute commute taking the B sixty Bus.

"Hey pretty girl!" I heard him say. He was fine, 5'9, Hispanic, and a little thick but built. He wore braids cornrowed to the back, and he smelled real nice. I can tell that he was much older than I was being still thirteen, but age no longer meant anything to me. He introduced himself to me and told me when I asked that he was eighteen years old. He said that he and his family lived in one of the other buildings on the other side, and then welcomed me into the neighborhood. He decided to be my "Bodyguard" while I lived there. He would go to the store whenever I needed something. He would make sure that I was inside the house safely. I had understood that that part of Brownsville was very dangerous. It was then and still is. I would call him Rich and he would call me China.

Rich and I had gotten acquainted real fast. I enjoyed our sexual encounters. When he first pulled out a condom, I didn't know what he was doing, so I jumped up. He then explained to me how the condom would allow us to have sex without me getting pregnant. Then I was definitely all for it. Rich and I spent most of our time together either in my (shelter) apartment or in front of my door. I had met some friends who lived in one of the buildings near the corner, and I would sometimes hang out with them.

One day while a group of us girls were hanging out in front of my friend Stacy's building, we heard "*POP! POP! POP! POP! POP! POP! POP!*" Everybody just started running for cover. Some hid behind cars, some ran inside the building, I just closed my eyes, dropped to the ground and played dead. The next voice I heard was Rich calling out my name. I lifted up my head and he helped me up from off the ground. But when I looked over to my left I started crying out loud. "O my god! O my god! Is that Stacy on the ground bleeding? Somebody call an ambulance. Call an ambulance! Somebody please."

That night when the ambulance arrived, it was too late for Stacy. We never found out who was the target. The talk on the streets was that it was just for fun. Wow! Just for fun! Rich had expressed himself to me regarding the death of my friend Stacy. He also said, "I told you it's crazy around here, for real! It's like niggers are getting paid to do crazy shit. Word! And for nuffin! I be glad when we get from over here." I told Rich that I was sure that we were moving soon because we never stay anyplace for long. Rich said, "Well if it's at night or during a time that I don't know about come back and tell me where y'all at a'ight?" Of course! I told him.

Sooner than I thought we were packing in the middle of the night. Becky and Bobby were scurrying through the apartment as if there was a fire. Becky didn't surprise me with us moving, I was just surprised by the urgency. We moved to Bed Stuy on Quincy Street in a studio apartment in the middle of the night. Now we are sharing the bathroom and kitchen with an alcoholic on the first floor, a drug addict on the top floor, and then there is Becky, Bobby and myself on the second floor. My life is getting crazier by the minute. The only sane or good thing I had going on was Rich.

I didn't even have to tell Rich because he followed us that night in his friend's car. He and his friend were sitting in a car talking when we came downstairs. When we pulled off they had followed us. Becky didn't know, but I kept looking behind us as we were riding, making sure that they kept up with Bobby. Rich and I didn't speak to each other that night because it was late and that wasn't the time. He just wanted to make sure that he knew where I was going. But, we did make eye contact, reassuring one another that we were okay.

"You gotta stop seeing that man. I know all about him, his wife, and his three kids. Um hum! Did he tell you that? Did he tell you he was married with kids? Did he tell you that he was a 28 year-old man? Did he tell you?" I asked my mother what was she talking about and she repeated it and said "Rich, Richie, or whatever the fuck his name is. The nigga you been seeing." I said, "Becky, Rich is 18 not 28, so who are you talking about? And he lives with his family, he's not married." "Girl you got a lot to learn. His wife is like his mother because she's 46, and takes care of him, and he has two girls and one boy. So he was somewhat right but wrong all day. And you need to stop seeing him. And I'm telling you now, I better not see him around here. I can get him arrested because you're a minor and I know y'all fuckin'! But if I see him, he gon wish that the police had gotten to him first." Now I was definitely confused because this guy, I consented to having sex with told me he was 18. And why was she so upset about me having sex for anyway, at least it was consensual. Honestly, I was really a confused girl growing up having no answers.

"Who is it?" I asked when the doorbell rang. To my surprise it was Rich. He said that he had waited for my mother to leave before he rang the bell, and that he wanted to spend the day with me. At that moment I had invited Rich upstairs and asked him about everything Becky had mentioned to me. To my surprise, he didn't deny any of it. Instead, he went on saying that he was in love with me, and that he only lied because he wanted to be with me that bad. I told Rich that I can't tolerate anyone lying to me and that we can't see each other anymore. But then he changed my thinking quick when he said, "Look here, I love you, and I'm sorry! But things aren't working out between my wife and me and we haven't slept together in two years. We just tolerate each other because of the kids. But baby, listen to me, and listen to me good! Sometimes it seems like I just can't get close enough to you because I love you so much! You and I are as close as two is three, and we're growing closer together. We found that magic seed, better than love, and it will grow forever and ever. Every day loves grows deeper and deeper. I just want to get inside of you. Oh baby, I wanna be more than a part of you, cause loving you the way that I do …"

At that moment looking at his handsome face, and listening to him made me melt inside, and I wanted him inside of me. He didn't have to say anything further. I was a believer that it was about me and him, and not his wife. So Rich noticed how weak I was for him, and he grabbed me and we started kissing and had sex right on the sofa where I slept.

-----------------

"Turn the radio up Joyce, that's my song. Come on Bobby dance with me…" Is what Becky said.

*"Inside of You"* Ray Goodman and Brown is playing on the radio

*"Sometimes it seems like I just*
*Can't get close enough to you*
*Because I love you so much*
*You and I are as close as two is three*
*And we're growing closer together*
*We found that magic seed, better than love*
*And it will grow forever*
*Everyday love grows*
*Deeper and deeper*
*I just want to get inside of you*
*Oh…I wanna be more than a part of you*
*'Cause loving you the way that I do…"*

You got to be kidding me? I had just been played! Oh, my goodness! That man rapped to me, saying the words to Ray Goodman and Brown's song **"Inside of You"** and I went for it! I went for it! I don't know if anyone has ever gone through something like that before, but I felt stupid! I felt so many different emotions--hurt, angry, sad, and lied to once again. And still I felt his presence inside of me that had my body at ease. However, from that moment I had made up in my mind that I was done with Rich.

When Rich came over to see me the next day, I spat in his face and told him to do himself a favor and stay away from me. I never saw him again. There was no room for any explanation, I was done! Shortly after that, I had run away from home because I was tired of being home alone! Tired of being hungry! Tired of taking care of myself! Tired of sharing the bathroom and kitchen with druggies and alcoholics! And tired of being me! I went missing in action for about a month. I ran away to a Group Home on East 10th Street on the Lower East Side. When my mother found out where I was she convinced me that things were going to change and to just come home. I came back home. Soon after, Becky, Bobby, and me had moved about five minutes away to a larger apartment in Bed Stuy at 373 Nostrand Avenue. This time I had my own room. Becky enjoyed reading books by Donald Goins. I wondered if that's where she had learned her hustling ways, because every one of his books was about pimps, prostitutes, hustlers, drugs, sex and welfare checks. I think she had all of his books. When she would read one she would buy another one. I would read it, and couldn't wait to read the next one. It must have been 25-30 books. I would find out later, that it was a good idea reading those street hustlers books. I just wish I had read them before I had met Richy.

# LISA CHINA WHO

During this time Becky and Bobby were still on some narcotic. She didn't know what I was doing in the streets. So I did whatever I did to survive. I would now meet this very handsome well-kept older man in his late forties, with a southern accent. Joe would treat me really nice. I introduced myself to him as Lisa therefore that's what he called me, and I had become who I wanted Lisa to be. I told him that I was eighteen, although only fourteen. It was easy for me to pull it off because I was tall and thick and very mature. Joe would take me shopping, and give me money. He drove a decent car and he would pick me up every night after he got off of work. Joe and I were sexually involved and I enjoyed every moment pretending to be his mystery woman. Joe practiced safe sex every time when he would go into me. We would drink and hang out almost every time we were together.

Joe and I enjoyed ourselves whenever we were together because it always seemed as if we both wanted to forget something or were hurting because of something. And together we were in a world by ourselves. Joe had light brown beautiful eyes that often seemed sad as I studied him. I didn't talk much about who I was because I pretended that I wasn't Joyce. Therefore Joe never knew the real me. He knew Lisa. Joe also kept his past to himself. We just communicated to each other the moments that we would share.

During Joe and I relationship, I would notice how Becky and Bobby were getting heavier into the narcotic. I continued enjoying another world being with Joe. After a while being with Joe I remember going to a bar for the first time with him. A song by Clarence Carter – *Strokin'* was playing and Joe grabbed my hand leading me to the floor to dance with him. While dancing he stuck his leg out which looked like an old man dance step. I didn't know if I wanted to laugh, dance, or run away. But I do know that I had all of a sudden felt shame. Still, I continued dancing but feeling different. I realized that I was dating a much older man. I mean, that's when it sank in. And after that night, Joe and I would enjoy each other's company indoors.

Soon after, Joe asked me to move in with him, and said that he would take care of me while I attend college. He said that I wouldn't have to worry about anything at all. And I believed him. But what Joe didn't know was that I was still in junior high school. Although it was a thought I couldn't take him up on it. Not for nothing. Becky wouldn't have gone for it. But then again!

I had told Joe that I appreciated the suggestion and that I had cared for him a lot. I had to flip the script and change his thoughts. I told him to bring his fine ass over here so that I can show him why what we had was good and we should leave it the way it was. Of course we stopped talking and went into the action mode of getting caught up into one another.

It wasn't long before I would meet people and become friends, being new in the neighborhood. I had decided to tell everyone I met that my name was China. However, to a selective few I would keep using Lisa. Cee Cee and I had become cool with one another, and one day while we were walking down the street her friend Tony was in a car when he shouted out to her, "Hey Cee Cee, who dat fine girl you wid?" Now at that moment I am not thinking that he was talking about me. Cee Cee introduced me to Tony and told me right in his front of him, "If I were you I would stay away from his ass. He is a playa playa, girl." I just started laughing and said to myself that he is one fine ass playa.

Cee Cee grabbed my arm and we started walking slow. To my surprise Tony started singing "Chi na is fine a than all …of the girls … I know…," and then he shouted out to Cee Cee, " Hook a bruva up!" Off the back I was diggin' Tony. He was funny and he made me laugh. I had never dated anyone as funny as he was, and I couldn't stop blushing.

That night Tony and I were standing in front of my building talking and laughing. Anyone passing by would see that Tony was rapping to me and that I was enjoying it! I was having such a good time talking to Tony that I had forgotten that Joe would have been by an hour ago to pick me up. I looked up and noticed Joe's car passing by and he was looking directly at me.

# HANDLE IT

I was enjoying Tony so much that Joe wasn't even an issue at that moment. I didn't want the laughter to end. I had finally taken a liking to someone who was close to my age. Tony was 19 and I was 14. For me, that was great! When I had the chance I would call Joe, but he would never pick up his phone. I even went by his house, and he wouldn't open his door. Sadly, I had never seen Joe ever again. Did I miss him? Hell yeah, I did!

Since that night, I didn't see Tony or, shall I say that Tony and I didn't speak to one another until three weeks later. Because we did practically see each other every day but it always seemed like he was ducking and dodging. I guess that was the "playa playa" part that Cee Cee had mentioned. I was kind of saddened by it, but I had adjusted. I'm my mother's child, and my life went on.

It's time for my Graduation out of Junior High School. I had asked Becky since Joe was no longer around was she going to buy me something nice for Graduation to wear. I had reminded her that my Graduation was one week away. She said, "Ya damn right I bought you a dress, a pretty one at that!"

I wore a pretty light blue and white dress with a belt around the waist, and a pair of my old burgundy sandals that needed a lift but didn't get one. But I Graduated with Honors and that was what mattered. The way I celebrated was walking across the street that night to get some Chinese food for dinner. I proudly said to the Chinaman, "Can I have Pork Egg Fu Young, Pork Fried Rice, an Egg Roll and a Welch's Grape Soda." This guy who was also inside the restaurant said, "Dang girl, I ain't never seent you round here. Where you from?" I looked at this country bumpkin and said sarcastically, "Across the street!" He said, "Where at? I ain't never seent you. Show me where you live. You gotta be new round here." I said, you could say dat, and then I asked where was he from because his accent was thick. At that moment the dialogue between him and I had gotten even funnier. He said, "Yeah my family from Charleston, South Carolina. girl I like you. As a matter fact, umma show you right na how much I like you. Ay ah Chink, um payin fo da bofe of us. Put dat dere bill wid mine. Mannn, I'm 'bout to marry dis girl."

At that moment I figured I got another shot at somebody wanting to take care of me. I was impressed when he paid for my food. Actually I thought he was funny. And that he was at least twenty five years old. We finally decided to introduce ourselves when he told me his name was Junior. When I told him that my name was China he shouted out, "Um in love wid China y'all! Um in love wid a girl named China!" I just couldn't stop laughing.

Not long after, I decided to introduce him to Becky. Becky said, "Joyce who's this country bumpkin of a man you done brought up in here? He hype as hell." Junior didn't know my real name so he said; "Oh, dat's yo real name Joyce, den where you get China from? Oh I know! It's dem eyes. You got some pretty eyes. Yes you do, and you my baby. You my baby wid pretty eyes." All I can do was laugh and shake my head at the same time. I guess Becky saw an opportunity so she jumped right in and suggested that Junior go to the store and get her a pack of Pall Malls, and a bottle of Wild Irish Rose.

He said, "Oh, dat's yo flava? Every time I come umma bring you wad ya like. I know if I keep the momma happy, I'll keep the daughter happy. We gon be one happy family. Umma go on ahead to da stoe so I can make ya daughter happy. China you just tell me anything ya want, and ya know I'll get it fo ya. Watcha need my China doll?" Laughing hysterically, Becky said, "Joyce where you find him at?

-----------------

Later on that night while I was outside on the block, Cee Cee asked me did I ever link up with Tony. I told her that we had only talked that night in front of the building and that was it. I said that he always looked like he's ducking people. Cee Cee said that was because he was a jive ass nigga that have too many women and everybody lives close to each other. Then she asked me about somebody named Country. I told her that I didn't know anyone named Country. She said that she had seen him leaving and returning to my building earlier. I asked what did he look like and she described Junior.

I said to Cee Cee that he told me that his name was Junior. And that he was at my house. Cee Cee said, "China, his real name is Junior but everybody call him Country because he is one fast talkin' slick ass dude. That nigga got six kids from his wife, dey live around the corner. He got two kids from this chick on Bedford Avenue and …" I was furious. I told Cee Cee that he was trying to get with me, talking about wanting to marry me and he didn't even know me. "Yeah, he wanna marry you a'ight! He about thirty five years old, you know!"

All I could think about was how I was about to be played again. I know that I was only 14, and that I had so much more to learn. But what was going on with me that I kept meeting these type of guys? I didn't have the answers. All I knew was that I felt I needed someone to take care of me because Becky still was not. I was so angry at Junior or Country whatever his name was. I had become furious.

Steph was my neighbor who lived directly across the hall from me, and we were at the beginning of our friendship. I had told Steph how this dude tried to play with my mind, and I needed some help in making a fool out of him. I told her that I would set it up with him to have sex, so I gave Steph my camera and told her that when I open the door and put his clothes in the hallway to come in and start snapping photos.

When Junior arrived he came with a bottle of Cisco saying that he had brought something for me. I said, "Well I'll be damn, what you want me to get drunk or something before I sleep with you?" He said Na, he just figured I would like a little taste was all. I told him that it was too early in the day to be drinking and I just wanted to get to us having sex while we were able to. So I took him into my bedroom and told him to strip so that I can see what I was working with and he did. While he was getting undressed he had the nerve to say, "Now you talkin, umma show you sumfin girl. You gon always want me to come and gid dis to ya."

I stood there for about ten seconds staring at his scarred dark worn body with disgust in my mind. I told him to go ahead and lie down and I would be with him in a moment. When he turned towards the bed, I picked up his clothes and walked to my door and put them in the hallway. All I can hear was Junior saying, "Come on China, let me give you wad you need!" Steph and I entered the room and she started snapping away. Junior was saying, "Wad da hell goin' on here? Wad ya doin' China? Ay, I know you! Why's y'all takin pictures in shit fo? I don't know wad y'all into, but ya bedda get ma damn clothes. Where ma clothes, ya crazy ass bitches? Where ma clothes?"

Steph had already taken the twenty five pictures that the instant camera held. At this time we both were laughing hysterically watching this country bumpkin scramble around my bedroom looking for his clothes until I decided that I couldn't take it anymore. I said, "Your clothes are in the hallway fool! Now go home to your wife and your children, and don't ever play another girl again! And by the way, should I give these photos to your wife or should I play you for some loot?" He said, "Oh China please, please, please don't show dem to ma wife. What ya need, just tell me please? But don't give dem to ma wife." I told his country bumpkin behind that that was just what I was going to do. Instead, I just let him think that I was going to do it without ever letting him know otherwise.

# MY FIRST LOVE

Tony was still playing the ducking game. I wanted him to stop and talk to me really bad. Sometimes I would just stand in front of my door because I knew I would see him pass me by. Finally the moment came when Tony and I would start talking again. We had become inseparable for many months to follow. Although Tony didn't have a stable job he always looked good being quite the dresser. He would always have money, and provide for me. Later I would understand that he too was a hustler. He would work some construction gigs whenever he could. But Tony was basically a hustler. Still, no matter what Tony did, Tony had become my first love. And boy, didn't I love that man.

It was October 31, 1981, when I knew that I had become pregnant with Tony's child. I was fifteen years old and pregnant by my first love. It was something about the way we had made love that Halloween night that allowed my body to feel so many sensations with him. The love making that night and throughout the night were feelings that I will never forget. It was the kind of feeling that makes a woman decide to do anything for her man. Tony handled me with extra care that Halloween night into the morning. And when I had missed my Menstrual and was constantly craving Banana Pudding, it had been confirmed. Now it was time to let Becky know that her fifteen year old daughter was pregnant, and that Tony was the father.

Tony and I had come up with a plan as to how to let my mother know. We had decided that I would go upstairs first and start the conversation and Tony would come upstairs ten minutes later. I needed to do it that way because I had never told Tony that I was only fifteen, instead I told him that

I was eighteen years old. So I knew that I had to strategize before it would all blow up in my face, because I knew that it was all about to go down.

When I got upstairs our apartment door was opened. Sometimes when Becky did cook she would open the door to our apartment to let some of the aroma out. She knew she had cooking skills and whoever would come into the building would always shout something out to her saying, "Hey Beck, you know I'm coming up for a plate!" or "Umm umm! You must be making some collards girl, wid some smoked neck bones! Save me sum a dat!" Becky never paid anyone any mind unless they came with a bottle or something. Preferably Wild Irish Rose or some Night Train. My friends were an exception whenever they were at our house. But grown folks had better bring a bottle.

"Hey Becky, I'm pregnant." I figured why hem and haw about it. Beating around the bush wasn't an option for me. I was overly excited, and I wanted to know my next step to motherhood. Besides, I had only 10 minutes to get out whatever was needed to be said before Tony would come upstairs. "What the hell you mean you're pregnant? You're not having no got damn baby! You're gonna finish school. I'll tell you what's gonna happen alright! You're gonna have a got damn abortion is what you're gonna do!" Those were the words that my mother shouted out when I told her that I was pregnant. She was furious!

I understood her anger and her frustrations because not for nothing my mother had high hopes for me. That's why she didn't want them to skip me when I was in the fifth grade. She said that she didn't want me to miss anything along the way. She would always call me smart, and she was proud of my educational accomplishments always being on the honor roll, and receiving all sorts of certificates. Although she was far from perfect, she parented me the best way she knew how. I will always believe that she was the best mother that she knew how to be.

Still, her fury was not changing my mind. I said to my mother that day that I was not having any abortion, because I may not ever be able to have another child. So an abortion was out of the question. Becky said, "You're only fifteen years old, and you think you can take care of a child? You are just a child yourself!" When I looked up, Tony was standing there shocked at hearing that I was only fifteen. Then he said; "China, you're only fifteen years old?" I looked at him, and said, "I sure am!" I think for a moment Becky thought that Tony was about to be on her side so she stood quiet standing there looking at him with her hand on her hip. Then Tony said while looking at me smiling, "All that is in a fifteen year old girl? Damn!" Then he said, Beck I'm sorry but I love China, and I will do everything I have too to take care of my son and China." Who in the hell said that he's going to be a boy?" Becky said. And that was the last time that I heard my mother mentioning an abortion.

Becky stepped in like a mother should during my pregnancy. She immediately took me to the clinic so that I could get the proper care starting with my vitamins, and she showed me how to look decent during my pregnancy. I said showed me because she would go with me and Tony when he took me shopping and she would help with picking out my clothes.

# SURPRISE

During my pregnancy, I had gone through some unfortunate situations. In the beginning Bobby and I had gotten along very well, until it became known that whatever narcotic he was using, wasn't agreeing with him well. The man had become what people call Shell-Shocked from being in the War. Bobby and I started getting into arguments over crazy stuff that I would see him doing. One particular incident during my pregnancy my friend Kimmie and I were walking down the street eating a chunk of welfare cheese. Kimmie was the same friend on St. Johns who had jumped me with her siblings, and now living in the same neighborhood as myself on Gates Avenue, we picked up our friendship as if nothing had ever happened. We were glad that we had lived that close together once again. Neither one of our living situations changed at all but we made the best out of it. Kimmie said, "Yo Chi," (short for China) "ain't that Bobby walking fast with your TV?" I couldn't believe what my eyes had seen. So I went upstairs to see if my TV was there and it was gone.

Now I knew for sure that whatever narcotic Bobby and Becky was on was one hell of a drug. So I figured that I'll play this game with them. And I did! I decided to see how they would feel if their TV was missing, because they were obviously losing their damn minds. Inside the house they kept a lock on their bedroom door. I never knew why because I never stole from my mother or anyone else, for that matter. So I decided to climb through the window from the fire escape. It was that simple! Kimmie and I came into their bedroom through the window. Kimmie did the lifting since I was pregnant and Steph assisted Kimmie carrying it down the fire escape through the front door into my bedroom and placed it on top of my dresser where my TV had originally been. I couldn't have done it without my partners Kimmie and Steph. We cut some more cheese and went back outside to enjoy our day.

"Honey, somebody took our TV, it's gone!" I heard Bobby say. Nobody but that damn Joyce did that shit. It's probably in her room. Becky said. Bobby came into my room uninvited and tells me that that's not my TV, and to give it back. I started laughing and said "How do you know it's not my TV have you seen my TV by any chance?" He just became enraged and started to take the TV. I stood in front of it and said, "You're not taking this TV until you return mine. Because If I can't watch TV nobody will and that's that! By the way, how much did you sell my TV for? I saw you. I saw you walking with my TV leaving the building." He got so angry and shouted out to my mother and said that he was about to whip my ass if I didn't give him back their TV. I was surprised when Becky said, "you ain't whippin' nobody" and shouted out to me to stop my shit, while walking into my room.

I had really started to get pissed off because I couldn't believe what was going on. I couldn't believe that it was being debated. And, I was missing the freekin' **"Cosby Show"**. So I said to my mother as intently as possible, "So you think what's going on is right? You know he stole my TV. I'm telling you now, if I don't have my TV ain't nobody gonna be watching TV in this house. Obviously, the both of you enjoyed the high off the sale price of my TV. So I'm assed out! Here take the TV! Oops It fell, I'm sorry. Now nobody can watch TV." "You are just an evil little bitch." Becky said. Bobby and I continued arguing, and I had ducked because he went to hit me and he missed. Then when my mother jumped in the middle of us, he tried to kick me barely missing my stomach. Well, Becky took over from that point because after all, I was carrying her grandson.

Shortly after, Bobby had died. I don't remember the exact cause of death but I do know that it had something to do with drugs. Becky and I both were sad as well as some of our family members because, in all honesty, Bobby was originally a good guy. That is before the narcotics!

Anthony was living with us from time to time, and we had gotten into a terrible argument. The argument was so ugly that I shouted out to my brother, "That's why somebody gonna shoot you six times cause you think you so damn bad. You just watch!" And he responded to me by saying, "Yeah, and somebody is gonna hurt you because of your mouth!"

That night the news had reached my mother through my brother's friend that my brother had gotten shot six times. I was six months pregnant, and I was devastated. I felt like somebody had taken my breath away. All I could do was cry. I was having a hard time eating, sleeping, and I wouldn't talk to anyone. I kept rehearsing in my head the terrible argument that we had earlier that day. I was feeling horrible. I'm not sure what the shooting was about, but I felt that it was because of me. Every day I would go up to St. Johns (Interfaith) Hospital on Atlantic Avenue to see my brother, and tell him how sorry I was and I didn't mean to say such mean things. I was never sure if he heard me because he was in a Coma hooked up to so many tubes that was scary to look at.

Then, to my surprise on a nice spring night in April while I was still six months pregnant I got to the hospital, and walked in my brother's room and every tube was out of him. He was able to see me, smile at me with his pretty white teeth, and speak to me. Then he said in a low voice, "You better learn how to watch your mouth!"

Walking home from the hospital I was filled with so much joy, and excitement. It was in the evening and it still felt nice out. I was smiling and speaking to people just because. I decided I should eat something while walking home so I went inside the store and bought a bag of Bon Ton Potato Chips. I figured that would hold me over till I got home and made dinner.

I was on the corner of my block still eating my chips when I saw Sheila and her friend walking towards me. Sheila was known to be the crazy lady who loved to fight. She had to be in her early 30's with a jacked up attitude that made people afraid of her. I was glad to see her because I wanted to straighten out a rumor that I had supposedly said something negative about her. I intended to tell Sheila that she had me mistaken, and that I didn't even know her, so therefore I had no problems with her. However, my attempt was unsuccessful, because I couldn't get all the words out.

As soon as she got close to me I said, "Hey Sheila, I wanted to tell you that…" And the next thing I remembered were stars flying around in my head. Sheila had slapped me so hard that I actually stood there for a moment and seen stars. However, Sheila's biggest mistake was waiting for me to snap out of my trance. I pinned Sheila up against the brick wall that was next to my building. I had threatened her friend to stay out of it. I started hitting Sheila nonstop until her friend decided to help her. I understood that because I wouldn't have stood by watching someone beat the hell out of my friend. Somehow I was able to knock her friend to the ground throwing Sheila on top of her and continued to punch her until she bit my thumb and held on to it. I continued to hit her so hard with my other hand until Sheila opened her mouth. I just continued hitting her. Eventually her friend just got away and stayed back and was shouting for me to stop. Still, I continued hitting her until I had nothing left.

I stood up and looked at the multitude of people just standing by. I walked into my hallway and started crying. Tony's oldest brother walked in behind me laughing saying, "What the hell are you crying for, do you know what you just did? You beat the hell out of Sheila!" I looked at him and wondered why didn't he break the fight up, and just shook my head went back outside in front of my door, looked at the crowd and said out loud, "It never dawned on anybody to stop this six month pregnant girl from fighting?" I'm certain my likes would have been off the charts if Cell Phones, YOU TUBE, Facebook or any other social media that's out today would have existed. The title would have been "Six months pregnant girl kicks ass after bees stop flyin'."I will never understand why we enjoy violence as much as we do. It's like animals enjoying ripping people apart.

I was still trying to calm down when my mother walked up. Apparently someone with some sense went to my mother's hang out spot on Lexington Avenue that was only six short blocks away and told her that I was fighting. Becky touched my stomach looked at me and asked me was I ok, then went directly to Sheila as people were trying to comfort her, and Becky knocked her down. When Becky was about to jump on top of her a Police Officer who was supposedly dating Sheila removed her. At that moment Sheila's friend came to charge at Becky and I gave her one of Sheila's slaps in return. The Police Officer said to me that he could take me in for slapping her, and I said, "Please do because I am tired!"

I didn't get arrested. Instead, my mother had taken me to the hospital to get checked out and to get a Tetanus Shot. The Doctor said that me and my baby were fine and said that it's always good to get a Tetanus Shot when you are bitten by a person. He said that human bites are worse than animal bites. Although my scar is gone, the memory of that night was filled with both joy and pain.

After the fight I had become this conversation piece from within my neighborhood. Females were telling their friends and friends were telling their siblings and cousins not to mess with China. It was spread all throughout Nostrand Avenue or NA Rock not to mess with Bony Tony because China will kick their ass. Although I had never said that, it was the word on the streets. The funny thing was some females were coming to me telling me that my Tony tried to rap to them, and they said they couldn't because they didn't want any problems with me. Females were telling on their own sisters and friends so that they wouldn't be implicated in Tony's madness. I would walk outside and people who never spoke to me before was befriending me. All I would simply say was, "What's up!" and kept it moving, because prior to the fight everybody hated the fact that I was dating Tony.

August 1, 1982 was my due date. Instead of being in the hospital giving birth, I was hanging out in front of my door with Steph and some other friends. Tony walked up drunk, and decided he wanted to argue. Here I was nine months pregnant and the father of my child had done lost his mind. His reason for arguing with me was that I was not carrying his baby because I was due to have the baby that day. Instead, I'm out hanging in front of the door. It was rather obvious Tony had drank and smoked some crazy shit that night! I tried to defend myself but realized my stomach was bigger than my punch. It was broken up by the folks who were out there but it didn't end.

Once again somebody had got the news to my mother and within minutes she arrived. Becky threatened Tony with all of her being. She said to him that night if it wasn't for her grandchild she would have taken his life, and I believed her every word. When I got upstairs I had cried myself to sleep. The next morning when I woke up I sat up in my bed. Then I said out loud that I am having my baby today. So I decided to make a noise as if I were in Labor. Becky ran into my room and started getting me together. She called the ambulance and before I got in the ambulance I said to my girl Steph, "Go find Tony, and tell him I'm going to St. John's (Interfaith) Hospital now." My mother just shook her head but didn't say a word.

My plan had to work. At some point on that day I had to give birth. I kept moaning, and groaning. Becky stood by my side saying, "You're going to be ok, just breathe." I kept on faking with the moaning and groaning. I had even brought out some fake tears. But through it all my Mom stood by and comforted me. All of a sudden, I guess I made the wrong sound or something because the Nurse said to my mother that she had to wait in the waiting room because she was not allowed in the room they were putting me in. Next thing I knew I was having real Labor pains.

On August 2, 1982, I had given birth to a 6 pound 9 ounce beautiful healthy baby boy. The joy that I felt that day had turned me into a woman and a mother at 16 years old. I counted 10 fingers and 10 toes. His body looked perfect. His complexion was almond in color and he was someone to love. My child! A child that I knew required more than what I had growing up. I knew that I had to give love, protection, and whatever I can. All I knew was that I had to be better at parenthood than my Mom. But at that moment, I looked into my son's eyes and felt a special love between a mother and her child. Steph had gotten the message to Tony because when I looked up, he was there with my mother. Later on Tony expressed how sorry he was saying that he was simply "fucked up!"

The following day when Becky came up to visit she took a look at her grandson, then took a look at Tony, and said "Ah hell no, I gotta shape my grandbaby's head because his head will not be flat in the back" she slapped Tony on the back of his head, "like yours!" Becky literally was shaping my baby's head going around and around and around. The outcome was that our son's head was not flat in the back at all. I think what my mother had done had some effect because after all, T.J. did grow up having Tony's body. And since the head is part of the body, had it not been for my mother, he would have had his father's head as well. A mother knows best! But, it wouldn't have mattered to me either way.

Bobby had died before T.J. was born, and Becky had asked that I give T.J. Bobby's name. Although towards the end of my relationship with Bobby, things started getting crazy between us, I actually had loved Bobby. I thought he was really a cool guy for my mother considering. It was the effects of the narcotics he was on that changed him as time went on. Therefore, giving T.J. his name wasn't a problem for me. But still I knew that it was only right to ask his father. When I asked, Tony was fine with it, and added his father's name, as well, giving our son two middle names without real meaning to either one.

As you know I was very young, still unaware how to find the proper bra size or knowing that flossing played a huge part in taking care of my teeth or better yet, not knowing that I was special. In between the things that I didn't know would later have negative effects that played different roles in my very own destruction. Had I had known the importance of a name when naming my child, maybe I would have made better choices. Maybe I would have said only yes to his father's entire name which would have left out everyone else's. There is strength in a name when the name is that of someone of influence and of purpose if instilled. I got nothing from nothing, I just said yes. I understood Tony's father was an abuser, and Bobby was a user. How much power was that to instill in a male child?

"Stop crying T.J., what's wrong? What's wrong with my baby?" T.J. was about six months old when I was petrified that something was terribly wrong with him. He was screaming and wouldn't stop. We rushed him to the hospital via cab. While at the hospital, the Doctor gave us the report that T.J. had needed a Spinal Tap. I said. Okay, okay then give it to him." Becky shouted, "Oh hell no he don't! Y'all ain't givin my damn grandbaby any got damn Spinal Tap!" That's when I learned to always get a second opinion. We left St. John's (Interfaith) and went to another hospital. But on the way in the cab to the hospital, Becky explained to me and Tony how serious a Spinal Tap is and what harm it can cause. Spinal Taps have caused many cases of Paralysis in adults, so a child would have been the same if not worse.

A Lumbar Puncture (also called a Spinal Tap) is a procedure to collect and look at the fluid surrounding the brain and spinal cord. During a Lumbar Puncture, a needle is carefully inserted into the spinal column low in the back (lumbar area). Samples of cerebrospinal fluid are collected. The samples are studied for color, blood cell counts, protein, glucose, and other substances. Some of the samples may be put into a special culture cup to see if any infection, such as bacteria or fungi, grows. It is done for the purpose of identifying possible symptoms caused by an infection such as meningitis, cancer, or bleeding in the area around the brain or spinal cord.

That was a deep procedure that I knew nothing about. I thank God for my mother that day because during her life experiences a Spinal Tap was not something that anybody easily accepted as their final answer. I truly believe that my mother saved my son's life that day. Oh, and by the way, T.J.'s diagnosis was an ear infection that was resolved with antibiotics three drops per day for 10 days. Thanks Mom!

# UNBELIEVABLE

Our home had become a real home after Bobby had died. Becky and I had peace. Tony was there most of the time. And the four of us were doing all right. I think that I was actually happy. Dinner was cooked every night by one of us. And we started looking out for each other. Tony and Becky had gotten very close. Tony was a clown, and my mother was a jokester, and sometimes they even switched roles and it all worked out well.

The funny thing between Becky and Tony was how they communicated. Becky had gotten so fat when she was with Bobby and Tony had given her a new name, "Hay hay hay! It's fat Becky." When she heard Tony say that for the first time she cursed him out in a joking kind of way that you had to know them to understand. However, she had her words for Tony as well. Whenever she didn't see him in the house or when she came into the house she would say "Where's that little bony motherfucker?" And she meant no harm when saying it. They really had a different kind of relationship. Hey, they both were street hustlers, and they both knew the lingo, the look, and the ways. All I knew was that I was enjoying the moment of peace, and enjoying how the four of us were okay.

Tony was a hustler by trade. One day Tony could be selling T-shirts, one day hats, one day, blow-up type beach balloons of all different styles. He would sell whatever he purchase in bulk that he knew people liked. He had no problem selling anything because he was handsome, had a sense of humor, a charm, and he was very flamboyant in nature. Tony was so good at gambling that he would use the money from his winnings and go on 14th Street to get his supply. Depending on the season he had a reason to sell something.

During this period in our lives, Tony was still a great provider. I remember one time Tony had come in the house with a bag full of brand new sexy stiletto shoes. Becky had fallen in love with a red pair and needed a size 8. However, when she did find an eight there was only one, and then she found only one size 9. We searched the bag for the same size but there was only a size 8 and a size 9 in that particular shoe. Becky said that it didn't matter to her, because when she put them on both shoes had fit her feet perfectly. We cracked up and Tony had given her a new name "One-Size-Fits-All" By this time, Becky had lost weight, and was looking good, and with her red pair of stilettos she was quite sexy with her new look and she knew it.

This was truly an amazing time in my life, Becky had for the first time seemed to have been trying as a mother to get it right. Sure she still hung out, and drank. But her behavior was well with me. She continued to help me take care of T.J., and teach me things that she thought I should know. When T.J. started talking he called Becky *Grandma Becky* and stayed with that name even as he grew. I enjoyed our late nights when we would stay awake watching TV in her room often laying across her bed then eventually falling to sleep together on some nights. Our favorite shows were **"Colombo"**, and **"Dynasty."** We even had a preparation before our shows would come on. If she didn't bring a box of cereal in with her, she would send me to the store for a box of Raisin Bran. For some reason Becky and I preferred breakfast at night, and I still do. Guess old habits are hard to break.

There was this one occasion when Becky had sent me out to the store to get a box of cereal. I went to the corner store, grabbed a box of Raisin Bran hurried up and came upstairs. Before I was able to eat my cereal, I had to do one last thing. Becky couldn't wait so she started eating before me. When I was about to pour my cereal, the box was almost empty. I said jokingly, "Now you know you ain't right! You ate almost the entire box of cereal, lady." I looked at my mother who was sucking her thumb sitting up in her bed looking like she was in her glory. All I can do at that moment was smile. I was just happy that we were together. However, I decided to see if I can possibly get at least a small bowl out of the box. I poured the cereal, and poured the milk and watched how another ingredient other than raisins would turn me off from Raisin Brand for many years to follow.

"Ooh, Ooh, Ooh! I'm so glad you were the taste tester and the greedy one. Maybe you should get "***Colombo***" to solve the case of "*Who put the ants in the box?*" Becky said "What you talkin' bout girl?" I brought my bowl of cereal to her and said if my small bowl have hundreds of ants floating in it, then your large three bowls had to have had millions!" She said, "What the hell!" I told her that it must have tasted like flavored raisins coated in chocolate because she never had eaten almost a whole box before. Becky told me to bring the box to her, and showed me that I had purchased an expired box of Raisin Bran. She wasn't even upset with me, she just told me to check the dates next time when purchasing anything, and that she would never eat in the dark again. However, she did say that's why it is always good to pray over your food so God can bless it. Afterwards, we just enjoyed our time watching our shows with an occasional laugh or two about the extra "raisins."

Still, Tony would be up to his old tricks. The day started out beautifully. As the evening followed, Tony decided to prepare a new dish for dinner. BBQ turkey wings, string beans, rice and corn bread. The apartment smelled like a soul food restaurant in Harlem. We couldn't wait for dinner. Tony had stepped out while allowing the turkey wings to simmer in what he called his "special sauce." He asked Becky to take them out within one hour. Becky had decided a meal like that required dessert so I had gone to the corner store to get some Hagen Daz Butter Pecan ice cream.

Before I could get across the street, a young lady about my age being 19 at the time approached me acting like a nervous wreck. I was looking at her like she was crazy. The girl started babbling, "No lie China, I didn't know! I didn't know! For real China, I didn't have nuttin' to do wid it. I told my cousin not to mess wid him. I told my cousin that he had a girlfriend, and a child. So when you see dem together, ask ha, ask ha China that I told ha 'bout you." I said to myself what the hell! I didn't know if I wanted to laugh, or ask questions because she was funny as hell.

When I came out of the store, a small crowd surfaced. Then the same girl said "China dere he is, he comin right now." To Tony's surprise, I was right in his face looking at him holding hands with this new chick. He didn't expect me to be outside since he left me in the house waiting for dinner. I'm glad my mother wanted some dessert. When he saw me, of course, he immediately let go of the girl's hand, and the girl had caught an attitude. I waited just to hear what she had to say and it was hilarious. "Why you's let go of my hand fo', um yo' girl now. I don't care about any Bitches!" Everybody cleared the way as if I was Oprah Winfrey in The Color Purple getting ready to hit the white woman. Tony even started babbling suggesting that the only thing she did for him was oral sex and that was it. Of course he said it the other way but I'm sure you all get it. Well to everyone's surprise, I didn't do the expected. I simply told the girl to please not to say anything else to me because it wasn't about her.

And before she can say anything else somebody immediately removed the girl from my presence. I took one look at Tony, and said, "Get your shit out of my house right now!" He started to curse me out, and out of nowhere a Rasta guy said, "Is everting good China, ya want I do sumffin fa ya?" Hell he scared me. Anyone who was there could plainly see that this guy was strapped and very dangerous, and I didn't know who he was but he knew me. I looked at him and said, "Na, I'm good. Thanks!" And Tony immediately kept it moving, and went up to my house to get his things.

I stood on the corner talking for a little while with the young lady who had warned me about the situation. She called her cousin over and said that she was the one she was talking about. Well, the young lady and I started chatting, and she said that she didn't know that it was me, and that she apologizes. She also had said that Tony had told her that he didn't have a girlfriend. An hour must have passed by and I looked over to my left and seen Tony walking up the block with a shopping cart with all of his belongings. Of course I was hurt and feeling sad. But I was also getting fed up. But even at that moment, every feeling that I was experiencing was all going to disappear when I bit into those BBQ turkey wings, green beans, rice, and corn bread. But first I knew that I had better not come upstairs with melted ice cream so I went inside the store and changed it.

When I walked into the house I can still smell the aroma. Oh, I was ready to go in! Becky was standing in the kitchen sucking her thumb looking satisfied, shaking her head and cracking up at the same time. I said to her, "Tony is crazy, but I'll fill you in after I suck down dinner." Becky started laughing even harder. While I was washing my hands, I was thinking she was laughing at whatever Tony might have said while he was packing. But to my surprise the joke was on me. I went to fix my food. I put the rice on my plate. I put the green beans on top of my rice. I cut me a big chunk of corn bread, and I went into the oven to get me some BBQ turkey wings and they were gone!

I looked at Becky and frantically said, "Where's the turkey wings?" Still sucking her thumb she said, "Girl, I don't know what the hell happened outside, but when Tony came in here, he got his shit, and grabbed his BBQ turkey wings and said "I guess I can at least enjoy my wings!" But luckily, while y'all were out there arguing, I saw y'all. I was in here eating. Damn those turkey wings were good!" I said, "The damn man took the wings out of the freakin' oven? Now that's a damn shame!"

That was just some of the foolishness that Tony and I went through. I have seven years of stories I could tell, and probably would have you laughing and or crying with me throughout every one. But through it all he was my first love. I was glad that my mother was there to help me get through that moment when Tony and I had broken up. Becky and I laughed a lot. She even hung out with me and my best friend Steph at our favorite spot the OASIS Lounge on Bedford Avenue. We were at a good place together. But I be damned, all good things come to an end! Now I got to put up with Inmate 000019820A who would now invade our space.

Rick was his name. He was an attractive brown skin old timer with a slick charismatic style that could fool any woman of a certain type in need of a man. Rick dressed to impress, and had a walk that was slick and sly. He wore his clothes well. He was about 5'9" weighing approximately 200 pounds, right. Rick knew how to bring it, and he brought it to my mother. Rick was also the only person that I have ever known that I actually hated.

Although my hate for Rick was growing, he and T.J. had exceptional love for one another, and I had never come in between their relationship, it was unique. And I never believed in putting children between adults' disagreements. It's just not fair to the child. Their relationship was the cutest relationship ever. What I remember most was that in the mornings T.J. would wake up, get out of the bed and go into my mother's room, bypass her and go to Rick and literally open his eyes with his tiny little fingers, and shout out "Rick! Rick!" Rick would open his eyes, see T.J. smiling at him and laugh. Then he would say "Good morning potner, how's my little man doing, you hungry? Let me get on up and fix something for my little man here."

It didn't stop there, Rick would go into the bathroom, brush his teeth, wash his face while T.J. would look up at him, and mimic everything Rick would do down to urinating properly. This was how my son learned how to go to the bathroom on his own. He learned by watching Rick which meant potty training was very easy for me. Then I would watch how T.J. would reach out for Rick's hand leading him into the kitchen. During this time Rick would share some kind of dialogue with T.J. that somehow created a breakfast that only they would enjoy.

My comfort was met through observation which never aroused any suspicion in me regarding the love that Rick had for my son. Trust me, I was an observing mother and I'm certain that it had a lot to do with my past. And because of my past, T.J. was given some early lessons on his privacy and what it means and what to do once invaded. I took that very serious. As you all could understand.

I had found out that Rick had spent some time being locked up because he too was a "hustler" of some kind. It didn't matter to me then that he had done some time, but what did matter was what he brought into our home. Rick had a dialogue that I had never heard. "Ah, ay uh Joyce did you ah, go in this here ah, bag? Ah, these things in this here bag is minz, and ah, it's per son al. Ah, that's why it's in a bag and thangz. So, when you see stuff like dis here, don't open it because like I said it's minz!" I said, "What the hell are you talking about? Are you kidding me? How in the hell is free cheese, free butter, and free got damn bread that I stood on line and got yours? What gives you the right to come into this house and start claiming shit that ain't yours?" He actually followed up by saying, "Ah due to the discombobulating, to the constipulation based on the situation, and thangz, ah because I live here, gives me the right to claim anythang in these here ah bagz." Really, I wish you would have heard how this man actually spoke. True story!

My mouth was fresh when it needed to be as you already know. "You are one ignorant bastard. You be using words that you don't even know the meaning to. Words that don't even make any got damn sense! I can tell you came straight out of prison you jackass! Comin' in here wrappin' food up, calling shit yours. Becky, I don't know where you found this cat at, but you can shore send his psychotic ass back! Let me get out of this house before I lose my mind." Before I would walk out of the door, I would tell the both of them to keep an eye on T.J. while he was asleep.

This type of communication went on between Rick and I for about a year. And I was to the point that I couldn't take it anymore. Every day we argued about food that was stored inside bags. Our refrigerator looked like a homeless person's shopping cart that was filled with bags, bottles, trash, and personals.

It didn't stop at just the food. I had to get a job because Rick had pumped my mother up to start asking me for $200.00 a month for rent, although our rent for the apartment was only $216.00 a month. Becky and Rick's relationship had started a whole new ballgame in the house. Once again, the drug style had changed, and their behavior was even more bizarre. I accepted the position at Wendy's Downtown Brooklyn on Fulton Street. I was given the early bird shift which was opening at 7:00 am and off at 12 pm. I figured since T.J. normally slept till 8:30, and wakes Rick up for breakfast, shortly after I would come straight home and resume my motherly duties. This way with my Welfare Check and the earnings that I received from work would help me temporarily through this path called life.

It wasn't Smokey Robinson's fault, but I don't care if I ever hear another one of his songs ever again. Every night since Rick moved in, between the hours of 10 pm and 4 am, Rick and my mother decided to clean the house blasting **"Being With You"** by Smokey Robinson. They played every one of his songs, but **"Being With You"** stood out the most. It was obvious that Rick was a Smokey Robinson fan, and maybe my mother was too at that point. I do understand that every woman of my mother's age was in love with Smokey. Such a beautiful song had turned ugly within my spirit.

My bedroom was next to the living room where my bed leaned against the wall. Directly on the other side was my stereo. The speakers that Rick had put into the drop ceiling would vibrate the entire apartment, which meant my head was also vibrating. I couldn't take it one night as I tossed and turned in my bed. All I kept seeing was the hours of the night going by and I had to be up in two more hours to go to work. I got up and started slamming doors, and sucking my teeth trying to give off a hint that I couldn't sleep. It didn't seem to bother T.J., because he slept right through it. I couldn't believe it. So

I spazzed out! I grabbed T.J.'s yellow hard plastic bat that was in the corner of my bedroom, and I went into the living room and started swinging at the stereo until it was completely trashed. Then I pulled Rick's speakers from the drop ceiling and said. "You fuckin' idiot!" Sure I got cursed out, but at the end of the day, my mission was accomplished.

Rick's favorite name to call me was *"Baby Huey"* which I didn't know the meaning of during that time. I just knew that I hated him calling me that. However, later on when I did the research on finding out what or who a *"Baby Huey"* was, I had disliked Rick even more. Baby Huey is described as a gigantic and naïve duckling cartoon character that was created by a gentleman by the name of Martin Taras. When I saw the picture of the duck I had actually laughed and said out loud, "Rick was a jackass!"

# PASS IT LISA

Sam was old as hell. He must have been about 60 years old and I was still 19. He was like an old fast talking slickster who a female in need could easily fall prey if they wanted a sugar daddy. Supposedly he was single, I didn't really believe guys at this point in my life, but I was sure ready to play them. I guess I had picked up some skills along the way from my everyday people. Sam had his own apartment in the projects down by Tillary Street in Brooklyn. And I was going through pure hell with my on again/off again relationship with Tony. I was tired of Tony being on the narcotic, and the drinking. I was tired of Rick with his psychotic ass. I wanted out! I simply wanted to take my son and get a freekin' life and I thought Sam was my ticket out.

Sam would ask me what did I need and how he could help me. So I didn't hesitate to say what I needed. I said get me and my son out of my mother's house before I go crazy. And then I think I had adapted a real way of not giving a damn what had came out of my mouth. I looked that man straight in his face and said, "And what is your old ass doing talking to me anyway. What, you want to be my sugar daddy?" He said he could be whatever I wanted him to be. He wanted to know what has gotten me all upset and said he could help me. At that moment all I wanted to do was eat something that didn't require me to open up another plastic bag. So I said to Sam, you can start off by feeding me because I'm hungry.

I hopped inside Sam's car, and he took me to the Chinese restaurant in downtown Brooklyn. Hell if I knew he was going to buy me Chinese, he could have just let me walk across the street from my house. This way he could have saved on gas. But I figured I would see how this was going to play out. I started laughing when he acted as if he was spending big bucks when he said, "Order wad you want, girl. Sam here is gonna take good care of you. Order wad ya want, girl." I know I had adapted a few names already but girl wasn't one of them. So I figured I better correct this man now because I didn't like it. I said, "I did tell you my name was Lisa?" He said, "Oh yeah, yeah, yeah, Lisa! I remember it's Lisa!" I never had another issue with the name again.

At that moment I felt like I can do this with Sam. That is to play him to get what I needed. I still wanted somebody to take care of me. I often wondered was I allowing myself to move forward with Sam because he reminded me of a father figure. Someone I had wished I had to take care of me. Sam watched me eat my food with enjoyment. I believe from that he thought he had this young girl in the palm of his hands. So of course, he started touching me and smiling. I had given him such a look, that if he touched me again without me inviting him to touch me, I was going to cut him. So Sam removed his hand and gave me a half smile.

When I was getting out of Sam's car, Sam literally had me cracking up by the way he spoke to me. "Lisa, dis is wad I want you to do on da morra. You come down stairs at 12 o'clock wid yo son and wut not, and umma be here watin' fo ya. Umma take you 'n da boy grocery shoppin so you can get some groceries. Den umma take you n him ta ma house 'n show yuz where you 'n him gon live. See Lisa, I told ya, umma take care a ya. Den da next day, you can go 'n pick out some furniture 'n wut not. Now come here n giv ya daddy some suga, 'n get on upstairs." I was so excited I said, "Really?" jumped out of the car without giving him any "suga" and said, "See you tomorrow!" He got away with smacking me on my ass though, shouting out the window saying, "Hey Lisa, don't hav me down here waitin' on ya either. I said 12 o' clock be down here!" with a little aggression added to it.

I was off from work the next day and I was ready to rock 'n roll. I had left T.J. with Rick because I didn't know if I would have to cut Sam or not so I played it safe going alone. After grocery shopping Sam walks me through his apartment showing me what he was offering. Sam said, "Dis here (pointing to the empty bedroom) can be da boy room. We can get some ah furniture fo it on da morra." I'm smiling at that moment because T.J. can have his own room. "Dis here is our room ya see it already got a bed so we don't need much mo furniture in here. We gon be usin' dat today too affer you put the food away and cook us suffin' to eat. You don had me food shoppin' and now I wanna eat and lay down fo awhile. Now gon and take care of dat in the kitchen."

I had noticed a pair of women's shoes in the corner on the floor but I didn't say anything. I also didn't say anything about the way he just spoke to me because I was still trying to take it all in. Besides, I was starving and I wanted to cook so that I could eat as well.

"Ay Lisa, make me da sausage, grits wid some cheese, some eggs wid some onion n green peppa. And cook some biscit too. I don't know wad you want, but dat's wad I want." After I finished cooking, I fixed our plates, brought the food to the table and sat down. Before I can put anything in my mouth Sam started his mess. "Lisa go get me some ketchup out da ah cabinet." I got up and got the ketchup and brought it to the table and sat down again. "Lisa go get me da ah hot sauce. Dat dere is in da cabinet too." I got up retrieved the hot sauce, brought it to the table and sat down again. "Lisa I need some butta fo ma grits, go and get the butta. Yeah, I like ma grits wid lots a butter." I got up, I went into the refrigerator brought out the tub of butter sat it on the table and gave Sam a look that showed a woman who was fed up. "Lisa, why didn't you pit ice in the awj juice? I want some ice. Go on in da kitchen and get some ice so ma juice can be good and cold. I can see I got's to train you suffin good!"

Apparently Sam didn't know the look. I got up, went into the kitchen, I got the ice and put some in a glass, and brought it to the table. Then I said. "Here is your juice you old ass bastard." I poured it on his head. "You think you were dealing with a stupid chick? You and that damn Rick must be related, you're just an older version. You got to be out your got damn mind if you thought for a minute you were gonna have me as your slave taking care of your old ass." Sam got ready to get out of his chair. I pushed his frail ass right back down, picked up the knife that was on the table, and in a threatening voice I said, "Sit down, old man, because you don't want this!" I grabbed a few pieces of bacon from off my plate. I grabbed my pocketbook and walked out of Sam's apartment. I had never turned back and I had never seen Sam again. However, now I know to bring or ask what condiments and what beverage the other person needs with their meal before sitting down.

# LOVE PREVAILS

So of course my crazy life continued but now Tony and I were seeing if we could work it out once again. He came with the pleading, with the gifts, with the serenading, with his charm, and not to mention his fine self. And of course, I was once again open to a love that I obviously didn't want to end. We were determined at that moment to make it work. T.J. was 3 years old, and I had to get out of that house with Rick and my mother.

November 16, 1984. It was Becky's birthday. Actually it was my mother's, my sister Sherlene, my grandmother and my stepfather Lem's birthday. Thus, it was also a day in 1984 that Tony and I would pound the pavement until we found an apartment. So our journey started from 8 am to midnight; Tony and I searched for an apartment and we didn't stop until someone had given us a yes. When T.J.'s little legs had gotten tired, Tony picked him up and carried him on his shoulders. Finally at midnight it happened. A Super of a building on Pacific and Nostrand Avenue had showed us an apartment, and said if we had wanted it it was ours for the taking with a rental agreement of $325.00 a month bringing it to $650.00 with the Security. He said if we can give him $325.00 at that moment to secure the apartment and the other half for Security by December 1st, the apartment was ours. I had $100 to give while Tony put down the $225.00. I had started crying because of the joy I was feeling about getting our own apartment.

On the way home Tony and I were laughing and talking about where we were going to buy furniture, and what color our bedroom was going to be. We were so happy. We couldn't wait to get home and tell Becky the good news. Now Rick can blast his music, they can get high all throughout the entire apartment, and Rick can unleash the food that was inside his plastic bags. On the way upstairs I grabbed T.J. from Tony and asked him to go to the store and get me a Pink Champ Ale. I walked through the door shouting, "Beck-ay! Beck- ay!"

Becky heard the excitement in my voice and came running out of her room. She was also excited because it was also the day that I would normally give her the second half of her rent, knowing that she and Rick used it to get high with. But to her surprise, the money that I had went to the Super as a down payment for an apartment.

Becky said, "What girl, what you all excited about?" I said, "Tony and I found an apartment tonight. And guess what, we are moving out December 1st. I know you're happy were leaving." Becky turned away from me, and walked into her bedroom. I went into my room and started taking T.J.'s clothes off saying to myself that that was odd. I heard her and Rick arguing but I couldn't make it out because he talked retarded to me. Next thing I knew Becky came back in a rage. She grabbed me by my neck, lifted me up from the floor and literally pinned me to my bedroom closet allowing her nails to penetrate the skin on my neck.

She started shouting out repeatedly, "You gonna pay me my rent Bitch! You gonna pay me my rent!" I was repeating my question asking her what was wrong with her, and to get off of me. She just kept shouting "Where is my rent money?" I thought I needed to get her out of her trance by saying. "It's me, Becky. Joyce, your daughter Stop it!" Tony walked in and shouted out, "Yo. Beck, what the hell is going on? Get off of her. That's China Beck!" Rick decided to come in the room and had the audacity to tell Tony, "Ah ah, you should stay adda dis potner, this don't have nuffin to do wid you ah." Tony said, "You sound like a got damn fool." When Tony was about to help get my mother off of me, Rick went to grab Tony's hand. Tony punched him and somehow got him in the hallway pushed him down the stairs and locked the door so we can work out the madness.

The pain had become too much when I looked over at T.J. watching all this madness crying. I grabbed Becky's hands and took them from off my neck. In doing so, I pushed her onto my bed. Then she shouted. "Oh you wanna fight now huh Bitch! You wanna fight?" I said to my mother that I will never put my hands on her. I just had to stop her from hurting me. She

# HANDLE IT

continued to be in a rage but calmed down enough for me and Tony to pack up some things while she was shouting, "Get the fuck out of my house, and don't leave nothing behind!" We grabbed what we could carry leaving behind everything T.J. and I owned. But that was the way it had to be I guess.

Tony and I didn't know where we would go that night with our son. We didn't have any more money because we had given it all to the Super. So we went to his mother's house on Pacific Street. Tony told his mother what had happened, but during that time she didn't really pay us any mind because that was during a time when she would get pissy drunk off of Path Mark beer. Really! She would get so drunk and curse you out until it was funny. Fortunately, Sylvia was very good to me. She stopped drinking a short time later, but initially she was hilarious!

The next day Tony and I decided to come to the house to get the rest of T.J. and my belongings only to see what wasn't sold was out on the curb for everyone to see. I stood there looking at the trash and how our things were set out, and I cried. I cried inside. I kept my tears to myself and I cried. Thankfully, I didn't bring T.J. because he would have probably tried to pull out his toys that were visibly in the garbage. I think that moment for me was more painful than when my mother spazzed out on me the night before. But it cut me and I felt the same pain when I told Becky what Thomas had done and she said or did nothing. I sucked up my silent tears, gathered up my emotions, took another look and handled it!

Tony continued to hustle so that we could get the money we needed for the apartment. On December 1$^{st}$, we were told that the Super had given the apartment to someone else. Apparently, someone had paid underneath the table. During that time that type of deal was done often. Tony and I were now introduced to it. Our down payment was returned to us, and we were back at square one. I was devastated. But still, it didn't take long for things to get worse. During my short stay at Sylvia's house Tony's drug and violent behavior started getting worse. Tony was now heavy on Crack Cocaine. Sylvia had loved me so much that she was willing for T.J. and me to stay at her house but would no longer allow Tony to come inside. I felt bad because that was his mother and no matter what I loved Tony and I wanted him to have somewhere to stay. So I thought if T.J. and I left, then Tony would be let in. I decided to take charge of my life and let the Welfare office know that

I was homeless and we needed somewhere to live. So at the age of twenty I would embark on another journey that no young girl should have had to go through especially with a four year old child.

# THE SYSTEM

Tony decided if I were to go through the system with our son, then he would go through it with us. He said in no way we were going down that road of homelessness without him. I was so glad because what we endured, I am certain that I couldn't have done the beginning stages without him. We went to my Welfare Center on Flatbush Avenue in Brooklyn. I was placed as the Head of Household on my case with Tony and T.J.. We were instructed to go to the EAU which is the acronym for the "Emergency Assistance Unit" on Willoughby and Dekalb Avenue.

EAU was a place where families would wait in a small space for a Social Worker to call their name letting them know where they would be placed for only one night. This step would repeat on the next day unless it was a Friday and you would then be placed for the weekend. It was shameful, demeaning, hideous, ridiculous and repetitious only to be mistreated by the workers that were there to supposedly help you. Everyday families had to come and repeat the steps all over again with their children and with all of their belongings.

The way it was done was that all family members had to be at their assigned Welfare Centers by 9 am. Your Case Manager would call you at 4:45 pm and hand you a check for food for a day and a referral to report back to EAU that evening. EAU would then have you sit there until 1 to 4 am, and they will give you tokens to get to the hotel and to return to your Welfare Center in the morning. They would also give a check to give to the Hotel Manager. The small hotels had gotten converted to being Welfare Hotels because of the amount of money they would get per person to house homeless families. These hotels benefited more by accepting families for only one night at a time, and our great city allowed it. However, if it were a Friday night the family was accepted for the weekend. Either way these people were getting paid.

The city paid these hotels $2,300 per person for one night a total of $6,900 for my family. These hotels or motels were often smelly, rat infested, and often very far from EAU. The smaller hotels chose the one night scam. And the larger Welfare Hotels preferred the big check for a stay up until 28 days at a time. I could never figure out why a person on Public Assistance was only given $215.00 per month to rent an apartment regardless of their family size. Yet, pay foreigners so much money to house homeless families temporarily. And still, it has not changed it is simply done differently. I didn't understand it then, and I still cannot understand the politics in terms of housing in this present day.

Often times we were sent to the Bronx, or Queens far out which always required us taking a train and a bus. And by the time we got to some of the rat infested hotels, it was time enough to bathe, change and return to the Welfare Center. Traveling to these hotels late and early morning Tony would carry T.J. on his shoulders while carrying a bag in one hand and holding T.J.'s legs with the other. For some reason they kept sending us to this particular hotel that was by the Belt Parkway in Queens. Traveling to this hotel had gotten to be a bit too much for us. The buses would stop running after a certain time and we would have to walk a very long way from the subway at 3 or sometimes 4 0'clock in the morning. The hotel was cleaner than the others but it was just too far. So I asked and I suggested to the owner if EAU were to mention my name to stay here I strongly suggest that you tell them no! Tell them that you will not accept Joyce Harriet and family ever again.

Well, of course the owner paid me no attention, because the amount of money he would receive spoke more volume than my quiet threat. We were sent there again, and this time before we left the room we literally destroyed it! We destroyed the walls, stopped up the toilet, cut up the mattress, cut up the carpet, and marked up the windows. Never again were we accepted to that hotel. As a matter of fact, the Social Worker at EAU had asked me what happened because of the way we were denied when they had spoken to somebody at the hotel. My response was simply, "I have no idea what you're talking about."

With that hotel being out of the picture, now we were only being sent to the rat trap where you can smell the rats as soon as you walked into the hotel. We had to go because if we didn't, EAU wouldn't serve us and we had to go along with this game for a minimum of 30 days. So we made the journey, gave the owner the check, about faced and went to the Welfare Center because it wouldn't be long before they would open. We would rest inside the Welfare Center because we knew that we would sit there all day. Because spending the night at the rat infested hotel wasn't an option. I did vow that me living among rats was over during the time when I was watching **"*Roots*"**.

It was a usual day for me at the Welfare Center. I was fed up, angry, and exhausted. I had looked at my child and felt horrible as a mother. My Case Worker came out to see if my entire household was together because if not she wouldn't have assisted us. It appeared that they all had taken pleasure watching family's lug their belongings and their crying babies just to sit there and wait for services. But this day my worker decided to call me in separately and sit at her desk. She wanted some more information, and she needed to give me additional paperwork. But during that time she also decided to give me attitude as if I had messed her life up, and the checks that she had to give me for food was coming out of her pocket. At that moment I decided I had had about enough!

My face got twisted while my heart was hurting. My eyes were red from lack of sleep. I looked at that woman and said in an angry stern voice, "Do you have 'any,' I mean 'any,' idea of what my family and I have been through?" She was about to say something and I shook my head letting her know that it still wasn't her time to speak. I continued and said, "Do you know what it feels like to be 'stripped' of everything? 'Stripped' of your womanhood without consenting? 'Stripped' of your happiness without thought? 'Stripped' out of a child hood? 'Stripped' out of your home? And now you think you can 'strip' me out of my dignity? Do you have any got damn idea? Because sweetheart if you 'ever,' and I do mean 'ever,' talk to me that way again, you are going to be 'stripped' of your life!" Then I sat back down and looked in her face. That woman looked at me in a daze for about five seconds and said, "I'll be right back!" I didn't care where she went or who she would tell, I was at a dangerous place in my mind.

"Ms. Brown here's your checks not 'check' here are the checks for you and your family. You are receiving a food allowance check, a check for carfare, and a check that you were due before but somehow didn't receive it. Also, I am sending you and your family to the Carter Hotel that is on 43$^{rd}$ and 8$^{th}$ Avenue in Manhattan. It is a permanent hotel that you and your family can stay there until you obtain housing. I wish you and your family the best and I am sorry!"

Have a good day Ms. is what I said leaving from her presence. And when I got to Tony and T.J., I couldn't wait to blurt out the good news. Now we were on our way towards stability. When we reached to the address, the building had looked like something straight out of the movie **"New Jack City"** and I was certain that there were some *"Neno Browns."* We moved right in the heart of the sale of Crack Cocaine, babies being sold, women screaming, babies crying, people stealing, it was a war zone. I would find out later that it was the worse and the largest city welfare hotel in history. I didn't blame the Case Worker because she wouldn't have known that. I believe that she thought she was helping by sending us somewhere permanent. But, oh my God, we were literally in the heart of hell. And it wasn't a place for a 19 year old girl with a three year old child, and a man who was at the beginning of a Crack Cocaine journey.

"Dis yo key Ms. You be in room 1808, and don't lose dis cause if you do, you gotta pay $10 to get anodder key. Go dat away towards the elebator." I looked at Tony and T.J. and headed towards the elevator. When we had gotten to our floor the hallway went in three directions, and the hallway was extremely long. The Carter Hotel had taken up an entire city block on both sides. Then some guy in a wheelchair with a Spanish accent asked what number we were looking for. Tony said in his humorous Spanish like voice "Poppy we looking for 1808." The guy said, "I know everydig da happens here. You lucky, you lucky! Dis you rite here. You's rite next to me. Come rite here." I didn't know if I should be afraid or safe because this guy was plainly carrying a shot gun while sitting in his wheelchair.

"You don't have to wordy about nuttin while you stay here. I patrol the hallway cause dese people rob quick. Dey crazy! Dey don't come bodda me cuz dey know I shoot dead. So you family no wordy okay, I say no wordy! You come you go, you sleep, no wordy. My name is Hector and you can call me Hector. Ok, welcome." Well, we introduced ourselves and that was that for the moment. I had to take all that in.

It wasn't long before I couldn't tolerate Tony. Maybe it was because of my pregnancy. I had just found out that I was five weeks pregnant, and I was devastated. Tony was already deep into the narcotic, and there were plenty of days that I didn't see him. Tony would stay out when he wanted and return when he wanted, sometimes returning high as hell. I couldn't have that around T.J.. I hated being around drunks and druggies as a child, and now I must subject my child to his father being high on Crack Cocaine and or often being drunk. Nah, I couldn't do that! It wouldn't be fair to T.J. So I decided to once again give up on us.

I thought about the situation that I was in, being homeless and pregnant. How I was barely able to provide for T.J. and myself. I thought about how I would take T.J. to nearby soup kitchens on 45th Street at a church to get food to take back with us. I thought about my life. I thought about what kind of parent I was becoming and bringing another child into this situation. I thought about us living in the worst Welfare Hotel where babies are being sold for crack cocaine. I thought about how hustlers were turning young girls into prostitutes. I thought about how I grew up. I didn't know what to do, so I had an abortion remembering the words of my mother.

I remember being told that it wasn't a baby and that it was just a clog of blood during the stage I was at. Then everything else was a rush and they got right to it. When I woke up I was placed in a room with other recoveries with tea and crackers alongside of me. I was told to drink, eat and get dressed. I did just that and left. I never thought about it again during those times. As a matter of fact, in my ignorance, I too had given the advice to others to have an abortion when I thought they shouldn't have their baby. The good thing was that no one listened to me.

I was sitting on my bed watching ***"The Jeffersons."*** T.J. was asleep, and there was a knock on the door. I got up to answer it passing the kitchen area and asked, "Who is it?" Hector the hallway patrolman said, "Mommy it's ok, it's u husband!" After three days of being away from us, Tony returns high and smelly. We stood by the sink which was our makeshift kitchen area and I said to him that he had to leave because he was no longer welcome to stay here. I told Tony that I no longer wanted the life that he was offering me and T.J..

"But I need you." he said. "I love you. I don't want you to leave me. If you leave me I will die." I told Tony that he loved that narcotic more than us, and while I'm out chasing him, he's chasing crack. Then he decided to take things further by saying if I were going to leave him, he would take the pills that was on the shelf above the sink. I don't remember what kind of pills they were, but it was probably some kind of antibiotic due to some infection that he had given me.

He said it again "China umma take these pills," and then he tossed his head back and threw the pills in his mouth. I shook my head and I turned on the water put some in a glass and gave it to Tony so the fool can wash all the pills he had just taken down. Then I walked to my bed and sat down just in time for George Jefferson to do his famous stiffing off dance. Tony came and sat on the bed next to me. I tried ignoring him while continuing to watch George and laugh. And then there was a loud thump! The fool had fallen off my bed unto the floor. I called security to call the ambulance because we didn't have an outside line. I explained what happened and the ambulance took him away to Bellevue Hospital. T.J. had slept through the entire thing.

# SOMETHING'S GOT TO GIVE

The next day I was watching TV and a program came on about Job Corps. It said "If you are a high school drop- out and you are between the ages of sixteen to twenty one, come to Job Corps where you can get your GED, a trade, job placement and receive clothing money and a weekly stipend. This is a two year program where you can get started today." I had definitely fit the description since I had dropped out of high school in the 10$^{th}$ grade. I looked over at T.J. and I smiled. Then I asked for an outside line and I called immediately.

Joyce- "Hello?"

Receptionist - "Hello, how may I help you?"

Joyce – "I would like to apply for Job Corps. When can I start?"

Receptionist – "Well first young lady, I would need you to come in and speak to one of our recruiters, and they will help you with that information."

Joyce – "Can I come in today?"

Receptionist – "Today is too late, but I do have an opening for tomorrow. What time would you like to come?"

Joyce – "What time do you open?"

Receptionist – "We open at 8:30 in the morning."

Joyce – "I'll be there at 8:30."

The Receptionist gave me the details regarding location and the documents needed.

Joyce – "Hello Sir,"

Recruiting person – "Hello young lady my name is Mr. Mack, and you are Joyce, correct?"

Joyce – "Yes! How soon can we leave?"

Mr. Mack laughs and gestures with his hands for me to slow down.

Mr. Mack – "Slow down young lady. First I must get some information from you for assessment. Then we will go from there. And what do you mean "we" young lady?"

Joyce – "I have a four year old son and I love him very much. We live in a welfare hotel. So, I want to do this and get it over with so I can take care of my son."

Mr. Mack - "OK Joyce, here is the thing; I can help you with a few things. But first I must tell you that we do not have a mother and child program."

Joyce – "I can't take my son with me? Never mind then forget it!"

Mr. Mack – "Wait, wait! Joyce, wait a second. Let me tell you the rest of the news. It's a two year program. You can finish the program sooner it is up to you. You can use your stipend to go home to see your son every weekend. We give you a check to purchase clothing, and a weekly stipend. You can use some of the money to take your son out when you go home for the weekend."

Joyce – "Mr. Mack, I don't have a home to go to! So please stop saying that! Look, did you say I can complete the program in less time? And if I do, they will help me get a job?"

Mr. Mack – "Yes Joyce! You are correct!"

Joyce – "If I get somebody to take care of my son can I leave tomorrow?"

Mr. Mack – "Oh, that's too soon. Paperwork has to be done and …"

Joyce – "Well how soon, Mr. Mack? Just tell me how soon!"

Mr. Mack – "The site that has a vacancy now seems to be Delaware Valley Job Corps Center which is located in Monticello, NY and if you bring in all your documents including who you are assigning temporary custody to, Joyce we can have you there in one week!"

# HANDLE IT

Joyce – "Wonderful, what all do I need?"

China – "Hi Sylvia, I signed up for Job Corps and I was wondering can you please take care of my son until I'm done? I will come to get him as much as I can on the weekends. And I will finish the program as quick as I can. Will you please take good care of him for me?"

Sylvia – "Yes, I will! And you let me know if you need anything while you're there. I love you China!"

China – "I love you too, and thank you so much! I have to bring a paper for you to fill out stating that you will take only temporary custody of him. I'll see you later."

Joyce- "Hey Sherlene, I'm going to Job Corps next week, and I was wondering if I can come stay with you on some weekends when I come out to visit T.J.."

Sherilene – "Yeah, I don't care."

Joyce – "OK, thanks! Talk to you later."

 And that's how it all went down. Sylvia helped me out tremendously. In all honesty Sylvia was there for me financially, mentally and for support. By this time she had stopped drinking. Not only did she take care of my son, her grandchild, but she would send me money, and packages. Even when I came home from Job Corps on the weekends I would help her where she volunteered at giving away clothing. I used to return to Job Corps with some nice pieces and shoes to match them. Sylvia was very good to me, and I had learned a great deal from her over the years. She was very knowledgeable and quite the thinker. I enjoyed those moments of playing Scrabble with her never being able to beat her, but instead I was learning from her intelligence of word choices. In all honesty I truly love Sylvia, and still.

 I was amazed when I had come home one weekend and Tony had surprised me. He had gotten an on-the-books job as a Messenger working in Manhattan around 34$^{th}$ Street. We went and hung out on 42$^{nd}$ Street and went to the movies and out to dinner that night. Next thing I knew Tony had proposed to me with a diamond ring. The diamond wasn't huge but it was given to me from the love of my life which made it the biggest diamond in the world. He had apologized for his ways and bad habits and told me how much he loved me and wouldn't want to live without me. Of course I had accepted and now we were on a new beginning once again. And I was excited. I returned to Job Corps twenty years old and engaged.

During my stay at Job Corps, I had met some cool people, but I had to stay focused. My only plan was to get my GED, a trade and get to my son. And I knew I couldn't get caught up with anything else. I needed to be there to watch and take care of T.J. So every day and every night I would talk to him asking him how he was really doing if you know what I mean. I was still on top of things although very far away. Truthfully, I never would have suspected anything perverted happening from Tony's family, but I had learned trust didn't come easy.

My Teacher Ms. Simmons said to me that I had completed all of the texts in just three months and that she had scheduled me to take my GED with the others who have been there for one year. She said that I was a determined young lady, and that T.J. was going to be really proud of his mother someday. After saying thank you to Ms. Simmons, I asked can I start training in my trade. She laughed very warmly and said that first I had to pass my GED.

Ms. Simmons – "When I call your names please stand, Erica Simmons, Simone George, Daphne Lewis, Earl White, Carlos Rodriquez, and Ms. Joyce H."

Ms. Simmons – "I have a letter in my hand informing me of the people who have successfully passed their GED examination. Congratulations!"

Joyce – (Excited!) "Ms. Simmons, can I start my trade now because I need to get to my kid?"

Ms. Simmons – "Yes Ms. Joyce, you may start working in your trade next week after the Thanksgiving Holiday. Meanwhile, I will get you on the switchboard for a little training to finish out the week. Crystal can use some help and you are such a fast learner."

Joyce – "Thank you Ms. Simmons. Thank you! By the way, did I tell you that I love you today? Because I do, you know."

Ms. Simmons – "I love you too Ms. Joyce, because you are something special."

# $27.00

It was Thanksgiving vacation and me and two of my Job Corps buddies agreed on a weekend plan. We had decided to go to spend the night at Pebbles' house on the first night, and then visit Janice's family the following day. I didn't have a place that they could come but I was cool with that for now. Then the next time we would all meet up would have been that Sunday following Thanksgiving at the Port Authority to return back to Job Corps. The first stop was at my sister's house so that I can drop my luggage off, and then pick up T.J. at his grandmother's house. I had already spoken with Tony and he was fine with it as long as T.J. and I was with him for Thanksgiving.

When we were leaving Job Corps we had received our stipend of about $67.00. We purchased our round trip tickets which was $34.00. I had wanted some extra money so I had asked Tony to meet me at the Port Authority at 3:45 pm, because our bus would have pulled in at that time. He agreed and gave me an extra $75.00 which had brought my cash flow up to $108.00. Since I had the most money before getting on the train with the girls, I decided to treat us all to a beer getting our vacation off to a great start.

The three of us was feeling good, and we were so happy this holiday weekend. We were looking forward to meeting each other's family members because we had gotten so close in Job Corps we were almost inseparable. Janice was a very large girl who was cute and funny as hell, and Pebbles was slim, attractive and hilarious. And then there was me. I never considered myself funny, but my personality was always considered uniquely sarcastic which made people laugh.

Riding on the A train, a woman leaned over me while we were sitting down. The train was getting kind of crowded so she was holding on the handle directly above me. Janice and Pebbles were sitting on my right side sitting side ways. The woman started talking to me noticing my luggage. I didn't mind speaking with the lady who had reminded me of my mother whenever she was on the narcotic and coming down off it. Still that wouldn't have stopped me from talking to her. Hell I was around that all of my life. The woman and I began engaging in a conversation that was all right. She wanted to know was I in school and coming home for the holiday. I had shared with her that I attended Job Corps and I looked towards my friends letting her know that we were together.

Pebbles had made a statement that I had ignored saying "Yo Chi (short for China) don't talk to that bitch she on some kinda drug or something." "So what, she's cool! Damn, I gotta to go to the bathroom." I guess the beer was starting to run through me. I said that I was glad that we were getting off at Hoyt & Schermerhorn because I knew there was a bathroom at that stop. I was the only one out of my friends who had known that because I was from Brooklyn, and Pebbles and Janice both lived in the Bronx. I also knew that the Police Precinct was directly next to the bathroom.

The woman responded to me by saying "Really? That's wonderful, because I gotta go myself. I had to get off at Hoyt anyway to transfer to the G train. I'll follow you and then I can get back on the train." And when she said that, Pebbles whispered in my ear, "Yo Chi, let's rob that bitch!" All I said was, "Cut it out, and stop talking crazy." I didn't take Pebbles serious at all. Besides, I had a plan. My plan was to attend Job Corps, get my GED and a trade. Then get a job so I can take care of my child.

Janice stayed downstairs on the platform with our luggage on the side of the G train which was the next train we would take to get to the Marcy projects to drop off my luggage. Pebbles and the woman followed me upstairs to the bathroom. I ran inside the bathroom and was urinating when I couldn't believe my ears. "They tryin to rob me! Help! They tryin' to rob me! Help me, help me! They tryin' to rob me. They are hitting me! Help me they robbin' me!" I was still urinating when I panicked and pulled up my underwear, came out of the stall and started hitting the lady nonstop saying; "Shut up! Shut up! Just shut up!" I couldn't stop hitting her. What did she mean by saying "they" I wasn't doing anything to her but yet I was being implicated and I had gotten scared.

Although I see the police I couldn't stop hitting her still shouting, "Shut up! Shut up!" The police separated me and the lady and the next thing I remembered I was being stripped searched then pushed inside of a cell, and now being questioned by a Detective. "Where did you get this money from?" I said, "I attend Job Corps. Before I left they gave me a stipend of $67.00. After purchasing a round trip ticket that cost $34.00 I had $33.00 left. Then my son's father who works on 34$^{th}$ Street met with me on his lunch break and he gave me $75.00. Then I had a total of $108.00. Then because I had the most money out of my two friends I treated us to a beer which cost me $3.76. And that left me with $104.24. Then I purchased a token for 75 cents. That is why I had $103.49 remaining of which was taken from me during the strip search. Now can I have my money back because I need it to take my son out this weekend?" Is exactly what I said to the Detective.

The Detective looked at me in a strange way but I didn't care. It almost appeared that if he didn't have to follow procedure, he would have let me go just for my accountability. But that was impossible for him to do especially since I was caught beating the hell out of the victim.

"Ms. Harriet, the woman, said that you and your friend robbed her and that you took all of her money. This is why I asked you about the money you were found with" "That's bullshit! I didn't rob anybody! I just want to see my son! Ask the lady to tell me to my face that I tried to rob her." The Detective said that was impossible to do because the woman had to be rushed to the hospital.

When the Detective returned me to my cell, I was still able to communicate with Pebbles because she was in the cell directly next to me. Facing us was this Caucasion Officer sitting at a desk without worries said, "You niggers are low life, and you are going to jail." I said to him, "The only nigger I see is you, dumb ass! And you can go straight to hell because you mean absolutely nothing to me!" My only interest at that moment was to get to Pebbles. I needed to be free.

I had come up with this story and I shared it with Pebbles as discreetly as I could without alerting the officer who kept getting up for whatever reason.

I told Pebbles to listen to me and listen closely. Because this will be our story until this is over. "The beginning pretty much stayed the same. We met this lady on the train and she was talking to me. You kept telling me to stop talking to the lady but I wouldn't listen. Because I was from the neighborhood I knew that there was a bathroom at the Hoyt & Schermerhorn stop. I said out loud that I had to go to the bathroom while we were on the train. The lady said she had to go as well. So when we got off the A train the lady and I went to the bathroom. And because you were concerned, you followed us to the bathroom without the lady knowing. You stayed out because the bathroom had stunk badly. Then you heard me yell saying "You trying to rob me," and you just jumped in and started helping me fight her without thinking. And that is when the cops came in. "Yo, the jerk is coming back…..you got that?"

A few minutes later Janice entered the precinct crying out loud calling our names. I had mentioned to the Detective that Janice was on the platform with our luggage and for someone to please locate her because it was up to her to take our luggage home with her. I felt so bad for Janice. The way she was crying was like we had gotten sentenced to life. But we were friends and we had a plan that we were all looking forward towards. Janice shouted out "China, Pebbles, y'all alright? Can I see them Officer? Umma take y'all suitcases with me. I love y'all." The girl was so distraught she left the precinct crying without giving me her address and I had never seen Janice again.

"Joyce Harriet this is your first arrest and also your mother is here for you. I am going to release you on your own recognizance and you must return on January 15, 1986. Stacey Bowans, aka Pebbles, you have a rap sheet on petty larceny but I will release you on your own recognizance until the next court date of January 15, 1986. You may leave my courtroom."

When I turned around I was surprised to have seen my mother and Rick. I haven't seen them since my son and I had gotten put out of our home. I was glad however that they had a car, I don't know how or where they got it from, but I was glad that I didn't have to travel on the train. The white Gloria Vanderbilt dungaree pant suit that I was wearing was now grey, and I was funky as hell. Pebbles and I never discussed anything while we were locked up other than the story I had concocted. I was just in survival mode. Becky had told us to come on and get inside the car.

Becky – "I don't know what you got my daughter into "

Pebbles –" I "

Becky – "I nothing! I know this is not my daughter's style. Mine yeah, but my baby, hell no!

Rick, there is a train, she can get out!"

Joyce – "I'll be back, let me walk her to the train."

Becky – "Yeah, handle your business!"

Pebbles – "Yo Chi, I got your cut. That lady had $27.00. Here, take your cut."

China – "Do you know that the Officer took every dime of my money. How do you still have yours?"

Pebbles - (laughing) "I hid it in my couchie Chi."

China – "Do you know that they gave me nothing back? They tell me I must wait until the court case is over! Do you know you jeopardized my freedom? Do you know that I don't have any money to take T.J. out? You mean to tell me that my freedom was almost taken from me for $27 mother fuckin' dollars? Where is the rest of your money Pebbles?"

Pebbles – "It's right here!"

Joyce – "Give me that shit! I'm taking my son out!"

    I snatched all that she had and kicked her down the stairs to the subway station. When I returned to the car, Becky asked me was I all right and I said, "For now!" When I had finally reached my sister Sherlene's house after being dropped off by Rick and my mother, I tossed my outfit in the trash and took the hottest and the longest shower ever.

    I had spoken to my sister and told her all about what had happened. She told me that Tony didn't believe that I was arrested and that he believed that I was hanging out with some other guy. I was furious when she told me that and immediately I broke off the engagement in my mind, and had all intentions on giving him back the ring. I had thought to myself, how could I marry a man that didn't trust me? How could he have those type of thoughts about me? I had never cheated on him. He was the one always cheating on me. But I guess that was his own insecurity based on his own demons. In any case, I realized that we were far from needing to be married.

-----------------

My court date in Criminal Court located Downtown Brooklyn had arrived. My fate was now in the Judges hands. "Stacey Bowans and Joyce Harriet, because the accuser never shows up to court, I am dismissing this case. Case dismissed." I looked at Pebbles as if I still wanted to snap her neck so Pebbles practically ran out of the courtroom, and she never returned to Job Corps and I never seen her again.

I returned to Job Corps and my Guidance Counselor was ready to send me on a job for my internship. I requested that if at all possible can they send me somewhere in New York. My Guidance Counselor stated that they had never sent anyone to New York for internship and that I had to go somewhere in town or on campus for my six weeks training. I questioned why it wasn't possible, and that it may only require a phone call. I also reminded her of the importance of me returning to my son, and this way I could be with him every night.

Well to my surprise, my Guidance Counselor made a few phone calls and called me to her office. She told me that I would be the very first one to work at the Department of Labor at 1515 Broadway in Manhattan. And that I can start on Monday morning if I chose to. I said, "Hell yeah!" I would start on Monday morning which was in four days at the Department of Labor as a Secretary. And if I did well, I might stay on permanently.

I worked directly under my miserable supervisor. She was demanding, condescending and very rude in nature. She spoke to me in a sarcastic manner, and she enjoyed every bit of her control. "Joyce, type this up before you go to lunch. Write this memo to all the departments. Take these papers and file them before you go home. Joyce I need letters for these individuals. Oh, and make sure you notify the departments for our weekly meeting." This went on for a while, and I kept up with it all. I understood that you had to do what you had to do as a Secretary. I understood that! But then I said enough was enough! Maybe had she asked me nicely, it wouldn't have been a problem instead, "Joyce, fix my coffee, and make sure you put three cubes of sugar and four teaspoons of creamer. Oh, and make sure it's hot!" Really!

The way I figured it out in my head. I do not and will not be anybody's dumping ground in any way again. And I couldn't stay there. I got the tools that I need to move further in life, so now let me move forward without the bull crap. So I left my internship telling my supervisor to get her own damn coffee. I also asked her what makes her think that her coffee would not have been compromised because of the way that she treated me. I told her that she needed to be mindful as to how she spoke to people because you'll never know what a person is capable of doing. I turned around and told her to kiss my black ass. And my foolish behind left the job that could have taken me where I needed to be much sooner in life.

I had left my internship without completing it. I could have gone back to Job Corps and waited for another internship placement, or leave and return for my graduation in a few months. I had already completed what I had come to do. Still, if I had returned to Job Corps I would have gotten more assistance with a job. I opted to get my son and do what I had to do. I had finished totaling six months and six days. I had my GED, and a Secretarial Certificate of completion, and a four year old son that I couldn't wait to take care of.

# FAVOR

I never forgot about that incident with the woman from the subway. I could have really done some time in prison for the role I played. I was guilty of hitting her repeatedly. This was the second time that I may have permanently damaged someone. Was the reason for her not showing up to court due to me hurting her? If I would have killed her I would have gone to jail for sure but what happened to her I will never know. I often wonder how she is doing and if she is still alive. I thought that if I ever had the chance to apologize I would. She was somebody's daughter, mother, aunt and possibly a sister. I had no right in putting my hands on her. Why did I black out like that? Couldn't I have just finished urinating and broke her and Pebbles up and then told the Police on Pebbles. Why didn't my mind work in the way of doing the right thing? I had choices, and it seems like my decision making through life was never good with the exception of giving birth to my son.

Even so, I was so happy with myself for completing Job Corps that I treated myself to a Queen Latifa show at Club Zanzibar in Manhattan. I had asked my sister Sherlene to babysit T.J. for me because my girl was in town. Everyone who knew me knew that I had loved me some Queen. I partied like a rock star that night. I stood directly in front of the Queen while she performed.

It must have been about 3:00 in the morning when I got off the G train. I know a young lady being 21 at the time didn't have any business in the street at that time alone, but I wasn't held accountable to anyone. I was exhausted and still a little tipsy because, of course, I had gotten my drinks on. After getting off the G train by the Marcy Projects where Shereline lived, I had to walk the long city block to get to her house. When I glanced across the street I had noticed an old dirty white van parked. I pretended not to notice it, but got scared because it didn't feel right. Then the person started driving slow before quickly speeding up and made a U-turn to come in my direction alongside of me. I took off my shoes and hauled ass cutting in between the projects. I wasn't like them scared chicks in the movies fumbling for the key and then dropping the key trying to get in. I pulled out the keys and opened the door. When I had gotten inside, all I could do was stand by the door breathing as if I was having an asthma attack. When I caught my breath, I went and hugged my baby boy while he was asleep.

Later on I realized that that was one of the ways people were being kidnapped. Because if I had not been alert, or not been paying attention, I would have been snatched up! And Lord only knows what could have happened afterwards. For this reason among many others, we must pay attention to our surroundings and be alert at all times. We must teach our sons and daughters about the seriousness regarding Human Trafficking. Children are recruited, transported, harbored, and transferred, for the purpose of being exploited. Exploited in brothels, strip clubs, personal sex slaves, sweat shops, etc. I'm certain that we are all seeing these words on more than just milk cartons. MISSING! One of the ways to avoid this disaster is to PLEASE teach your son's and daughter's to pay attention while outside. They must stop talking and texting on their cell phones and not pay attention to their surroundings. These kidnappers are quick and they are watching our children. If caught teach them to kick, scream, yell, bite and fight. #MYFIGHT.

# HERE WE GO AGAIN

Now that I had completed Job Corps, I knew that I had to start the process of being homeless all over again. Taking the chance of living with a family member wasn't an option. I had to become independent and begin to build a life for me and my child. So I told my sister Sherlene and Sylvia thank you for everything. Tony and I had talked and he reminded me of what that process was like. He said that he will not allow T.J. and I to go through that without him. You see he was my first love, and the father of my child. I knew that Tony wasn't a bad person. He had all good intentions to protect us as much as he could. He desired to do so from within his heart. And in my mind, he was in control of his habit. Not to mention, I still loved him.

When we arrived at the Welfare Center my Caseworker sent us to Cumberland, which was a shelter sectioned off from what was then Cumberland Hospital. I was already warned about Cumberland Shelter so I immediately told Tony to follow my lead. Once inside, I acted as if I had a mental condition. Constantly shaking my head and repeating myself. Tony then repeated what I was doing and T.J. must have thought that we were playing and started laughing hard. The intake person had a frightening look on her face and denied our stay and told us to return to the Emergency Assistance Unit "EAU." My plan had worked. I had really learned a lot from my mother over the years.

After spending three months here and there in numerous welfare hotels and a few family shelters we were sent to the Saratoga Family Inn in Jamaica, Queens. We were one of the first families to live there after it being turned over from the Holiday Inn. The three of us were finally at a stable, comfortable decent place. Once we were stable, I was finally able to get to the Doctor and get checked out only to find out that I was pregnant again. And once we became stable, Tony again started to wander and have disappearing acts. Therefore, once again I did what I knew best because although we were in a better situation, we were still homeless. So I would have the second of three abortions by Tony, while homeless.

We were prohibited to cook in our rooms at the Saratoga Inn. However, for me that was a hard rule to follow, especially since neither T.J. nor myself liked the food they served daily. I would study the staff that were on and befriend them. Monitor their daily security checks on the different floors and the sides of the building. And allow that window of opportunity to work for me as I pulled out my hot plate, and prepared my meals. We enjoyed a three-course dinner. My dinner often consisted of BBQ chicken, fried chicken or steak. The vegetables would be either, corn, green beans, spinach or broccoli of which T.J. always called trees. And because there were so many flavors of Rice-A-Roni, we would have a different flavor every night.

My friends and I would often help each other out in many areas. We shared our days of cooking to kind of throw people off. We always shared what we had to survive while we were there. Whatever one person didn't have and needed, the other person would supply it if they had it. We celebrated our children's birthday by helping out in all ways of preparation because regardless of our situation, we would always give our children a party. We were there through all of our baby daddy drama because unfortunately, we all had the drama. We were all real close and came together in a healthy way. I lost touch with one of the young ladies over the years, but through Facebook, I am now in touch with the other who is doing quite well for herself, and she did a great job raising her children.

During my stay at the Saratoga Family Inn, there are memories to remember as if they were yesterday. One of my friends was dating her Case Manager, and although there wasn't supposed to be any fraternizing, they couldn't stay apart. They had become somewhat inseparable over time. Tony was on and off of the narcotic that sometimes he was there and sometimes he wasn't. But for me life had to go on. When he was there everybody loved him. The children loved him most because he would talk like Donald Duck to them and they were fascinated by it. Tony was always great with children because he was a child himself in his own kind of way. My friends were very fond of Tony. They just didn't like his disappearing acts.

I would move forward because I had to. It was always very easy for me to find work. I had found work inside the Mall on Jamaica Avenue during the Christmas Holiday so that our present situation wouldn't ever dictate our financial happiness. For the remainder of our stay I had gotten a job at the JFK Airport as a Security Agent. I remember working at the airport one time and I saw Linda Lavin from the TV sitcom **"Alice."** I was so excited because that was one of my favorite shows growing up. I walked quickly towards her and I shouted to my co-workers, "Look y'all its Alice!" She responded to me very nasty saying, "Yeah sure, let everybody know it's me!" I paused for a half of second and then shouted, "Actually, I don't watch the show because of you because you're not funny. Mell is!" I know it wasn't nice, but I felt I had to come back with something. And I never watched the program again.

During one of Tony's disappearing acts, I had decided that I wanted him out of my household. I couldn't put up with him anymore. I was pregnant and fed up. Therefore, he was no longer allowed inside the shelter. I remember this one day T.J. was in daycare downstairs in the building and, I had already made dinner and I was relaxing with my back towards the door sitting at the table with my red painted toenails that shined beautifully as I propped my feet up in a chair while reading a book.

It was normal for my Case Manager to pay a visit to see how things were going. He announced himself and I summoned him to come inside and have a seat. He sat in the chair on the other side of the table and started asking me questions regarding my case. I continued to be comfortable with my feet up while talking to him. Then it came a point that he was just writing notes and I continued reading. To my surprise the man had stopped writing and started sucking the toes on my right foot. I lowered the book and watched how he was going in and it was feeling so good. I had never had anyone do that before, and it felt real nice. I pretended to continue reading when he stopped sucking the right foot. I kindly lift up my left foot and let him continue in giving me an experience of a lifetime. He was enjoying himself so much, he must have forgotten that the door was open because neither one of us had closed it.

When he was done, he looked at me and I looked at him. I left my feet propped up on the chair and I said, "That was cute!" He just smiled at me and asked could we go out sometime. I told him, "I'd rather not being that you have a wife 'n all." Besides, he wasn't quite my type. Although attractive! That was the only time for toe pleasure between us. However, he did allow me to experience another side to my sexy.

During my stay realizing that it was only temporary, I began to utilize my Secretarial Skills to write a letter to Mayor Ed Koch about housing. By this time I had known that the Housing Specialist at the Saratoga Inn did not like me at all, and I knew that I had to help myself. I also knew that it was a good time to start applying for City exams.

Normally, it would take people years to get into the Projects. It had taken me three months since I had written my letter to Mayor Koch. After all, our Politicians are there to help us. When I received the letter of acceptance to move into the projects, I decided to pay the Housing Specialist a visit so they can "close" out my case. I went down to their office with my Walkman and headphones on, bopping my head pretending to be listening to my music.

Secretary – "Ms. Harriet is here!"

Housing Specialist 1- "I'm not helping her get nothing. She walks around here thinking she's better than everybody. Shucks, she can find her own apartment for all I care. I can't stand her."

Housing Specialist 2 – "Yeah, her Case Manager be praising her like she don't belong here or something. Sometimes I think he likes her."

Housing Specialist 1 –"I know Peters, that other Case Manager, likes her too. Her and her friends get on my nerves acting like they are goddesses of the shelter."

Housing Specialist 2 – "Oh, we better call her in before she leave. Cause you know the bitch will leave."

Housing Specialist 1- "Hello Ms. Harriet, you can come in now."

Housing Specialist 2 – "Hello Ms. Harriet, how are you today?"

I said "Obviously better than you two miserable bitches. I just wanted to let you know that I have found my own apartment without the likes of your help. Y'all take care now, ya hear. Oh, and by the way my battery's been dead since yesterday," and then I sashayed out of their office.

With the exception of the miserable Housing Specialist, my stay was pretty good at the Saratoga Family Inn. I could have gotten very comfortable and stayed there much longer than one year, but I had other plans for my life. I was surrounded by two good friends as well as T.J. having their children as his friends.

# R U KIDDEN ME?

I had told Tony the good news about getting an apartment and he insisted that we give our relationship another try. Of course, I agreed. You see when you love someone it's hard to say no and mean it forever. Especially when you know another side to the person that is beautiful. Therefore, the three of us moved into our very first apartment together. It was a one bedroom apartment in East New York Brooklyn in Unity Plaza Housing projects. The name sounded good, and I didn't know much about Brownsville or East New York. I was just glad to have an apartment of our own. We lived on the fifth floor next to a Spanish family who was very nice. We agreed to give T.J. the bedroom, since we had accumulated so much stuff for him. I had purchased a day bed where Tony and I slept in the living room. Overall, it was a cute apartment that I furnished well, and kept clean.

A short time later once we were stable, Tony started his shenanigans again. T.J. and I had returned from spending the night out at my sister Sherlene's house. When I put my key inside the door, I heard moving around inside the apartment. I knew that it wasn't Tony because I had taken my keys from him due to his disappearing acts. I told T.J. who was six years old at the time to go inside the neighbor's house. When I got inside our apartment I noticed that we had been robbed, and they weren't done because there were still items placed by the window for pick up. I thought that I had checked the window gate and thought that it was locked. Obviously I was wrong. Then I thought that they were still inside when I was putting the key in the door and they couldn't have gotten far.

When T.J. walked in it hurt my heart to hear him say, "Mommy they took my bike. Mommy and my clothes, and they took my new leather coat

Mommy they took it." I felt that we had both been violated. And now being violated had become a pattern in my life. But it angered me that I couldn't protect my son from this violation. They had even taken the food from out of our freezer. That's how I knew it was somebody on Crack.

I was furious, and immediately thought that the neighbors in the connecting building that shared the same fire escape as me had robbed us. I was fearless, and climbed right into their living room window walking through their apartment and was searching for my belongings saying; "Y'all wanna rob somebody? Y'all think I don't know y'all just robbed me? Where is my shit hah? Where is it at? Y'all didn't get enough time to sell it yet, where's my shit?" Then I had walked into a room filled with guys, and I realized that that was too many for me to handle so I said, "That's all right! If I ever catch any of you with mine or my son's shit, I got you. Watch, damn, y'all wanna rob me! Ya fuckin' Crack Heads!"

My neighbor had stood there looking at me as if I was crazy when I had returned. When I asked her what was wrong with her, she told me that she wouldn't have never thought that I was crazy enough to go inside someone's apartment the way I did. She told me that she understood that I was upset, but I had done a dangerous thing. My only response was that they robbed us. They took me and my baby's stuff. I feel so violated again! I worked hard for what we have, and they gonna come and take it. Damn! I grabbed T.J. and held him, reassuring him that we were going to be okay.

My mind had started to play tricks on me because although my neighbors were the closest and the most obvious, why didn't I see anything inside their apartment? I started to think that Tony had robbed us. Or was it inside the room with all the guys? Did Tony do it? I remembered when Tony had robbed the owner of the bar from directly under where we lived while living with my mother. Tony had taken the owner of the bar's DJ equipment. He had brought it all upstairs to our apartment. The bar owner had known my mother, so politely he knocked on our door at 7 0' clock in the morning because he was notified that he was being robbed, and told my mother that Tony was seen robbing his bar. He asked my mother can she please tell Tony to return his things.

When my mother came into my bedroom and seen all the equipment in there, she screamed on Tony and told him to take it right back downstairs. Then she told him that he wasn't a good thief because a good thief would not have done it that way, and they wouldn't have gotten caught. Afterwards, my mother had given me a lesson saying, never "allow" anyone to take your freedom with what they decide to do. Do not be an accomplice and have nothing to do with it, because I could have been the one left holding the ball. It was a lesson well taken and received. Therefore, knowing that that was a "crack head" move, I had thought of Tony. Although I never found out who did rob us, my suspicions of it being Tony had faded away.

-------------------

Who in the hell is knocking on my door at 6 0' clock in the morning? "It's me, Tony." When I opened the door I leaned on my wall and said, "I haven't seen you in days. Look, I packed your clothes and you can turn right back around because it is over between us. Tony raised his voice and looked at me and said, "You think you can just leave me?" He grabbed the police bar that locked the door and pushed it straight into my throat. I tried to pull it out and he fell on top of me in the closet. Meanwhile, Tony continued to push while I pulled. Then I heard T.J's voice after dialing 911. Then I heard him dial his grandmother Sylvia. "Help, my Daddy is a Crack Head and he tryin' to kill my Mommy. 410 Williams Avenue between Dumont and Blake Apartment 5 B grandma, grandma, my Daddy is tryin' to kill my Mommy." Tony got off of me and ran out of the apartment.

I was able to get the bar from out of my throat, and before I knew it Sylvia was there with the ambulance. T.J. was crying and asking me was I okay. All I can do was shake my head yes, and hold my throat with a cloth. I went ahead in the ambulance while Sylvia stayed with T.J. The ambulance had taken me to Brookdale Hospital. To my surprise, Abby came and was furious. She was angry as hell and wanted to put a hit out on Tony. But first she wanted to get me out of Brookdale. So we immediately left, and went to a hospital in Manhattan.

The Doctor stitched me and bandaged my throat and told me the proper way to take care of it, and that nothing was damaged. I was back to normal within a very short time only having a scar to remind me on a daily basis. Often times I think back to that day and how it all had happened. As I reflect, I can truly, honestly, without a shadow of a doubt, know that an Angel was assigned to me. And every time I look into the mirror I thank God again and again. Writing this piece also reminds me that I should ask T.J. if he ever had nightmares or reminders of that day because he too was terrified. He was six years old and he was my Hero.

Afterwards when we realized that I was okay, Abby wanted to put out a massive search for Tony. She had wanted him dead for what he had done to me. But somehow, I had convinced her that it wasn't Tony and that it was the narcotic he was on. I told her I knew that if he was in his right mind he would not have hurt me. It was the drug that had changed him. Besides, although she was upset and I understood why, I didn't want her to take my son's father's life. He was doing a good job of taking his life on his own. For that reason Abby agreed not to continue on her search, but she did say if he ever were to put his hands on me again that there wouldn't be a rock that Tony could hide under. I had taken all that Abby said very serious, because I knew how my sister got down, and I knew that she loved me.

-----------------

Around the corner on Dumont Avenue was a real nice development. I wasn't sure what kind of facility it was so I stopped in and asked. To my surprise, I was told that it was a Tier 2 Shelter just like the Saratoga Family Inn. I immediately asked were they hiring and I was told that they were and to drop off my resume. I hurried up and went home and pulled out my old fashioned typewriter and utilized my secretarial skills and typed me up a nice resume. I was so thankful that the thieves didn't take it, although they were about to as it sat by the window for the next pick-up. Then I walked it right back around that corner and handed it to the person who said they would forward it to the right person. And he did. I was hired shortly after on the overnight shift as a Family Center Monitor at HELP 1 USA.

I had gotten to know a teenager who lived on my floor named Drina. I was kind of fond of her. She was 17 and she was going to go away to college in another year, and I never saw her involved in any trouble. I asked around a little bit about her, and I didn't get any bad reports. So I had asked her would she like a babysitting job overnight inside my apartment. I told her that I would be there in time to take him to school. She agreed. I told her my rules and my requirements. One being, once I leave for work she was not to open my door for anyone. Whatever she had to do she had to make sure it was done before I went to work. My shift would start at midnight so T.J. would have already been asleep. I had prepared his clothes for school which was directly across the street, and all she would have had to do was get him up and he would get himself ready for school. T.J. knew how to bathe himself and get dressed so he didn't need Drina's assistance in that. I felt confident that Drina babysitting T.J. was good because T.J. had liked Drina always saying that she was really pretty.

It's Mother's Day and Malcolm who I now work with brings roses and a cake to the two women on his shift. Ms. Harrow and I were very appreciative for Malcolm's gift as she already known that he was a special kind of gentleman. And now I was sure to experience his kindness. During the night into our shift, Malcolm had asked me out to breakfast following our shift. Of course I welcomed it and thanked him for the roses and the cake. From that moment on Malcolm and I began a relationship that was life changing for me and one that I will never forget.

Breakfast was postponed because I was asked to do overtime on the 8 - 4 pm shift. I could have definitely used the extra money so I said yes. I called Drina to tell her that I needed her to take T.J. to school, and to use the spare key that I gave her for one lock to lock the door. I asked her if she wasn't able to pick him up at 3 0'clock to let me know but she agreed to do so. However, if she had said no, then I wouldn't have been able to work the shift till 4 pm, I would have gotten off at 3p.m so I could have been able to pick him up myself. When I came home that day T.J. was sitting in the hallway in front of our door.

Mommy – "T.J., why are you sitting in the hallway? And where is Drina? She is supposed to be watching you?"

T.J. – "Mommy, have a seat. I got something to tell you. So please have a seat."

Mommy – "What's wrong?"

T.J. – "Ok, you can't say anything until I'm finished, ok?"

Mommy - "OK baby, I'm listening."

T.J. – "This is what happened Mommy. You told Drina to watch me. Drina told her mother to watch me because she had to go someplace. Her mother told me to stay inside the room with all the other kids while she stayed in her bed. So, they asked me to play a game. I said ok. Then somebody put a blindfold on my eyes, and then said now open your mouth. So den I put my hands out and it felt like my thing and I took the blindfold off and seen that the boy was going to put his thing in my mouth. So I kicked him, then I pushed him out my way, I did most of the things you told me to do when somebody is trying to hurt me. Den I ran out the house. That's why I was sitting in the hallway waiting for you to come home."

Mommy - "What? Stay right here!"

I was furious! I went and pushed their door open, and I began beating the hell out of every boy that I had seen inside the house and cursing and threatening until the mother asked what was going on. I looked up and started choking the mother while cursing her out. I said," What kind of damn place you call home? Did you know these damn nasty ass kids tried to get my son to suck somebody's dick? Did you know that? Or you just stayed your fat ass in the bed eating cake and ice cream? When I see your daughter Drina I'm gonna punch her dead in the face because she was supposed to be watching my baby." Next thing I knew I was being handcuffed while the Police were telling me to calm down. Then while handcuffed, they asked the mother who was in the house what had happened.

I said, "I'll tell you what happened! This fat ass, got all these foster kids living here, and all of them are perverted. They tried to get my six year old son to suck some boy's dick. That's what's going on. So now what y'all gonna do? Because when her daughter comes home, the bitch that was supposed to have been watching my son, I'm gonna punch her dead in her face! Remove those kids from that house is what y'all need to do." The Police Officer asked was the mother pressing charges and she said no. Obviously she was hiding something because I was whipping some ass in that house. The Officer took the cuffs from off of me, and told me to go in the house. And that is exactly what I did.

I went inside the house and grabbed my baby and commended him on his bravery. I hugged him so tight and apologized for leaving him with someone. I told him that he had done a very good thing by telling me what happened, and that he was a very brave little boy, and told him how much I love him. I also reminded him if anybody ever tries to touch him (pointing to areas on his body) or tell him to touch them, that he had to make sure he get away from them. I reminded him to kick, scream, yell, run, bite if he had to, but get away from them, and always tell me what happened. Because nobody has the right to do anything to him that he didn't want them to do. And then I asked him did he get what I said? He said, "Yes Mommy, I got it."

Then this little six year old boy had the nerve to ask me to do him a favor. He asked me to please stop dabbing my finger with my saliva to wipe his face. Then he showed me exactly what he meant by putting his finger to his mouth, dabbing it with his saliva, then came towards my face to simulate him wiping a spot off of my face. I had to smile and say, "Yes I'll stop!" But I had also used that as a teaching moment telling T.J. why I did that to him. I told him that my mother used to do that to me and I hated it. But somehow, although I hated it, I didn't think not to do it to him. I vowed that I will never use my saliva to wipe anything from off of his face again. But then I pretended to do it again and he ducked, we laughed and hugged and I asked him did he feel safe and he said "yes Mommy."

After the incident with my babysitter, whom I had never seen again, I was glad that my mother had come back into my life. Supposedly Rick had killed somebody by "accident" in the hallway of the building, and my mother and him had to leave the apartment leaving everything behind. Rick had gone to stay with his brother in the projects, and my mother didn't want to stay there. Anyhow, we both had understood that we needed each other. She needed a place to live and I needed a babysitter that I can trust. Besides, she was always good with her grandson, with the exception of putting the both of us out. Babysitting would not have been much anyway because T.J. would have been asleep before I had left for work.

I did have a few rules, and one of them was absolutely major. I had told my mother that under no circumstances did I allow Rick inside of my house. After coming home a few times noticing that she disobeyed my wish, I had told her that she could leave. When my mother realized how serious I was, and I reminded her that I can walk around the corner at any given time to check, my mother started to respect my wishes or else she too would have been homeless. I had really despised that man. And I knew that he can no longer be a part of my world.

I was no longer concerned about Tony coming around because he had signed himself into a Drug Treatment Program. He said when he had heard his son say that he was a "crack head" when calling the police that morning, it had ripped him up inside. He said that he had signed himself up for a two year program. When I had spoken to him, I had wished him the best throughout his recovery, and told him that as long as he did better for himself that I would be there for him as a friend. And whenever possible, T.J. and I would visit him. He welcomed it and I could tell that he was very shocked at my response. After all, remaining friends with my son's father was not a bad idea. Tony was a good person who needed help as well as myself. We were both acting out in harmful ways without realizing it. His may have appeared more dangerous and obvious than my behavior, but clearly we both had some issues that needed to be addressed. I'm so glad that I didn't allow Tony's dark moments to affect such a bright future between the three of us. I never believe in putting children in the way of adult problems. And I definitely wasn't going to be the one to keep T.J. from his Dad. Especially since I know what it feels like not having one.

Shortly after Sherlene and I were called to enter the Academy for the Department of Corrections I was informed by my Gynecologist that I was 5 weeks pregnant. We were being told in the academy that a lawsuit of some kind was against the Department of Corrections due to my exact situation. The outcome of the law suit was still pending so I wasn't sure how to handle my situation. The Training Captains went on to say that Correction Officers had to start the process over if they became pregnant during the Academy stage and during the probation period. I became afraid about what to do. Should I have the baby or should I have an abortion? I had really liked Malcolm and I wanted to give him a child, but I really didn't know what I should do. I did know that I didn't want to stay a Family Center Monitor if I didn't have to.

I had told Malcolm about the baby and he was overjoyed. He told his mother, who was also excited. Meanwhile, I was having my own sense of feelings of confusion. I wish I had known who to talk to but it seems as if I have been making my own decisions for so long, that I had to come up with this one as well. I didn't want to wait too long to decide because after all there was a baby growing inside of me. So once again, I thought that having an abortion was the best decision at that time. God, I wish I had known better. All I knew was that this was a great opportunity for me to give my son and myself a better life. Meanwhile, there was a young lady who was in the Academy with me throughout the entire time pregnant. She did all of the class work, but didn't participate in the physical aspect of it all. She's not aware of it, but I admired her. And I will make a point in telling her that the next time I see her. And today when I look on Face Book and see the picture of her daughter it actually brings tears to my eyes knowing that I too could have had a child her age.

My decision didn't only affect me, it had affected Malcolm, his mother and the way she treated me afterwards. His mother and my relationship had changed, and at that point I had felt that she disliked me from then on. Why didn't I think about the effects that it would have had on them? As I write this book tears flow from my eyes realizing the hurt that I have caused other people because of my spontaneous decision making. I have once again deprived my child of a sibling. I have deprived Malcolm from giving him his first child. I have deprived his mother of giving her her first grandchild, and of course, his siblings, and their expectations.

First: At three weeks your baby-in-the-making is a ball of cells called blastocyst. The blastocyst already contains a full set of DNA (Deoxyribonucleic acid, a nucleic acid that contains genetic information) from you and your partner, which determines sex, eye color, and other traits.

Second
At four weeks the ball of cells has officially become an embryo and is about the size of a poppy seed. Over the next six weeks, all of your baby's organs will begin to develop, and some will start to function.

Third
At five weeks your baby's tiny heart begins to beat at twice the rate of yours. His entire "body" is only about the size of a sesame seed.

Fourth
At six weeks facial features (like eyes and nostrils) are beginning to form, and little buds appear where arms and legs will develop.

Fifth

At eight weeks, arms and legs are growing, and your baby now has little fingers, as well as a nose and upper lip. He's moving quite a bit now, but you won't feel it. He's about 5/8 of an inch long and weighs hardly anything - four hundredths of an ounce.

And it goes on, but need I go any further? I had killed four of my babies without even knowing it. In my ignorance, I had even told my niece to have an abortion when she had gotten pregnant at a young age. I had loved her so much that I wanted her to get a shot at being a child, and make a better life for herself. I'm glad that she didn't listen to me because she's doing well for herself and she's a great mom. However, it pains me because of what I know now. I have taken lives that weren't mine to take. Once conception takes place it is a living soul. I was told at the clinic and by others when I had my first abortion that a baby didn't form yet. I was deceived, but I blame no one. I was simply misinformed.

The schedule while in the Academy would shift from week to week. From 8 - 4 pm and 4- 12 am for eight weeks. Before we knew it my sister and I had to pick up our crispy Class A Uniforms for our Graduating Ceremony. The both of us were so excited about our new careers. A few of my co-workers and I were traveling home on the same train one night after the 4 -12 am training. Sherlene and I were on two different tours and we didn't live in the same part of Brooklyn. Therefore, we never traveled to the Academy together nor did we leave together. However, there were a few of my co-workers that would ride the same train as I did. Malcolm would always pick me up after the 8 - 4 pm shift. But on the 4 – 12 a.m. shift he would be just starting his shift at my old job.

While on the train, I had noticed this deranged looking man watching us very closely. I'm not sure if the others noticed him, but I kept an eye on the man who was keeping an eye on us. Soon enough, I was the only one left on the train with the man still watching only me. I was sort of frightened because I had to get off on Julius Street in Brooklyn, and I always thought that to be a dangerous train stop, especially coming down that extremely long flight of stairs, being without light to lead my way. When I decided to get off the train I noticed that he started following me. While I was walking down the long flight of stairs he slowed up. With my heart pumping and my street knowledge creeping in I turned abruptly as if I was deranged also and said; " What! What! What the hell you following me for? You want to see crazy? I'm as crazy as they come, jack! What?' I said all that while shaking as if I had the Tourette's Syndrome Disorder.

That man looked at me and ran past me down the stairs. I stopped and held my chest and regrouped before continuing my journey home. When I reached home, I noticed that it was pitch black and the elevator was not working. I prepared myself mentally to walk up the stairs.

While walking up the stairs, I smelled Marijuana and heard males in the hallway. Although afraid, I continued to walk up my five flights. When I had reached a group of guys in the hallway sitting on the steps, they all lit their lighters when one of them said, "So who you, 5/0?" I wasn't crazy so I decided to make a funny and said, "Na, but ya'll weed damn sho smell good; ya need to hook a sista up!" And then started laughing and continued walking up the stairs holding my chest. That's when I knew that I had to move and move quickly.

When I got inside the house Becky was up waiting for me because she wanted to see my uniform. When she opened the door she said I had looked like I had just seen a ghost or something. I told her about my night coming home. I had demonstrated to my mother exactly how I transformed into a crazy woman. Becky was cracking up and told me of a similar story that had happened to her. Now we both were laughing hysterically.

Then I told her how the man ran past me and left me the hell alone. And I told her how much I had appreciated reading all those books by Donald Goines that she kept in the house. I said that I wasn't crazy but I sure as hell can act like I am when I have to. I had Becky almost in tears while laughing then she called me a sick child. I told her that I wasn't sick, I was a survivor.

I continued sharing my nights' events. I told Becky that it didn't stop there. I told her about the hallway situation. Again we started laughing and Becky reminded me that if Malcolm didn't work nights he would have definitely come and picked me up from the Academy because he wouldn't want anything to happen to his Precious. I started laughing and said that's right because he loves him some Joy. Then I started to get excited showing my mother my Class A uniform for the upcoming graduation ceremony. Becky was so excited because both of her girls were graduating from the Academy together. She just wanted to know how she was going to wear her hair, and finally she decided that she wanted braids. I told her that both of us can go to the salon and get our hair braided together.

My mother and my relationship was building back up again. She had come back into my life during a time that a girl needed her mother. She was there for T.J. while I worked. She helped me with the cooking, the cleaning, and we were finally mother and daughter. I had my mother back to when things were good between us. I took care of her. I had a great job earning a decent living, and there wasn't anything my mother needed that she didn't get.

Eventually, Malcolm and I were spending more time together and he began helping me out with T.J. Becky started to stay over Sherlene's house to babysit my niece and nephew as she had needed help as well. Shortly after, Becky was accepted into "NYCHA," New York City Housing Authority in Brownsville. She was so happy to have her own apartment again. I was just as happy for her, and took her furniture shopping. The smile on her face filled my heart as she picked out every bit of furniture, in addition to picking out her own washer and dryer. She was so happy and I loved being able to put all those smiles on her face. From that moment on, taking care of my mother was a pleasure and I wouldn't have traded those moments in for the world.

# TEARS THAT NEVER DRIED

Malcolm and I were happy together despite what his family may have thought about me after having the abortion. Although we lived at two separate locations we shared a good life together. He still lived with his mother, and T.J. and I lived on Lafayette Street in Bedford Stuyvesant. We enjoyed traveling with family and spending time with friends. I was well past the probationary period with the Department of Corrections when I would discover that I was pregnant with his second child. The three of us were so excited. T.J. had looked forward to his baby sister or brother. Malcolm was overjoyed once again. I was even more excited because now I was in a place that I was able to provide very well for my family, and I really wanted T.J. to have a sibling in addition to be able to give Malcolm what I had took away from him.

I was six months when I had to go to the bathroom in the middle of the night. When I got up my water had broken. I shouted out for T.J. to call the Ambulance. When I received the news that I had a Miscarriage, I was devastated. When I had to tell T.J. the news, part of me witnessed a sadness that had come over him that would stay with him for the rest of his life. Telling Malcolm was more difficult because it seemed like he had loved me so much that he was only concerned about me. And for some reason, I needed to see his real emotions. Malcolm would always just want to make sure that I was ok, without expressing his true feelings. But I realized that it wasn't what I thought I needed to see from him, it was more about the comfort he had given me.

One year later I was given the news that I was pregnant again. His mother was looking for a house for all of her sons to live with her. After agreeing on a house, Malcolm decided that T.J. and I should come and live with him. He wanted to make sure that I had followed the Doctor's orders by being on strict bed rest. I agreed knowing that his brother's had girlfriends who also had children that were around the same age as T.J. that would live there as well.

While there, I would always prepare a snack for when the kids came out of school. While in the kitchen I was standing up and once again at 6 months my water broke. I had already known what had happened. I shouted out "It's happening again!" I don't know who in the house called the Ambulance but someone had called and I was off to the hospital again. No one had come with me to the hospital, which had saddened me more. Malcolm wasn't home now that he was working the 8 - 4pm shift on his job since being promoted to Shift Supervisor.

Words couldn't express what I felt, so I said nothing. I didn't know what I was doing wrong. I thought that I was doing everything right. The Doctors couldn't even give me an explanation as to why this had happened again. I was sad also because nobody had come to visit me from his family's house nor did they say anything to me when I returned home. For days I watched how another Miscarriage had affected T.J. and Malcolm, but all I could do was say sorry.

I tried to find answers and ask questions why was I having Miscarriages. What was happening to me that I couldn't keep my pregnancy past six months? I tried to think of everything. What was I doing? Did I reach too high? What? I couldn't put anything together. Then I remembered that even the Doctors couldn't give me an answer so how can I come up with an answer. They were the ones with the medical degrees. But then, I realized that I must have gotten more damaged having abortions. Those Doctor's and Nurse's were ripping those babies from out of my womb destroying my body without worries. And of course another Doctor recognised another Doctor's work, so why should they tell me the truth. That was the way I started thinking. At that moment I became more depressed and no one knew it. I started thinking about how I wasn't good enough for Malcolm because I couldn't even have his child. I started thinking that I was damaged goods and he deserved so much better than me. I thought that if I couldn't give a man as good as Malcolm a child then I was no good to him or any other man.

Malcolm was just that kind of man that had good and happy spirits all the time. He was really a diamond in the rough. Under no circumstances did he ever allow me to feel unloved by him. It was my self-pity that would come into play in my head. Valentines' Day was approaching and all of the couples decided to get away to the Poconos. I believe there were six or eight couples who came on the trip. We were all enjoying dinner when to my surprise Malcolm popped the question. "Precious, will you marry me?" I had to say yes, but I was still very depressed.

However, by this time, my desires were changing. And because I had a love and a deep respect for Malcolm, I had decided to tell him the truth. Tell this man that I couldn't marry him. My closest friend at the time said "Joy, don't tell him. He loves you so much that you can have your cake and eat it too." But I said no, and that he deserved better. He deserved a woman that can give him babies, and love him just as much as he loves her if not more. I had to tell him that I no longer could be with him because I had now wanted to be with woman. This way, I wouldn't have any challenges regarding having a baby.

Malcolm was a good man. I think he was the most kindhearted, giving, respectful and loving person a girl could have. He was a handyman and didn't mind doing any kind of work or chores. He was a provider, and he provided security. He was good to me, my son, and my family loved him. But, once again my decisions were not always the best. I had let go of a good man.

Of course Malcolm didn't take what I said well, but at that moment there wasn't nothing else that I could do but move out and wish him the best. A few years later Malcolm met him a wonderful woman who gave him lots of beautiful babies, they had gotten married and moved away, I think to Atlanta or Virginia. And believe it or not, I am so happy for him because if there ever was a man that deserved happiness it was him. Meanwhile, after Malcolm and I break up, T.J., and I moved to Coney Island where another half of my journey would begin.

# NEW BEGINNINGS

I was out on sick leave at the time from The Department of Corrections, due to the route bus crashing into a pole. For this reason, I had been home a lot. Now that Malcolm and I were no longer together, I jumped right into the next thing. I used to think that I was afraid of being alone, but I realized that I simply didn't have to be alone. I wasn't sure how to go about meeting someone who was Gay, so I decided to go through the personals in the Daily News. I had come across a section called Alternative Lifestyle. In no time a young lady responded to my ad. She knew me as China, and she and I would talk for hours on the phone every day and every night. She told me that she was Hispanic but the girl sounded black over the phone. We were both very talkative and vibed very well.

Cozy said that she worked Construction, and we would often talk on her breaks. She told me that she had a daughter and her daughter's father was a Cab Driver, and that although she was Gay all of her life she wanted the experience of having a child. She had asked her friend who was a Cab Driver if he was willing to father her child. He was willing, and it was understood that he wouldn't share any parts of her life.

We had already fallen for each other deeply, so it didn't matter what we had looked like. T.J. had wanted to spend the weekend at his cousins' house, and I was looking forward to being with Cozy for the first time after talking on the phone for weeks. I think that was literally the first time I had wanted to get rid of my son for a few days. It was the blizzard of 1992 when I would see her for the first time. I didn't think that she would come because the subways and the buses had stopped running. She lived in Crown Heights and I had lived all the way in Coney Island. I guess that's a one hour car ride, and about two hours via subway and bus because you would have had taken both to get to my house.

When I opened the door, I saw this 5'6" Spanish aggressive female covered in snow almost up to her waist. Her face looked frozen, and her first words were, "I walked!" She was frozen. I peeled her clothes off and for the entire weekend she would make me want her more and more. For that weekend all we did was make love, and the only time we stopped was when we fell asleep in each other's arms or bathed. We both should have loss weight because we literally didn't eat any food.

I knew that I had to talk to T.J. about this new lifestyle that I was in. So when he came home I sat him down and said, "I'm not sure if you will understand what I'm about to tell you because you are only 11 years old. But, I'm going to explain it to you as best as I can. So Mommy needs you to listen." He said, "Ok Ma." I said to him, "You know that I love you, and you know that no one will ever come between us. You know that Malcolm and I are no longer together. T.J., your mother is in love with a woman. I no longer want to be with another man. I have my reasons, and maybe later on you will understand why. But, the truth of the matter is I have met a woman who makes me feel the way I want to feel in a relationship. She is the same person that you heard me talking to over the phone for the past few months. She has a two year old daughter, she works in Construction, and I really enjoy her conversation." I looked into his eyes and waited for his response or a reaction. "Mommy, as long as you're happy, I'm happy. I will love you no matter what because you are a good Mom regardless." I said I was glad he said that because I will be introducing him to her the following weekend.

It was very easy talking to T.J. about my new way of life. I decided to share it with my family now although nothing ever seemed to matter with us. I called my mother first:

Joyce – "Hi mother, I'm calling to tell you that I am Gay, and the woman that I'm dating name is Cozy."

Becky – "Baby that's just a faze"

Joyce – "Hey Sis"

Abby – "Hey girl what's up?"

Joyce – "I'm just calling to tell you that I am Gay, and the woman that I'm dating name is Cozy."

Abby - (Excited) "What, I can't believe you came out before me!"

Joyce – "Hey Sis"

Sherlene – "Hey, what's goin on?"

Joyce - "I'm just calling to tell you that I am Gay, and the woman that I'm dating name is Cozy."

Sherlene – "Is it because you work in a women's jail?"

Joyce - "Hey, I'm just calling to tell you that I am Gay, and the woman that I'm dating name is Cozy."

Anthony - "It don't matter to me, I'm gonna love you regardless, Sis."

    The four of us had become a family. I loved her Mom, and her Mom loved me, and T.J. I had a great relationship with her family as she did with mine. I had a two bedroom duplex apartment. T.J. had bunk beds in his room and Rissa slept on the bottom bunk while T.J. slept on the top bunk. Everything had really seemed to be going very well. My friends loved her, as I would often have company.

Cozy - "When I get off from work, I'm gonna go to the Barber Shop. When I call let me know what you want for dinner, so I can pick up whatever we don't have before I come in. I'm cooking tonight Ms. China."

China – "Ok! You don't have to go all the way to your barber because there is a good one right downstairs from us."

Cozy – "I don't let anyone but John cut my hair. I've been going to him since I was 16 years old. He cuts it just the way I like it can't do it Babe. I'll call you later."

"Ring, ring, ring "

Maria - "Hi China, how you doing?"

China – "Hi Maria, I'm fine how was work? "

Maria - "Work was fine. How is my grandbaby and T.J. doing? And are you guys going to get Rissa dressed at your house for her party tomorrow or over at my house?"

China – "They're both fine. We can dress her at your house since the party is in your backyard. This way she won't get dirty before people see how pretty she's going to look."

Maria – "Did Cozy tell you that Rissa's father is going to be there?"

China – "No, Cozy didn't tell me."

Maria – "She's there at the Barber Shop now he is supposed to give her money for the baby too so she can pick up some more things for the party tomorrow. He helps out a lot especially since he knows Cozy isn't working."

China – "Maria, are you telling me that Rissa's father is the barber. The one who cuts Cozy's hair? And are you telling me that Cozy don't have a job?"

Maria – "Oh my goodness China, Cozy didn't tell you who Rissa's father was? And she told you that she was working?"

China – "Yes, Yes, Yes, yes, yes, and yes! I'll be damned!"

Maria – "Cozy is going to kill me, I didn't know. I thought that she would have told you. I thought you knew she was on Public Assistance and that Rissa's father gives her money all the time for the baby."

China – "She's on Public Assistance too? Oh boy this keeps getting better! Maria I gotta go, I'll talk to you later, ok?"

When Cozy had gotten home that day, we talked about all of the lies. She had said to me that she didn't want to tell me the truth because I wouldn't have wanted to date her. I had now a change of heart about our relationship and we were just hanging in there at that point. I was so disappointed in her, and I was furious. It made me feel like our relationship was a lie. Sure we made beautiful love together, and that I loved her daughter and her family. Sure we had good times together, and enjoyed each other's company. But I couldn't tolerate being lied too. Especially since we had met over the phone and the truth should have been easier since we weren't face to face.

I had got even more furious when I remembered listening to conversations that she had with T.J. about her purchasing something for him. I would hear her say, "Umma buy you that! Umma buy you that! Oh, and we could go here and umma take you there!" I had realized that T.J. wasn't communicating with her as much because he had realized that she had been lying to him as well. I realized at that moment that she hadn't purchased anything, nor have they gone anyplace other than her mother's house together. I didn't want T.J. to experience any more lies being told by the people that I brought into his life. I was already dealing with the lies that his father was now telling him during his early recovery stages.

Tony had completed his two years in recovery and he wanted to do a lot for T.J. He had felt that he had already disappointed him in many ways, but Tony thought that he was able to step up and be a father. However, Tony's way of doing things started out by making promises to T.J. that he didn't keep, and would often disappoint T.J. It would bother me whenever that happened, but I would continually instill in T.J. that his father was still trying to find his way. Still, it would make T.J. more upset with his father when he watched him take care of another family.

So when I found out that Cozy was also lying to him, I knew that our relationship was over. It was different when I found out the truth about her not working and who her daughter's father was because that was more directed towards me. But then, when T.J. was caught in the lies I had to end it.

Gay pride was approaching and I was excited for the first time to be in the mix of it all. Cozy didn't want us to go, but she couldn't stop me from going. We were no longer together. So it was inevitable for new prospects to enter our lives. One month later, Cozy and I went to the Gay Pride Parade together. That's when I would meet a woman who caught my attention. She was beautiful. She wore a baseball cap with a long ponytail, she was chocolate like me. She wore a dungaree shirt with the top two buttons opened that showed her sexy. I had fallen in love. I was having the time of my life. I had never been to the parade before, and I was enjoying every minute of it with my second female love. I had forgotten all about Cozy whose feet was hurting and now sitting on the curb with a friend of hers. I came out to have a good time and that was what I did.

Tiffany lived all the way in Charleston, South Carolina. She would occasionally come down to New York when she wasn't in the Army Reserves.

After the Pride Parade, Tiffany had planned to return to South Carolina. Separating was very hard. Neither one of us wanted to say goodbye. We made several attempts until finally we made it a permanent call. The next day we talked on the phone almost the entire day. We had even come up with our theme song every time we spoke. ***"Someone to Love."*** by Kenny G and Baby Face.

Tiffany – "And you gave me someone one to love and you gave me someone to love"

China – "And you gave me someone to love and you gave me someone to love. Oh Yeah! Oh yeah"

We couldn't take the fact that we were so far apart from one another. I wanted her here with me, and she wanted to be with me. Our hearts wanted to be close to each other, as we longed to be next to each other in our thoughts. During this time my friend Steph had also been living in Coney Island and we were still very close. I had even gotten Steph to love our favorite song because she would join in when she heard me sing it over the phone. I wanted to be with this woman. It wasn't enough that she would come down and visit. The both of us could no longer stomach being apart. So we decided together that she would come to live in New York with me.

Tiffany – "I got some good news. Eric is coming down here to get me."

(Eric was a very close friend of Tiffany's that lived in Brooklyn)

China – "For real, you and David are coming down here to live with me and T.J.?"

(David was Tiffany's son)

Tiffany – "That's what we want right?"

China – "I'm coming down with him. I'm coming to get my baby girl."

Tiffany – "What about work?"

China – "You know me, I'll work it out! I am so happy right now."

Tiffany – "I don't want you to get in trouble on the count of me."

Sadly, I wasn't even thinking about my job. I knew that I was out on sick leave and that I was allowed certain hours outside of the house. I was willing to take a big risk to get this woman, knowing that I was jeopardizing my job. But for some reason, I knew that I could go and get her and return without anyone coming to my house to check on me. A wiser person just would have been there waiting for her when she and her two-year old son arrived.

As I sit back while writing this book, I realize the many decisions that I made in my life were done without thought. I acted on impulse many times. When things came to my mind, I reacted without spending a pittance of thought to figure it out. At any time did I put any of the lessons I learned about my childhood into practice. I had now begun to repeat who my mother was in a different light. I hated watching the different people come in and out of Becky's life. I had become my fearless mother in almost every way. But yet, without thinking, I had inflicted this same behavior on T.J. Sure he loves me, but what was I really teaching him? To him he says that I am the best Mom. In my thinking, I did him a disservice.

--------------

Tiffany and I would only attempt to have sex when the boys were asleep. David had the bottom bunk but he never slept in his bed. It seemed every time Tiffany and I would get ready to make love, David would start crying. Tiffany would call him out and ask him what was wrong. That's normal for a parent. I would have done the same thing as well. But what happened next would blow my mind. She would then hold him and put him to sleep right between us every time. I would turn over and go to sleep mad as hell. This would happen every night.

Finally, one night when David started crying, Tiffany and I was about to get physically involved when that annoying cry would appear. And like always, Tiffany would call him into the bedroom, and place David right between us. I was furious and said "Are you serious right now? The boy is not even crying. Every time he makes a sound you baby him up, and let him block us. He has a bed right in the room with T.J., what is the problem Tiffany? I didn't sign up for this." "I know, but if I don't he's gonna tell my mother when she calls and speak to him. And you already know what my mother is thinking," is what Tiffany said to me.

"Yeah, that's another thing, you a grown ass woman and you're worried about what your mother thinks? Almost every day for the past three months your mother sends you a box of mail talking about sin. So she must know that you're, Gay, but yet you say she doesn't know? And every time we want to make love, you get on top of me and hump as if we're doing something. I past the humping stage when I was eight years old. I'm a grown ass women. I'm telling you Tiffany, I can't keep this up. If you're not gonna make love to me, then we're gonna have some problems. And let the damn boy sleep in his own bed and stop spoiling him. He don't even be crying, he's just making a whole lot of damn noise and I'm sick of it!"

I had finally returned to work, and I was standing at roll call admiring this Captain who I had a crush on ever since I came on the job. I had just kept it to myself because I was with Malcolm, and then with Cozy. But now, I felt like I was ready to let her know because I didn't know what Tiffany and I were doing. So I decided to write this Captain a letter. I knew that she was dating someone, but I wanted to put it out there to her that I was now in the "life" hoping that when we were both single she would consider giving me a try.

Tiffany and I were going through the drama of her mother sending boxes of reading material about sin, hell, and Salvation. Then I would listen to the drama while her mother would question David over the phone. Not to mention the drama regarding having no sex, and David blocking us every night. It had become unbearable. And I didn't know what else I can say to change that. So from that moment on, I would get off from work in the morning, call Tiffany, and say that I was doing overtime and go to Cozys' house and we would make love to one another until we fell asleep. Then I would wake up, take a shower and be home by 5 pm in time for dinner. This behavior would be on going for three months until my doorbell rang and T.J. said that it was Cozy. Tiffany was angry as hell and said, "Who, what the hell she coming here for?"

At that moment I didn't really care. I knew that Cozy still loved me, and I constantly was letting Tiffany know how I was feeling. I kept telling her that things had to change but it remained the same. I knew that Tiffany loved me, as I too had loved Tiffany. But I had also missed the way Cozy would make love to me, and I yearned for that feeling again. In all honesty, Cozy had taken me sexually where nobody ever has. I never lied to Cozy. I told her what was happening with me and Tiffany. I also told her that I wasn't leaving Tiffany. And she knew that I wasn't coming back to her and right now it was just about the sex. I never lied. I wanted things to work out with Tiffany and me.

Instead, I was able to receive what I wanted from Cozy and get it, and still maintain Tiffany and my relationship up until now. Yeah, I was being selfish but I came to realize that that was who I was. It was all about China, Precious, Joyce, Lisa….whoever the hell I was.

China – "What are you doing here?"

Cozy – "China, I'm in love with you. And I know you love me too. I can't take it any more being without you. I love you so much! I'm here to tell Tiffany that I want you and that's it!"

Tiffany – "What the hell are you doing here?"

Cozy – "China is gonna be with me, and that's it"

China – "Where did you get such an idea from? I never said that to you."

Cozy – "You come over my house every morning after work, and we make love. I know you love me and want to be with me. She can't make you happy like I can."

Tiffany – "What do you mean she come over your house every morning after work? China you tell me that you're doing overtime so which one is it? And you are still sleeping with her?"

Cozy – "Tell her the truth China, Tell her that you are tired of her just humping on you and you need a real man!"

Tiffany – "Yeah China, tell me…"

China – "You happy now Cozy? Are you happy? You came all the way over here to break up my relationship with Tiffany. Are you happy? I'm damn shore not gon stand here and lie. I kept it real for the most part with both of y'all. Tiffany, I kept saying that shit had to change in the bedroom. I kept saying it but you ignored it, and still till this day you wanna hump. And your son sleeps with us. And Cozy, I never told you that I wanted to leave her. I told you that I loved her. I was just tired of not getting laid. You and I can never be a couple again. You lied to me. You just comforted me every time I needed you to. I'm sorry that I involved you, but you allowed it. I never lied to you about how I felt about Tiffany. And yes, Tiffany there was never overtime for me. I went to Cozy's house because I needed her touch. So now that the cat is out of the bag, Cozy you gotta go, and Tiffany, the next move is up to you."

I really wish that it hadn't gone that way. I never intentionally wanted to hurt anyone. But like I said earlier, I made decisions without taking a moment to think about them. I didn't think about the danger I could have caused myself or others. I didn't realize until I started writing this book that I was a selfish person. I was Selfish in ways of wanting things to go my way. But, again I wasn't looking to hurt anyone. Tiffany and I had broken up and she returned to the South. That day was sad for the both of us. But it was also understood for the most part.

If you ever read this book, Tiffany, I want you to know once again that I never meant to cause you any harm. When I saw you for the very first time, your beauty in itself captivated me. You have a smile that would light up the world. During our time together we sang together and we danced. We laughed and we cried. You brought out a song in me that till this day means a whole lot. "Someone to Love." Nothing that we went through and experienced together was a lie. I just had a crazy tolerance level, that I think only I understood.

Years later in 2012, Tiffany called me and let me know that she was coming to New York and that she wanted to see me. Tiffany had also said that she wanted to see my sister Abby because back in the day they were cool with each other as well. I thought it was a great idea, and I had looked forward to seeing her. It happen to be the same day that me and my girl Vee planned to hang out, and Vee was also cool with Abby. So I decided to call Abby and have everyone link up at her house, and as always, she was down for the cause.

During the time we were all together, I noticed that Tiffany was throwing a lot of shade around and we all caught it, but only Tiffany and I knew why. I was like really! After all these years, really! Tiffany was still hurt behind what I had done, and I guess her seeing me brought it all back as if it were yesterday. I had gotten so tired of the shade after ignoring it for a while and shouted out a few times, "I'm sorry! I'm so sorry! I am sorry!"

By that time I was at a different place. Therefore, my attitude was different. For some of us we can easily tell someone else to let it go and that it happened a long time ago. Get over it! But that's not fair for anyone to say. When a person gets hurt by someone that they love, getting over it is not something that's so easy to do. There was so much about love that I didn't understand. However, when I finally found out what love really is, it makes me feel hurt because of the ones that I hurt in my ignorance.

Later on I would understand that Tiffany really didn't want to disappoint her Mom and Dad. They were both spiritual people with morals and family values. None of which I had aside from when I was five living with my aunty and uncle. Tiffany had an understanding of things that I believe she fought with on a daily basis. I, on the other hand, had no direction, no morals, no guidance, no structure, no stability, no wisdom, no one to be held accountable to, and sometimes I didn't even use common sense. Hell, I didn't even realize that my parenting skills were shot.

# DANG

Yes, I am my mother's child. Years later T.J. and I had now moved three times since Coney Island within a two year period. I don't know what was I thinking when I decided to pack our things and move from Coney Island but again my thinking process wasn't right. I was not only unstable in my living situation I was also unstable in my thinking. One of the reasons we moved was because I had decided to help Abby and move into her apartment due to a situation she had encountered. When my services were no longer needed, my son and I moved into Harlem on 145th and St. Nick. I had truly loved that apartment. T.J., on the other hand didn't like the fact of living so far away from his cousins and friends, so whenever possible he would go and spend nights on the weekends.

During this time I was enjoying the Gay life. I was still hoping for an opportunity to get in with this Captain at my jail. I was still finding ways to let her know that I wanted to be with her. To my surprise a common friend of ours was having a fishing trip, and I enjoyed fishing. So of course, I found out that she was going and I was excited! Especially since I found out that her and her girlfriend had broken up. I wanted her so bad, and she knew it. I even felt that she had let her friends on the job read the letter that I had written her. But still I didn't care. I had never paid anybody at work any mind anyway.

I often think that I was there as long as I was because of her. I hated that job. I hated to see how the system was failing people of color. The consequences were different from their white counterparts. I viewed prison as another injustice. I started to become numb feeling like I was doing time as well. I started feeling like I was living in my own world and the only people who were in it was who I had let in. I was in charge of my life, and right at that moment the only people that I cared about was my son, my family and this Captain.

Evie – "Joy, can I use your towel for a minute?"

Stell - "Yo nigga, don't be asking my girl for her towel, find your own towel."

They both started laughing. I was shocked as hell that she called me her girl!

Stell – "You having a good time?"

Joy – "I sure am I like fishing and the company is great!"

Stell - "I see you don't have no problem putting those worms on the hook either. Acting like you a pro at this. Let's see what you got and catch some fish."

Joy – "You ain't said nothing but a word!"

Stell – "A'ight!"

After laughing and enjoying ourselves, as it was getting closer to dock it was down time and I had gotten tired. I had told Stell that I was going to sit down while she continued fishing. I had found a seat near this guy, and I sat next to him. I was exhausted, and I just needed to sit for a while. Well Stell had come over about an hour or so later and seen that I was sitting next to a guy. I was so tired all I did was look up at her. She continued to stand there, and then suddenly she walked away. Without thinking about anything, I sat there until the boat docked.

Before we had started fishing I had asked can I ride back with them, and Stell said sure. We walked to the car and I sat in the back. The only words that I heard from Stell was; "You can get out here!" At that moment, I realized that chick was definitely pissed with me, and I had no idea why. She didn't even care where she was dropping me off at and it was about midnight if not later. Thank God her friend Evie said "Nah, were not gonna drop her off here. Where exactly do you live?" "On 145th and St. Nick," I said. Evie said "We can drop you uptown." I had felt so bad. I had finally had a chance to be with this Captain and somehow I had blown it.

Nobody had spoken another word the rest of the way while I was in the car. I'm sure they had their jokes when I had gotten out. I was broken! I was so sad. I didn't know what had happened. Like what did I do wrong? We were having such a good time. Was that the Gemini in her that flipped? I was not only embarrassed but very hurt! At that point without spending too much time trying to figure it out, I knew that I had to move on because I just didn't stay single, I didn't know how to do such a thing.

However, I still always kept in my mind the possibility for another opportunity to be with that woman. Man, I had never wanted nothing or nobody as much as I wanted her. It wasn't her facial appearance because she wasn't pretty, or fine, but she looked damned good to me. She was tall, skinny, very neat and professional and her personality was the bomb to me. You can tell she was educated, and down to earth. She was the real deal as far as what I thought an Aggressive Gay Woman should be.

-----------------

Cozy – "You know I'm missing you so much. My mom, my aunt and my grandmother asked about you. And you know the baby misses you."

China – "I miss everyone too, and I think about you all a lot. Damn girl why you had to lie to me, you know that's when things went downhill for us."

Cozy – "I don't know why I lied. I can probably give you a million reasons, but then that would be a million more lies. All I know is I can't get you out of my mind. I can't keep a girlfriend because all I do is talk about you. China, please take me back."

China – "I have never stopped loving you and I can never get the feeling away from me as to how you used to make love to me. I think you got a degree in lovemaking and you made an everlasting impression."

Cozy –"I can still make you feel that way. Can I come see you?"

China – "Honesty from here on in. Are we going to go into this relationship with the truth, because I really can't stand being lied to"

Cozy – "Yes, let me prove it to you how much I want to be with you."

China – "I'm going away for five days with my buddy Cathy. We are taking our kids on a little vacation. How about you come to my house next Friday and stay the weekend with me. I'll give you my address and I will meet you at the subway. This way we can rekindle the spark we had from the beginning."

Cozy – "I remember it like yesterday. That was one of the best times of my life."

China – "Good, I'll see you then!"

Cathy and I had become really good friends. We started in the Academy together. As a matter of fact, we sat directly next to each other in class. After the Academy, Cathy and I were assigned to two different facilities. But shortly after she had come to the jail that I was working in and we worked the same post together on the same tour. We had become really close as we often enjoyed hanging out and traveling.

The time had come for me to meet Cozy at the train station on St. Nick. I was excited. I couldn't wait to see her. I knew that we were going to have a beautiful time together. All I wanted to do was get the night started with her because my every being had longed for her in a special way. When we saw each other, we greeted each other with a gentle hug and a good kiss. Then we started to walk the one block to my house.

Cozy – "Look at you, all the way out in Harlem now."

China – "Yeah, I'll tell you the story behind that later. But, I'm so happy to see you."

Cozy – "I'm happy to see you too. I couldn't wait for this day to come."

China – "Are you okay? You seem nervous!"

Cozy – "I am, China, I did something so stupid. I don't know why I put myself in a situation that I shouldn't of, but I did China. I was there and I was so scared. I'll tell you about it in the house. It's a lot going on right now and I'm scared shitless."

China – "Ok, well here is my humble abode."

When Cozy and I got in the house, for some reason we forgot about everything and everyone. We just started loving each other as if it were the very first time. Nothing else seemed to matter. It was just she and I in the house, and it was beautiful. She caressed my body in a way as if it were going to be the last time. She made love to every part of me allowing me to enjoy every moment. Tears fell from my eyes as I was being filled with pleasure. We didn't talk at all. Our lovemaking spoke for itself. The weekend had gone by in an hour. Before we knew it, it was Monday morning and she had to rush to get her baby girl off to daycare. We had planned to meet up later that day to go out and have the conversation that she was trying to talk about when we had first seen each other on Friday.

I couldn't wait to see her again. When the time came for us to meet, I couldn't reach her. I waited, and waited and waited until I finally called her Mom, and she said, "Hi China, Cozy got arrested when she went to pick Rissa up from school. She's arrested, China."

All of a sudden, it hit me. Cozy was trying to tell me what happened but we had gotten so caught up in each other that we didn't talk about it. That thing hit me like a ton of bricks. My heart felt like it had dropped. I had longed to be with her again. I needed my Cozy. As time was going on I couldn't try and communicate with her because she was now in the jail that I worked in. I would only hear from her mother who had been updating me throughout the year while she was going back and forth to court. I had realized that there wasn't anything that I could do but move on with my life, although I was silently weeping.

Luckily, I had worked midnights and had a steady post, which meant the chances were slim to none that I would see her unless she got into a fight and would come to the Bing area. The Bing is a Special Housing Unit that housed inmates who would get into fights or have Infractions of any kind that required lock down. There was only one person who knew Cozy was there and could connect me to her and she said nothing to no one. My partner Cathy didn't even know because she and Cozy had never met.

# SWITCH OFF

Nice summer evening, hanging out at the Pier in the Village with Abby, my friends Kit, and Rosie. Shortly after, Trina pulled up in the car with a few of her friends. When this dark-skinned woman with a nice haircut stepped out the car I wanted to know who she was. By this time I think I had outgrown China so now I'm just Joy from here on in. I walked up to the car, said hello to everyone and then I had to give a special shout out.

Joy - "How you doing Ms. Lady, my name is Joy."

Jazzy – "Jazzy."

Joy – "Jazzy, I like that, and your name fits you well. So what's up with you these days?"

Jazzy – "I'm in the Air Force and I'm only here for the weekend. I go back tomorrow."

Joy – "Word! So that means you and I gotta stay up all night and talk because I really would like to get to know you better before you leave me."

Jazzy – "You talk as if you know I don't have a girlfriend or something."

Joy – "You do now!"

Jazzy and I had an interesting time together. What attracted me to her was her looks and she had a certain kind of coolness that intrigued me. Jazzy was twenty eight years old. She wore a bob style haircut. She was my complexion, my height and about my weight. She just had more of a shape than I did being nicely built. She wore black Levis, black boot-like shoes, and a blue Levi denim shirt with the top two buttons open to show her sexy. Sounds familiar? Oh well!

During my time enjoying what she looked like, she began to smoke a kind of cigarette that I had never seen before. When I inhaled the aroma of it I loved it and for some reason, I really wanted to get to know her more. When I asked her the kind of cigarette she was smoking the way she said, "Djarum" had turned me on. I know, it didn't take much for me. However, it was her uniqueness that I had liked.

Jazzy had to return to the Air Force. Of course we exchanged all of our information and promised one another that we will stay in touch. We did however enjoy a kiss that said "I will see you again!" The departure appeared to have been rather sad for the both of us. And obviously everyone else noticed it because they were all having jokes saying "Jazzy don't go, please don't go!" We all started laughing as if Jazzy and I had fallen in love and everybody knew it.

# MOMMA BECK

Often times I would enjoy having gatherings with friends and family. T.J. was at the Marcy Projects with his cousins so I decided to have some adult fun. About 10 people from my job had come, including my partner Cathy. Abby who I always partied with had come as well. My ex-girlfriend Tiffany from South Carolina was there, and to my surprise, Becky had come to visit her baby girl. I had introduced my Mom to everyone and asked that they all give her a shout out and everyone held up their drinks as if giving a toast. I had a good crowd that night in my Harlem one-bedroom apartment. I had plenty of food and drinks so there were no worries. Whenever I would look around everyone was conversing with one another, laughing, drinking, eating and oh yes, some found room for a dance or two. We were all having a great time.

Tiffany had stayed after everyone had gone that morning. She was returning to South Carolina and she needed some rest before she took the drive. Before she left we had a great conversation. It had been mentioned to her through some common friends that Cozy had gotten arrested. However, she didn't know all the particulars. I had told Tiffany what I had known and she wished her well. We continued updating each other regarding other people that we knew and then Tiffany thought it was best for her to be on her way. We said our goodbyes until the next time.

Later on that evening Jazzy had called me wanting to know how the house gathering went. I had told her that everything was really nice and that I wish that she was there. Jazzy and I enjoyed talking to one another and we had missed each other more and more, and we both were feeling it. Later that day I received a telephone call from Becky. She told me that she was in the hospital and that the Doctors were running tests on her. She told me that she wasn't feeling well and she knew that she had to see a Doctor. When I asked Becky what hospital was she in waiting on these tests, she told me St. Mary's Hospital. Immediately, I said to her that I was on my way, and that I was taking her to St. Vincent Hospital in Manhattan. St. Mary's was the Hospital that I wouldn't have recommended anyone to use their bathroom, so of course I didn't want them to take care of my mother.

Room 721 was the room to be in. Becky was diagnosed with having a Rare Lung Disease. She was told that she would need a Lungs Transplant and would have to eventually be placed on a list. She had a room to herself. The leather green comfortable recliner had become my bed for six months. Her room was always decorated with cards, beautiful flowers, plants and lots of love. Some days my siblings and I would be there together with our children and some days it was just me and T.J. However, who came and how many had come didn't matter. We all had made our mother's hospital stay a good one.

In between hospital runs, work, and all else that mattered, I found out that there was a birthday party being planned for me by my partner Cathy and my boy Ace. Ace and I were also co-workers who had grown to be very close. Ace and I had gotten so close that our secrets had become the glue that kept us together. Often times he would come to my post and we would play checkers all night and laugh and talk. Ace would tell me some stories that kept me laughing hysterically. He had become like a brother and best bud all in one. We were friends and that meant a lot to me.

To my surprise, my party was being planned around Jazz's next visit. By now, Jazzy and I were seeing each other for about seven months, and loving it. Our communications were mostly over the telephone with maybe two visits at best. We would always write letters to one another and send photos so that we both can see what had been going on in our lives and talk as often as we could. I wasn't able to call her, but Jazzy would always give me a time and a day that she would need me to be by my phone, and I would be there most of the time. I had looked forward to her celebrating my 30th birthday with me.

# HANDLE IT

The music was pumping, the backyard was filled, and we were partying. It was good to see so many people turn out to come celebrate with me. To my surprise while in the middle of Jazzy and I dancing, the music had stopped. Jazzy shouted out how much she loved me and proposed to me with a diamond ring that very moment. Oh my, I was surprised. Of course I had accepted the proposal. Everyone congratulated us and we continued to party until some craziness broke out with Jazzy and some guys.

Supposedly someone who wasn't part of my party group had taken the liberty to touch Jazz's behind, and Jazzy had smacked the hell out of the guy and all hell broke out. It was eventually contained, and the guys left. I still don't know what had really happened that night. And I still can't figure out how I lost a great friend in the same night. Ace and I had not spoken since, and we were really cool friends. On that note, hey man, I still love you.

I couldn't wait to tell Becky the good news. When I got to the hospital I had told Becky everything from the beginning to the end. I told her that many pictures were taken and that I had to get them developed so that I can show them to her. I told her what Jazzy and I wore, and how surprised I was when she proposed to me. I told her about the craziness, and how Abby helped shut it down. We even talked about how later Jazzy will be upgrading my ring to a diamond that I can see. But for now it was all in love and I was very appreciative. But still, I was with my mamma, and we always kept it real with our jokes.

Doctor – "Hello Ms. Rebecca, how are you feeling today?"

Becky – "I'm fine, and how are you Dr. Spooner?"

Doctor – "I'm well thank you! Well after all of the tests, after all of six months of treatment, we believe without a Lung Transplant Ms. Rebecca, you only have six more months to live. And, we will be discharging you to a Nursing Home because we have provided all the treatment for you at the hospital. Now the only thing left to do is to have a Lung Transplant. I'm sorry to be the bearer of bad news but as discussed before Ms. Rebecca, your Lungs were really bad. We have contacted Tisch Hospital and they have set you up with an appointment. They will be working with you from here on regarding putting you on the waiting list for a Lung Transplant."

Joy – "So Dr. Spooner, what you're saying is that you guys are kicking my mother out of the hospital. What type of Nursing Home do y'all plan on putting her in.? Better yet, can I get a little time so that I can find a Nursing Home for her myself? I need to do some research on the one I think is best. So can y'all give me one week before y'all just place her some place? All I'm asking is for one week."

Doctor – "Honestly, for insurance purposes, I can stretch out three days. Her time as per Medicaid is actually up today. I truly do apologize! Ms. Rebecca, there is really nothing else we can do."

Joy – "No problem, I guess I better get on it right away then because you are not going just any place. And by the way, Becky you have more than some six months to live. You're gonna be ok, you hear me. I'm gonna find you some place next to me in Harlem. I gotta go and work this whole thing out. I'll be back, I'm off tonight. Love you."

Becky – "I love you too! See you later."

    I went home and got on the computer, made some phone calls and set up a few appointments back to back. Finally, I visited a Nursing Home on Riverside Drive in Harlem that I found to be decent enough for my mother to reside in for one month while I find a house to bring her to. I was excited that it didn't take me much time and that I was pleased with what I had seen, and the location being very close to where I lived. I had linked the Director up with the Social Services Department at the Hospital. I had made all the arrangements for my mother's arrival. Sanitized my mother's room, and notified cable TV assistance within the Nursing Home so that Becky could just come on in and be as comfortable as possible. She was now ready for her move-in date within the time period that Dr. Spooner had given me.

    That evening Jazzy had called me and I had told her all that I did and why I had to do it. She had already known my mother's situation being in the hospital but I was now updating her. When I told her that I had to go and find a house for us all to live in she had become very excited. Jazzy said that she wished she was no longer in the Air Force and that she wished that she was there to help me get situated. Jazzy even expressed how she wanted us all to be a family. I would say to Jazzy how much I wished that as well, but I also understood that she was enlisted for a few more years and I had accepted that.

I notified my siblings of the changes and everyone came up to the hospital to help Becky transition and to show up at the Nursing Home as a family. While still at the hospital it was thought of as a sad time because there were Nurses who had gotten very close with Becky and with all of us. Becky had shed some tears, as well as the Nurses. At that moment I realized that there are some Nurses who enjoy what they do. They brought not only their skills, but love, smiles, kindness, and comfort to our family. And for that they will be missed. They were a wonderful team of people that helped Becky get through.

Off to the Nursing Home with my siblings. I needed the staff to know that our mother was not just a drop-off, because I was well aware of what goes on in some of those places regardless of how they appear. I wanted them all to know that our mother has family, and this is only a temporary stay not exceeding one month. And they will see me there every day!

After getting Becky situated we all had made our rounds individually getting acquainted with staff and procedures of the residence. We introduced ourselves to some of the residents and we even participated in having a few jokes with some of the staff. We needed to let them know that Becky was our mother and she may not be treated like everyone else. That would have only applied to staff who was lacking in humility, compassion, and/or care. I only needed them to have at least one quality.

We spent the entire remainder of the day and evening there. Then I realized that tomorrow would start a new day to work hard looking for a home. Before leaving, I asked Becky was she okay being there, while reassuring her that it was only a temporary stay. I needed her to trust and believe that my words were promising as I walked out of the door leaving her in an unfamiliar place with unfamiliar people that were much older than she was. It felt nice when she looked up at us and said, "I love you all, and I'll be just fine!" Then she said, "And y'all better bring y'all butts back up here because y'all know how these places can be!" And then we all started laughing when Abby said, "Trust me, they already know!" We all had understood that while Abby made her rounds, she must have dropped some "inspiring" words. And then we all said that we loved her too, before leaving.

In less than two weeks Sherlene and I found a Two Family House in Brooklyn on St. Nicholas and Fulton Street. The ground floor had a backyard and three bedrooms so that we each can have our own room. The second floor accommodated Sherlene and her four children well. What a fit. We felt we had to take it, it was the perfect setup. The only thing left to do was agree to take it and sign the paperwork.

Jazzy had called and I was excited to tell her the wonderful news that my sister and I had found a house and that I was moving forward with all the paperwork. Jazzy was more excited than I expected. But to my surprise, Jazzy said that she was being Dishonorably Discharged from the Air Force due to her being Gay. And that she was coming home the following Friday, which was one week away, as she had to complete her discharge papers. I asked was she okay with their decision, and how did she really feel about that. I even asked how in the hell did they find out. All Jazzy let me know was that she said they had been watching her, and when asked, she didn't deny it. The question that stayed in my head was what were they watching her doing? Still, at that moment I wasn't going to make it about me or Jazzy. I needed to get my Mom home, and I had much to do.

Jazzy had seemed fine with the decision. Therefore, I wasn't going to prolong the conversation regarding it. Jazzy asked for the new address, because she was coming home. Jazzy and I had talked about living together and now it was about to happen. So we talked about her finding work, because it would be great for the both of us to bring in income. We talked about how we can work in shifts helping out with my mother since I had worked overnights, she would find a day job. We talked about sharing the load in the house with cooking and cleaning, and making time for ourselves. It was like two children sharing a fairy tale together. Although Jazzy was twenty eight and I was thirty.

After returning from the sign-in, I went to the house stood in front of it and was daydreaming. I immediately snapped out of my joy, and started planning and figuring out all the medical equipment that Becky was going to need before coming home. I had to call for her to get her medical bed set up, and the Portable and Electric Oxygen Tanks along with picking up her medications. I needed to go to my mother's apartment and gather some of her things to add to her new room so she would feel more at home. And then I had remembered to call St. Vincent's Hospital so that Social Service can assist with providing a Home Attendant. There were things that needed to be done, and I had to do them.

As time was approaching quickly, Jazzy had come out of the Air Force on time to assist with packing and moving from Harlem to our new home. I had hired some movers and because they were being paid by the hour, there was no time to waste. The crazy thing for me was although I was moving about in and around getting things done, I watched Jazzy do a very seductive body movement in front of the moving men that had me perturbed. However, the only thing that I said was, "Jazzy I can really use your energy up and down these six flights, because time is not our friend right now." I didn't think she heard me so I shouted, "I don't know what ya doing but I can really use your help right now!"

Afterwards, I just kept that in my head and never mentioned what I had seen. However, her behavior made me go back to the night of my party. I had wondered, was she doing something like what I saw that gave the guy the impression that she wanted him to touch her. Because I never understood what made that dude think it was okay to do what he did at such a gathering. But like I said, I will never know what really happened that night at my party. Although, I had started to believe that it was actually, Jazz's fault.

We arrived at our new home. It was getting dark. In all the planning, I forgot to get in touch with Con Ed. I started laughing because I had realized that I couldn't think of everything. So we set up what we could, and we did what we did to prepare ourselves for the night because with or without light, this was our new home. We had the entire weekend to clean up, put away, shop for furniture, receive deliveries and prepare ourselves for Becky's move-in date which was the following Monday.

Exactly one month to that day Becky had moved into the Nursing Home she was now leaving. Without missing a visit, it was time to go. The look on her face when I came to get her to enter our new home had lit up my world again. Becky's pecan tan complexion with her mole on her right cheek was glowing with happiness. My mother was coming home. She was coming home to a place that was new and inviting and accessible for all of her family to visit her, including her mother. We were on our way to new beginnings again.

During the times that I had visited Becky, we shared many conversations regarding Jazzy. I kept Becky updated with everything. Besides, Becky was still her same self it was only her Lungs that had the issue. Her brain, sense of humor, and sarcasm was still the same.

I had finally taken a moment to myself. I had gotten scared. It was 1996, and I have purchased a home at Thirty years old. Didn't know what to do with a house, didn't ever want a house. A Loft was all I ever dreamt of and still to this day. What I did know was that I was going to take care of my mother, be the best Mom that I knew how to be and everything else along the way I would just have to learn.

The time had come and I had introduced Jazzy to my mother. They both seemed excited somewhat but also uncertain. I couldn't figure it out then because I didn't want too. All I knew was that everything had to work because we were all together. I did know however, that T.J. didn't like Jazzy at all. He thought that she didn't know him well enough to come on to him strong like a parent. He thought that she needed to chill a little bit and get to know him first. And I understood that, so I told Jazzy to take it easy.

Everyone had gotten comfortable in our new home. Sherline had moved upstairs with her family. And we were working things out. I continued working nights, and making sure that the home was taken care of. Becky had everything that she needed and all of what she wanted other than new Lungs and a man. I told her that I could get her one of those vibrating toys to help her along the way. Becky started laughing and said it might feel too good and make her stop breathing even with the Oxygen. So we both looked at each other and said, "Nah, you don't need it." We kept up our sense of humor because like I said before, Becky was still alive and very much herself.

My Aunty Brenda would make it her business to come to the house and help out with Becky. They were sisters and best friends. Aunty Brenda would come in the mornings and sit with Becky and all you would hear was laughter coming out of my mother's room. I was sure that they shared many stories from back in their day. Sometimes she would stay all day and leave in the evening, and sometimes she would leave and come back. Often times she would cook something and we all would enjoy it because Aunty Brenda was a great cook. I would put my bid in and she would always make it. Either way Aunty Brenda would come and be with my Mom, her sister and her best friend until her passing.

When Aunty Brenda had died, I noticed a different type of sadness in my mother. It was a sadness that was understood because like I said they were best friends and they had definitely gone through a lot together. Knowing that my mother had to be hurting, members of the family would visit more frequently. I thought the cutest moments was how my little niece who lived upstairs would make sure she came downstairs every day to ask my mother, "Are you okay? Are you ok grandma?" and she would sit in my mother's room on the floor and play by herself.

# CRAZY IS AS CRAZY DOES

Jazzy had asked that we go and see her parents together because she would love for me to meet them. She said that she would set it up soon because they needed to know that she was no longer in the Air Force. Also she said that she would use that opportunity to tell them that she was Gay. I suggested that she tell them that on her own without me being there but she said no, she wanted me with her.

The day had come. It was on a Saturday that I would meet Jazz's parents. Off to Canarsie we went. Right before we reached the house, Jazzy asked me was I ready to meet her parents. I wasn't sure then why she'd ask me was I ready to meet her parents, but I found out later that day the reason behind the question. However, the question should have been is it all right for you not to meet my parents? Certainly after the visit, Jazz's identity had been revealed.

What the hell did I get myself into? Jazzy and I walked into the house that she grew up in. Her dad seemed to be cool, but her mother was like some prima donna, crazy Step Ford wife, pretty but yet a scary evil woman. She had some serious control over Jazzy even in her adulthood. I watched how Jazzy was intimidated by her mother's every word. Jazzy was like this little child who was scared of her mother. Scared to speak, scared to eat, scared to laugh, and scared to cry. I sat there as if I was watching a freekin' movie called "Who the hell is this? And what did you do with Jazzy!"

After a moment, I couldn't take too much of the degrading, the fakeness, nor the air. I had to go. And everyone who knows me, know that I am not staying anywhere that makes me uncomfortable. It could be a friend, family, foe, job, or relationship. So we left. She didn't have to leave but I certainly was. While traveling home Jazzy let the cat out of the bag about her childhood regarding the beatings she would get, and then later signing herself into the Air Force to get away from her life. I thought at that moment that "we are what we eat. We are a product of our environment." Or "the apple doesn't fall far from the tree." There are several metaphors that I can use, but at that moment I had realized that she was bringing it into our home. Why else did T.J. say that he didn't like her? I knew it had to be a reason behind it, and now I was able to see where it had come from. At that moment I realized that I had damaged goods. But once again, I decided to give it a try because, after all, we were supposed to make a new life for ourselves in our new home. However, I "stressed" to Jazzy to be very mindful how she speak to T.J. because he will not be her target.

I always made it a habit to cook full course meals when I had become a mother. Sitting down at the dinner table to eat together was normal for my household. Now that I was taking care of my Mom, the meals had gotten a little better because she would sometimes direct me with the seasonings. I know not for nothing T.J. appreciated that because his mother was no Chef. This day however, I decided to make two of my specialties, Lasagna with Garlic Bread, and for dessert Banana Pudding. When Becky heard what I was cooking she started laughing and saying that was the reason she was getting so fat. During these stages in my life I didn't know much about the effects of fatty foods. Or shall I say that it wasn't a thought of interest to me. I didn't have a thought about Cholesterol or how to make better choices when cooking. I cooked, and whatever I used, we ate. Being healthy wasn't an issue or a thought. However, when I was growing up, starving was.

Becky would often give great dinner ideas. We loved it when she would have me make Lamb Chops and for dessert her famous Bread Pudding. Now I know why today my son and I both have High Cholesterol. All the fatty foods and shellfish we would eat on a regular basis. Hell, I was killing all of us slowly. It seemed like now that I was no longer deprived of food, I was going in on a regular basis with whatever we wanted to eat without limits. I'm not saying we were gluttons, and just ate. No, it wasn't like that. I'm simply saying that food in my home was never an issue. I never wanted my child to be deprived of what I was deprived of growing up, and food was one of those things that I vowed would never be an issue. And it wasn't.

Every day when I would come home from work, Jazzy would be sitting in a different spot in the living room with The New York Times, a cup filled with some sort of beverage, and a cigarette. Actually all through the house Jazzy would leave her signature of mess. She was a damn slob. And messy is something that I am not. My mother had mentioned to me one day that she didn't take her medicine because Jazzy had ignored her all day. She also said that when Jazzy would pass her room she would turn her head letting my mother know not to ask her for anything. I didn't understand why she was doing that because we had agreed on her assisting my mother until the Home Attendant showed up. But Jazzy wasn't assisting in anything at this point. She didn't cook, clean or anything else. She just ate, drank, and smoked.

Joy – "Hey Jazz, how is the job search coming along?"

Jazzy – "Still at it!"

Joy – "What types of jobs are you looking for, because you have been looking in The New York Times for three months now, and as far as I know, you haven't had an interview yet. Have you ever tried The Daily News?"

Jazzy – "The Daily News don't have the kind of jobs that I'm looking for. When I was in college my Professors always said The New York Times is for scholars."

Joy – "Well 'scholar', excusez em moi! But you shouldn't limit yourself. And why are newspapers, cups filled with juice and ashtrays that need emptying everywhere in the house? I had told you that we should only smoke in the living room with the door closed or in the hallway. My mother has an Oxygen Tank in her room."

Jazzy – "But I don't sit in the living room all the time, and the papers that are around are there because I change my position."

Joy – "Well can you clean up after you 'change' your position? Jazzy, I don't know what's going on with you but ever since we came from your parents' house three months ago, you've been acting strange and I don't like it. And another thing, check the freekin' Daily News, you might find something for a beginning 'scholar!' You sit around here moping, making everybody in the damn house depressed. Fix whatever the problem is, and don't stay there.

Jazzy – "What happened to us, Joy? What happened to us? We never spend time alone. If you're not working, you're entertaining T.J., or your mother. It seems that you never have time for me. You wanted me here, remember?"

Joy – "Yeah, you got damn right! I work then I might work overtime. Then I come home and cook so everybody can have a decent meal. I clean because I can't live in a nasty house. I make sure that all the bills are paid, the front of the house is clean, my Mom is good, and my son is on task. Then I go back to work and it all repeats itself. What the hell do you want from me? Because if you noticed everything I just said was I."

The next morning when I came home from work I asked Becky how she was feeling?

Becky – "I'm ok, can you give me my medicine please, and I'm gonna need you to give me some bread or something so I can take that new medicine. It says I have to take it with food."

Joy – "I got you. Wait a minute, why didn't Jazzy give you your medicine yet? You were supposed to take this at 8:00 a.m. it's now 9:30 a.m."

Becky – "Joyce I've been calling Jazzy and she wouldn't answer me. I don't know where she went. After T.J. left to go school about 7:45, Jazzy came out the room, and I haven't seen her since. I even tried calling her because I had heard some noise in the basement. It sounded like somebody was banging something."

Joy – "Let me fix you something to eat."

Becky – "What's wrong with the girl, Joyce? Something is wrong with her. I don't like her for you, she ain't right!"

Joy – "Hey Jazzy, where you been? You couldn't have been far with your pajamas still on."

Jazzy – "I was in the basement looking for something."

Joy – "I'll be finished in a minute. I need to talk to you. I'll meet you in the bedroom."

After I had fixed Becky something to eat and gave her, her medicine, I went to talk with Jazzy. I reached out to hold her shoulders and turn her towards me when she flinched. I went to hold her again and she flinched again. I didn't t understand why she kept flinching, so I tried again to hold her and she flinched even more. I asked Jazzy what was the problem? She said that she had fell and bruised herself. So of course I wanted to see the bruises. She tried to stop me from taking off her pajama top, I was like, "Are you kidding me? I have undressed you plenty of times and you never stopped me, so don't stop me now. I want to see the bruises!"

Joy – "What the hell, this ain't from know damn fall. What the hell is going on Jazzy? Don't start crying. Tell me what the hell is going on."

Jazzy – "I went in the basement and banged myself on the wall because I was angry."

Joy – "You did what? Oh shit, that was the noise my mother heard. You bruised yourself because you were angry. Well, what the hell makes you think I can sleep next to someone who would do that to themself? I wouldn't be able to sleep. I don't know what is wrong with you, but since this is how you do things, Jazzy you gotta go. I love you, but you gotta go. I can no longer leave you here with my mother, and my son. I'm sorry baby, but this didn't work out. I'm gonna let you stay in my mother's apartment until you get on your own. Don't worry about the rent, it's a small amount and I'll continue to pay it. But you have to leave today, sweet heart."

Jazzy – "You're kicking me out?"

Joy – "At least I am giving you another place to live. But I can't have you stay here, I'm sorry. I don't mean to be cold, but that's dangerous what you did, so please pack up so I can take you where the apartment is. "

That was the way that it had ended between Jazzy and me. Sure I know that was cold and a harsh and maybe inconsiderate the way I dealt with the situation. But I was putting safety first for my family. And besides, I was a 30 year old woman not having that kind of experience. Therefore, my spontaneous decision making kicked in immediately once again. I had to do something and quick because I had to work that night and couldn't call out. I knew that time wasn't on my side. She couldn't stay there with T.J. and my Mom. Jazzy had literally freaked me out. She gathered her things and went to my mother's apartment. I changed the locks on the doors, and I got ready for work, and moved on with my life. Was I sad about the situation? Yes! Did I wish things were different? Yes! Did I love her? Yes! Could I have dealt with someone like that? No!

It didn't take long for me to meet Jean. Jean was a Parole Officer 15 years my senior. Very intelligent, and she intrigued me in a different way. She had it going on for herself and I appreciated that. She had a Two-Family Home of her own, well into her career, a nice bank account and a Benz to blend in with the coolness of her personality. I thought to myself finally, someone who was literally holding down their own. Jean was my complexion with a head full of hair that she would only keep styled one way. She wore her hair curly going to the back. She was 5'8" and weighed about 155 pounds. Everything blended in well for her character and her role as an Aggressive Gay Woman.

The Home Attendant assisted with Becky five days a week 9 - 5 and sometimes 10 - 7 pm. After going through a few, I had finally gotten a really good one. Becky really liked her. She and I used to work together and I asked would she take on taking care of my mother and she accepted. Meanwhile, Jazzy had raised my stress level because I had been trying to reach her for a week just to check on her because I wanted to give her more money for food and whatever else, but she wouldn't return any of my calls. Being that Jean was now the new woman in my life I thought it was the right thing to do by letting her know that I was concerned about my ex-girlfriend and that I needed to check on her. Without hesitation, Jean said, "Let's go!"

After several times of me knocking on the door and getting no answer, I entered the apartment. Clothes and newspapers were everywhere. A stench whispered throughout the apartment. It looked like whoever lived there was a depressed, deranged person. All I could do at that moment was cry because I was truly concerned about her. Jean noticed my deep concern and suggested that we drive around to see if we would see her.

We drove around that day and other days but we'd never seen Jazzy. I had gone back to the apartment on a few occasions but still no Jazzy. Eventually, I turned the keys into the Housing Management office and gave up the apartment because at this time I knew that my mother will be staying with me permanently.

I remember seeing Jazzy about a year later. I had gone to B52's which was a club in lower Manhattan that was a Gay hangout spot known for karaoke. I'm not sure if it is still, but I certainly had some great times there. I enjoyed having a good time and getting my dance on whenever I could. That night, I had been dancing for like four songs straight with people, and I needed to sit down for a while. I was so danced out that when I came and sat down, I put my head down and placed my hands on my lap trying to regroup.

Finally when I had gotten it together, I looked to my right and noticed Abby sitting next to me. But when I looked to my left I had a fear come over me. It was a spooky feeling. To my surprise, it was Jazzy. Her locks that I had started had grown uncontrollably and she didn't quite look like herself. All I can say was hello, and all Jazzy did was look at me with an uninviting eye. Of course I let Abby know just in case anything jumped off.

I didn't stay sitting there because I had felt too uncomfortable. Abby and I had kept our eye on Jazzy because you just never know how these things could play out. With that being said, I didn't order another drink because I needed to be in my right mind, just in case. But honestly, I felt bad. At that moment I really felt that it was my fault. Jazzy had allowed herself to love me. Jazzy wasn't a bad person, I just think that if our past isn't dealt with in a healthy way, our future becomes unhealthy to ourselves and others. In both Jazzy and my case, we had a very unhealthy past that clearly neither of us dealt with. Therefore, we continued in our own self destruction while inviting others.

# A LITTLE BIT OF THIS, A LITTLE BIT OF THAT

"You're busted! You two are so busted! I knew the both of you were giving Becky sweets on the side. You are so busted. T.J., you went to the store to get it, and Babe you were in on it. Y'all are so busted." The three of them started laughing uncontrollably. While Becky was laughing she said that it was just a little something sweet and that was all. When I tried to respond regarding her Diabetes, T.J. reminded me that it was no different when I become Betty Crocker in the kitchen making Banana Pudding, Bread Pudding and baking cakes. I said that I had a method to my madness. I give her a little dessert after dinner. Then, I give her medicine so it kind of mellows it all out. I said "you guys give her sweets after she done had her medicine. Y'all better cut it out, and Becky I know you be puttin' your bid in for something sweet." We all just laughed it off because we all wanted to keep Becky happy in our own way.

---

"Jeanie, Jeanie, are you okay? I'm calling the ambulance." Becky shouted, "What's wrong?" I said that Jean was having an Asthma Attack. To my surprise, Jeanie was also very sickly. She was a good person to me and my family. She had it all together in many ways. Still, I had come to realize as much as I wanted her in my life, she needed me in hers. I wasn't sure if I was ready to take on such a responsibility always running to the hospital with her, and watching over her. But within such a short time Jean and I became very special to one another.

"Jeanie, you shouldn't be smoking when you have Asthma. The Doctor said that when you go back for your next appointment, you better had quit smoking. I know he's a good Doctor because he helped T.J. with his Asthma, and he's not having any problems." Jean's response to me was that it wasn't that easy for her to quit smoking. And then what she would do is redirect the conversation by mentioning shopping for my favorite item, which were shoes. And she knew that I would get excited about that and forget about what we were talking about until the next time an episode occurred.

Over a very short period of time I found myself at the hospital with Jean quite often. I had called out sick one night because I didn't want to leave Jean home alone after we had returned one day from the hospital. Although it was against my better judgment by calling out, I felt my presence was needed. Besides, Jean always had a way of letting me know that she needed me and I couldn't find it in me not to stay. Luckily, I had taken heed to her request because shore enough, I had to call the ambulance for Jean to return to the hospital.

While at the hospital with Jean all I could think of was this being the day that I was caught out of the house without proper reason. The New York City Department of Corrections allows employees out of the house during certain hours while out sick. If caught outside the house when you are not allowed, you can be brought up on charges. I was very much aware of it, and from time to time I had taken my chances. I would later find out that night wasn't a good night to take chances.

Waiting for Jean to see the Doctor, my pager went off and I called home. T.J. said that two Captains from my job had paid me a visit and instructed me to call when I reached home. I had gotten busted, and knew that I had to suffer the consequences. I just didn't know what. For a while nothing would happen.

I had planned another vacation by way of doing Mutuals. Mutuals are working your shift and working someone else's so that you can have a certain number of days off consecutively. As Correction Officers you needed and appreciated having the option to do that. I had done enough Mutuals that had given me two weeks off. When I returned to work, I was assigned another post. I was surprised because I had a steady post for seven years. To my surprise, I was taken off my steady midnight post, and was placed on what they called the Wheel. The Wheel is rotating shifts. Four straight days on the 7 - 3 p.m. tour with two days off. Four straight days on the 3-11p.m.

## HANDLE IT

tour with two days off. And four nights on the 11 -7 a.m. tour, and so on. I hadn't been on the wheel in years and with my lifestyle being a single parent who was very active in T.J's life, taking care of my mother, taking care of the many issues that I had with my house, and taking care of Jean, it had become increasingly overwhelming.

When I inquired about the reason or reasons being placed on the Wheel, it was said that I was under Investigation. That response alone didn't set well with me because I knew that I hadn't done anything to be under Investigation. Upon my further investigation, I found out it was when I was caught outside of my home when I was on sick leave. Five months had passed sense then and I had forgotten all about it. Obviously, the department didn't forget. I had put in writing, a request to return to the midnight tour for a hardship while I was being investigated. I was having an extremely hard time on the Wheel trying to maintain everything. I was granted a hardship to remain on the overnight shift for six weeks. However, I was not to return to my steady post.

While at Roll Call the Captain who I still had a love crush on assigned me to the 6 Upper A Post. My stomach dropped! 6 upper A was where Cozy was. Her case was so intense that she was still being held there two years later. At this point was I supposed to say to the Captain that I couldn't work that post because my ex who is not really my ex because we never officially broke up, is now living in Six Upper, or should I just go to my post was the question that I had silently asked myself.

The A post is inside the housing area and that officer has visual of the unit. The officer assigned to that post controls the doors, gates, answer the phone, and call in the count, along with other duties. The B Officer works on the floor with the inmates. For the first time in two years Cozy and I had seen each other since we had gotten back together. I turned to my left and there she was. She looked up at me and simultaneously we both shed tears. The only thing that was separating us was Plexiglas. We didn't say a word to each other. She put her head down while her tears flowed and walked to her cell. Me, my tears fell for the remainder of the night.

The following night I was sent to 6 Upper A post again. This time the tears from both of us were uncontrollable as we locked eyes. She said, "China

I mean Ms. Harriet, I didn't do what they said I did. I really didn't and you gotta believe me. They are offering me 25 years. I wish I could do it all over again. I was so stupid! I froze at first and out of fear I reacted. I was so scared China I mean Ms. Harriet." I could not stop crying. But at that point we knew that she had to return to her cell. I was speechless. I think my tears had spoken for me. I couldn't stop crying throughout my entire tour. I was a wreck. My eyes must have been bloodshot red. I avoided direct eye contact with anyone who had to talk to me. I thought I was having a nervous breakdown right on my post. I could barely breathe.

The following night Captain Bryce (Stell) assigned me the same post. I started to think that somebody was up to something. I couldn't take seeing Cozy locked up anymore I said, "Captain, can you please assign me another post? I can't do it! I can't go back to that post! My ex-girlfriend is in there, can you please assign me another post?" I didn't have any worries of her understanding that because her ex-girlfriend had done some time in this prison as well, again and again.

Soon after, the decision was made to place me on the wheel my hardship had ended. I tried it for a while, but then I couldn't take it considering all that was going on in my life. I couldn't allow myself to feel trapped, and out of control with my space and time. I wasn't going to allow the department or anyone to have control over me in any kind of way. After all, I had promised myself never to allow anyone or anything to make me feel other than myself after what my cousin had done to me, and how others had treated me. After growing up with that guilt and pain, and having no one to go to, in my mind I felt the need to always be in control, and I felt that I needed to be free.

I was ending my 10th year as a Correction Officer. I had just finished a meal relief. While I was walking down the corridor I had this sudden urge to leave and never return. I no longer wanted to be a Correction Officer. I started feeling like I couldn't breathe, and I needed air. I didn't say a word to anyone. I walked to personnel asked for resignation papers, filled them out, cleared out my locker and kissed Riker's Island goodbye.

Immediately after, I had gotten a job as a Supervisor at a Group Home for at-risk boys. After six months on that job, I had gotten fired. I had to rush home because the lights had gone out. There was a Black Out in certain parts of Brooklyn and my home was within the area. All I thought about was Becky and her Oxygen. I called my Supervisor several times to let him know that I was leaving a co-worker in charge who often stepped up as Acting Supervisor. I had never gotten a return call from my Supervisor, so I left work to go home. I notified Channel 7 News and they were at our house within 20 minutes. I wasn't sure as to how long the lights were going to be out. But I was sure that my mother would need more Portable Oxygen tanks just in case. Mission was accomplished! Becky had gotten a delivery within one hour. Thanks Eyewitness News, because I didn't have time to take a risk like that. I understood why I had gotten fired, but I also understood why I had to leave.

It had now been close to two years since Dr. Spooner had given my mother six months to live. Becky was still continuing to enjoy life with family. It seemed as if twice or three times a week another family member would come and visit with her. Becky was having more company than T.J. and I put together. She was enjoying frequent visits from her mother and their relationship seemed to have been really working itself out. We had back yard BBQ's and evening rides in her wheel chair. On one occasion we took the drive out to Long Island to spend the day with Aunty Beverly and Uncle Jay. Whatever Becky wanted to do, I did everything in my powers to make her happy.

Becky and I would sometimes have personal moments when we both would share what was in our hearts. She said that she knew something was wrong with me and she wanted me to tell her about it. I said that I was feeling overwhelmed and I had needed a break from everything. I had felt like I was still a child dealing with big time grown folk stuff, and it was sucking the breath out of me. I was feeling like whenever I thought I was okay something else would happen.

My basement would flood every time it rained. The first time it flooded I had lost everything personal that I owned as well as many brand new household items. I would call Plumber after Plumber and all they would do was unclog the drain. I notified the City and they sent someone out. The City said that it wasn't a City problem so I was back to square one. Rats would flood the basement. I had paid out a lot of money to different Plumbers. I was stressed out. And I had no answers.

During this moment with Becky, I expressed everything to her and I cried in her arms for the very first time. Becky said that she was proud of me. She said that she thought that I was doing a great job as a mother as a daughter, as a sister, and as a friend. She told me that she loves my caring heart and the way that I take care of her. Becky had thanked me for helping her now and earlier in her life when we used to go shopping and go to the hair salon. She thanked me for taking her furniture shopping when she had finally gotten back on her feet. She told me that she loved me. Then what surprised me was when my mother told me that she had forgiven her mother and that she wanted me to forgive her too.

I looked at my mother I told her that I had loved her also. I gave her the biggest hug and smiled. Then I told my Mom to find us a movie to watch while I get us a snack. That night Becky and I enjoyed ***"How Stella Got Her Groove Back"*** and we laughed throughout the entire movie. Becky said that she was Stella and she planned to get her groove back after she got her new lungs. I said all right now!

May 18, 1999 at 4:46 a.m. Becky's Pager went off. The Pager was specifically for the hospital informing Becky that it was time for surgery. We had already known that when the Pager went off to get to the hospital ASAP! Therefore, there was always a set of clothing prepared and an assignment for everybody so we can leave quickly. That was the phone call that we had been waiting for. They have Lungs for my mother. Jean, T.J. and I are rushing to get her ready. We were so excited, as well as nervous. T.J. notified Sherlene upstairs, and off to the hospital we all went. While at the hospital, I notified my grandmother and my mother's siblings that the day had finally come for Becky to get her new set of Lungs.

Several hours later the Doctor came out and said that the Lungs were too big and Becky's body was rejecting it. Words could not express what I was going through at that moment and a long time afterwards. I couldn't explain or express what anyone else was going through because I couldn't see past the excitement of the Pager going off. The next thing I knew, I was told that my mother had died because they had turned the machines from off her. REALLY! Nothing else was ever said. At 10:30 a.m. May 18, 1999, Rebecca was pronounced dead.

# HANDLE IT

After my mother had passed something had left me as well. I couldn't quite put my finger on it at that moment. Cathy couldn't make the funeral because she was giving birth to her youngest son. However, there were a lot of people from the Department of Corrections to support both me and Sherlene including the Captain (Stell) that I still had my crush on. Malcolm and other old friends of mine that I haven't seen in years had come and gave their support. Many of my siblings' friends and family members were there. People showed up to say goodbye in record numbers.

However, I wasn't myself at the funeral and I felt it. I just didn't feel right. I kept asking myself what happened. I felt like I was in the Twilight Zone or something. Why did they call her for the Lungs if they were too big? They had done all the measurements that they needed. We were reassured on a few occasions that we would "ONLY" be notified with the right set of Lungs for Becky. We were told how these procedures was time sensitive so they had to be accurate before making the call. We were confident because these Doctors have done these procedures quite often. Why my mother? I just couldn't figure it out. I would smile periodically because I was reminded of the talk we had a few nights before the Pager went off. And how much we had enjoyed our last movie together ***"How Stella Got Her Groove Back,"*** I am still so thankful for that night because the memories from it still makes my heart smile. But still, it remains a mystery.

Becky was Cremated because those were her wishes. I realized later that the only reason those were her wishes was because she didn't have a Life Insurance Policy, and she thought Cremation was inexpensive. Still, Sherlene and I with the help of Jean paid for what an average funeral would cost. Obviously something else had gone wrong, but the money didn't matter. However, I will always stress the importance of Life Insurance. If you don't have it get it and that's that!

My siblings and I had spread her ashes over the waters from on top of the Williamsburg Bridge. That was because for many years almost every day Becky had walked that bridge, and for me spreading her ashes over it symbolized her finally being free. And that's what I felt when I held her ashes in my hand, letting the wind take hold of them. I felt that my mother was finally free.

# R U KIDDIN ME

Sherlene had moved out from upstairs with her family she had decided that she didn't want to stay in the house anymore since our mother had passed. Jean had suggested to me that I rent out the upstairs in rooms like her mother was currently doing at her home. I thought that was a great idea so I did just that. There were four bedrooms upstairs and I rented them out individually.

Things were going well upstairs for a year. T.J. was about to go off to college in less than a year, and I didn't want to stay there alone. I rented my apartment out to a married couple with three children. By this time Jean and I were very close, and we spent much of our time together. We were enjoying ourselves with friends and family "mines only" and still going to the hospital often due to her Asthma. The decision was made for us to live together at her house, until I decided what I wanted to do. Jean was very accommodating to me and T.J. She and I shared her room, and T.J. had his own room before leaving off to college.

I had come to realize that Jean would treat me really nice by doing things for me just to get the attention off of her. I would watch Jean and sometimes feel like something deep was going on with her, but I couldn't figure it out. After being with Jean for six months, I would now understand that Jean was still in love with her wife. She made it appear to me that she hated her wife and she never wanted to see her again because of what she had done to her. To my surprise, Jean had still loved this woman with all of her heart and we all know if someone has your heart no one else can. Besides, who wants to share that space?

While we were asleep Jean's cell phone rang, Jean got up from the bed went into the kitchen thinking that I was still asleep to have a private conversation with her wife. "I still love you, why don't you just come home and we can start all over again. I love you honey and miss you so much, please come home." At that moment, I was frozen like I was when I noticed Thomas on top of me. I pretended that I didn't hear a thing. I had just heard Jean tell her wife that she can come home. If she can come home then where were my son and I going? What the hell was happening? Every part of my being wanted to scream!

Jean walked back into the room looking as if she wanted to cry. I asked Jean why wasn't she honest with me regarding still being in love with her wife? Hell I was still in love with a couple of folks my damn self. I just had to walk away. She could have told me that she was still trying to get with her wife. I wanted to know why couldn't she just tell me before I uprooted my son and came to live with her and rented out my house. At that moment Jean started crying hard, and said she was so sorry. She said that she didn't know why she didn't tell me because she really wanted to hate her wife for leaving. Then Jean finally said that she was still in love with her wife and didn't know what to do. And because of her feelings that was the reason behind her seeing a Therapist every Saturday for the past two years because she was still hurting. I didn't know what to say, so I said absolutely nothing!

Jean had assured me that in no way would T.J. and I have to leave. She knew that her wife would never return to that house because her wife hated it there. Jean said that she wants me there just as much as she needed me there, and that we had no worries. I believed her, but I did still have a home to go to and I thought that I needed to return to it. So I decided to let the tenants upstairs know that I will be moving upstairs and that they had a certain amount of time to find another place. I knew that I couldn't move downstairs because I had just rented that out to a family with a two-year lease, and it had only been six months. Besides, I didn't want to live downstairs I thought it would have been too hard.

The strange thing was, I didn't get upset and I knew because of the relationship she needed me, and part of me had now started to need her. So we remained friends, and nobody from that moment on understood our relationship. A relationship that was strictly platonic. No sex, and no kisses, but lots of hugs, letting each other know that we have our own kind of love for one another. A friendship! But something was now happening to me again. My Mom had died, and I was unemployed.

# HANDLE IT

On top of that my tenants had refused to move. They said that I was renting my house illegally and they had rights. I didn't know what rights they thought they had but I went to the courthouse only to find out that it was illegal to rent rooms. So then the tenants upstairs conspired with the tenants downstairs and then nobody was paying me rent. The house was categorized as illegal because I had rented rooms. Meanwhile my mortgage and other bills with the house had to be paid. Now at thirty three years old, I was completely lost for words. If I had known that it was illegal to rent out single rooms, certainly I wouldn't have done so. I had listened to Jean thinking she knew best because her mother was doing it for years as well as other people.

I went to get my rent from the tenants downstairs and the youngest daughter who was about six or seven years old had come to the door with her hand on her little hip. This little girl looked me dead in my face and said, "Wad you want?" with attitude! I was lost for words again and the mother had come to the door with an attitude as well. At that moment I had realized the games had begun. I didn't quite know how to deal with it all, so I started court proceedings.

Meanwhile, as time went on Jean and her wife would have conversations and periodically have weekends together at a hotel. Jean would always be respectful and never allowed me to hear their conversations. However, I would always know when a weekend with her was coming up. Jean would go about things differently. She would want to go clothes shopping for us, food shopping and give me extra money to have while she was away. I had no problem going along with the flow.

Often times what would bother me was when Jean would return home sometimes and get deeper into her depression. I used to get so upset that she was so in love with someone who didn't love her the same way. Sure, their business was their business but my friend was suffering right before my own eyes, and it was sad for me to watch her in so much pain. However, those depressed moments still existed after every return from being with her wife.

It's Saturday night, Jean is with her wife, and I am preparing to go to my favorite spot. Before I go I decided to fix me a White Russian drink while preparing to go to "**Nannies.**" **Nannies,** was a Gay club in the Village where I spent many of my Wednesday evenings, enjoying Karaoke. I decided to go out solo and I was feeling different. Couldn't put my finger on it, but there was a difference. I think I was finally affected about Jean being with her wife and not me. Was it finally sinking in that she lied to me when we first met? I didn't want to think about it anymore so I made another drink and started enjoying the music playing inside the house. It had become quite the norm for me to mask my pain or my feelings with drinks, sex or from time to time Cocaine that I smoked in my cigarettes when I felt like it. It was even better when I enjoyed all three at the same time.

When I finally reached **Nannies,** I was already in my own world. I didn't visualize anyone's presence but my own. I was sitting down inside the club with a drink in my hand enjoying the music, bopping my head. I noticed this woman trying to get my attention by dancing in front of me, but I ignored her because my mind wasn't right and I wanted that time alone to just enjoy the music. So I continued to act as if no one existed. Although I would get up to dance alone, someone would always join me. And although noticing others I didn't acknowledge them when I walked off the dance floor.

I was about to light up a cigarette when the woman who was dancing in front of me decided to do it for me with her stylish lighter. It had a design of two women hugging or something.

Joy – "Thank you!"

Vee - "You're welcome, now can I have a dance?"

Joy – "Would you be upset if I said maybe another time?"

Vee – "I won't be upset if you would at least give me your number."

Joy – "Wow! Aren't you straightforward?"

Vee – "That's the way I like it! My name is Vee."

Joy – "Joy! Well Vee, I'll make sure I'll give you my number before I leave. Is that cool with you?"

Vee - "It's cool with me as long as you know I'm not letting you go until you do."

I admitted to myself that the woman was very attractive. She was thick, my height and complexion. She had long hair, and a beautiful smile. I smiled and continued to enjoy myself alone. As I was leaving, Vee had decided that she was leaving as well, and we exchanged numbers. Vee was very outspoken.

Whatever she wanted to say, she said it. After she had given me her number she said, "If you don't call, I will come and find you because I really want to get to know you!" I smiled and said "Damn, it's like that? aight!" And we went our separate ways.

It was Sunday night when Jean came home. Whenever she had her weekends with her wife she would return around 7 or 8 in the evening because she had to get ready for work the following day. This time when she returned she really didn't seem like her depressed self. This time she seemed angry. So I asked did she want me out of her home so that her and her wife can reunite.

I didn't normally ask about anything pertaining to her time spent with her wife. But, I needed to know, because like I said this time she returned with attitude. And it started to get on my damn nerves. I started thinking was she angry because she didn't know how to tell me to leave because her wife was returning, or what! So I asked, because I really needed to know.

And boy didn't I get an answer. Her response to me was in such an angry voice when she said, "Why you ask me that for?" All I could do at that moment was make a cat sound and say, "I'm just asking if you guys are planning to get back together because I would have to move. I wouldn't want to be told at the last minute." Again, Jean shouted in an angry voice and said, "She is not coming here. She hates it here! That's one of the reasons why she left. You don't ever have to worry about leaving." So I had to ask "Is there something else you want to tell me then, because every time you come back from you guys' weekend excursions, you come back depressed. Jeanie what's going on? Because frankly watching you being depressed is starting to depress the hell out of me and it's not my damn problem."

I didn't mean to make her cry, but I was truly being affected behind everything that had happened and all that was happening. However, I cared enough to follow through so I asked Jean to please tell me what was wrong. I needed to know how she could get past this because it was truly affecting the both of us at that point.

Jean finally broke down and said, "I can't take it! I can't take it! It's like she says one thing, but then she shows me another. It's like I'm being played with sometimes. I get my hopes up then the hopes are gone. Then she would call, and I get my hopes up all over again. Why am I allowing her to do this to me?"

At that moment I sat next to her and she vented to me and cried out loud and all I could do was listen and hold her because I felt that she needed it. I kept thinking to myself if it were the same kind of love that I had for Tony and if so it was understood why she tolerated the emotional abuse. Jean and I must have sat on the edge of her bed for about three hours while she cried and shared the pain that was inside of her heart. I had understood her pain. At that moment the both of us realized no matter what, we were always going to be there for one another no matter what. My friend was hurting. She was still deeply in love with a woman who she had married in her parents' home. And on top of that she was still a little girl who missed her Dad, and was still grieving his death over 15 years ago.

Afterwards, when Jean had gotten it all out, she looked up at me with eyes of a sad little girl and said, "Wooka gonna fix Babe?" I smiled and said to her, "Hell yeah! We gonna get through this just as long as Babe wanna be fixed!" I had suggested to Jean that she get actively involved in something. I mentioned ACORN which is the acronym for Association of Community for Reform Now. I had told her that it was a community based organization that advocated for low and moderate income families. I had told her that T.J.'s grandmother was also involved with the organization for years. I thought that would have been a great way for her to meet people and get involved in new things.

---

My friend Cathy had purchased a house up in Rockland County. She said that she didn't mind driving to and from work because the drive was maybe an hour and half one way. I was happy in one sense because she was now a Homeowner, but sad in another sense, because my buddy had moved so far away from me. When she lived in Harlem I would simply get on the train whenever I felt like it, and we would always meet up and do things. Now she's in Rockland County. I was sure that it would only be on certain occasions that I would visit. But still, knowing that friends can live a distance from each other but still remain friends if that's what they were. So I had no worries. I had loved her, and I knew the feeling was mutual. Years later as things began to change in my life, our friendship had changed as well. And because of the challenges and changes, she and my sister Abby had become

# HANDLE IT

"best buds." Was I affected behind that? Yes! It hurt my heart. Did I get over it? Yes. I had to *"Handle It!"*

During the summer, Jean and I would try and hit as many street fairs as possible. The one street fair that was mandatory for us to attend was in Brooklyn at Atlantic Antic. People would come from all over to enjoy it because it was the largest yearly street fair. Jean and I would walk slow, laugh, talk and look for certain things that stood out for us to purchase. It's not that we would buy much, we would find little things, like candles or magnets that we didn't have. And Jean would always find a belt or something simple that she couldn't find in the stores. We mainly went for the Corn on the Cob and Funnel Cakes that we would enjoy like children.

This particular time at the street fair was the following week after meeting Vee. As I said Atlantic Antic brings people from all over and that year it brought Vee and her friend from Harlem. Vee seemed to have been very surprised when she saw Jean and I together. Often when anyone would see Jean and me together one would always think that we were a couple. But, it was nothing for me to introduce the two of them since I wasn't in a relationship with either one.

Vee's approach had seemed a bit disappointing because of her assumption. I really didn't know anything about Vee, still, later on as we did get to know each other I had ralized that Vee was very much like myself. And with that being said we couldn't date. Instead, Vee and I had become great friends. We hung out a lot, and had much fun together. She would have her jokes from time to time but we would laugh them off and keep it moving. Over the years and still, Vee and I are very close friends. She was one of the people who had learned Jean and I and had understood our relationship. Actually, not too long after Jean and Vee met they too had become good friends. Jean would often get a kick out of Vee, because Vee was funny and she used to make Jean laugh all the time.

I must admit having a friendship with Vee is like no other friendship. The love she and I grew to have for one another over the years is impeccable. I wouldn't trade her in for a million dollars. True story!

# NJ KIND OF LOVE

Tess – "That was a nice shot! I see you know a little something."

Joy – "I try! You up next"

Tess – "Yeah, I feel like puttin' something on you."

Joy – "Oh really?"

Vee – "Oh, it's like that?"

Shay – "Yeah, it's like that!"

Vee – "Wait hold up, you kinda cute, what's your name? I know she can't be your girl cuz you all up in my grill. So wud up, what's your name?"

Shay – "Shay"

Vee – "My name is Vee! So what's your name?"

Tess – "Tess."

Joy – "I'm Joy, show me what you got, it's on you."

Tess – "I see I'm a have to shut this down you been playing for too long!"

Joy – "Don't talk about it be about Ms. Tess."

Tess – "Damn I can't believe I missed that shot!"

Joy – "Yeah, I have that effect on people. You like that right? I surprised myself on that one."

Tess – "I see you got a little skill, but I'm shutting it down right now! And if I don't, breakfast is on me."

Joy – "If you do, breakfast is on you!"

Joy- "Where are you guys from, because I never seen any of you at Nannies before?"

Tess – "We live in Jersey City."

Vee – "Oh, I got me a Jersey chick."

Shay – "You don't have me yet."

Tess/Joy - "Yes she does."

Joy – "What brings y'all to this side of town?"

Tess – "You, are you seeing anybody?"

Joy – "Now I am. I guess I'll be getting familiar with Jersey City."

Vee and I were hanging out at Nannies playing a game of pool. And Tess came in with her buddy Shay, and that was how we kicked it from Nannies to the restaurant and then to N.J. It was as simple as that. Tess was cool as hell. She was about 5'7", thick and my complexion. She wore glasses and she had short hair, and was definitely attractive. She had a very unique style to her that stood out with an awesome personality, and a great sense of humor. How could I go wrong? While Vee and Shay were getting to know each other, Tess and I were doing the same.

During that time I was attending my first semester at New York Technical College on Jay Street in Brooklyn. Jean would normally drive me in the mornings because she worked up the block. By this time Tess and I were seeing each other on a regular basis so I would drive my own car. She worked Tuesdays through Saturdays from 5-2 p.m. and I didn't have a job. However my classes were Tuesdays, Wednesdays and Thursdays from 8:45 a.m. - 2:15 p.m. Tess and I would plan for me to come to N.J almost every weekend since we had met. I loved it because I enjoyed her company so much, as she enjoyed mine. I also enjoyed being around Tess's daughter Tyra. Tyra was 12 years old, cute, and she had quite the personality.

But then without thinking, I was being very inconsiderate, and I guess disrespectful. I didn't think to tell Jean that I was staying out, I just did. One day while at Tess's house, I got paged by Jean. When I called her back we had gotten into an argument. Jean said that she was worried about me, and

I should tell her when I decide to stay out. I said that I didn't have to tell her where I was going and who I was going with since she and I was not in a relationship. Jean repeatedly was trying to explain to me that out of courtesy I should. I didn't understand why what I did was an issue. In my way of thinking, we were both adults living together with separate lives.

However, although that was true, respect for one another was also very important and that was something I didn't have. At least not in that way because I was always so used to doing my own thing my own way whatever and whenever I felt like doing it. I adapted that attitude since I came to live with my Mom at six years old. What Jean taught me at that moment was some serious interpersonal and communicative skills. Skills that I had needed to develop. After that moment, Jean and I had climbed to higher depths regarding a friendship.

Although I knew part of Jean's concern and attitude was her being upset because I had obviously found someone, and she didn't like it. I also knew that she was 100% right, and I should let her know when I decide not to come home, out of respect. Besides, I would have been furious if she had done what I had done to her.

Meanwhile, Tess was wondering was Jean and I still in a relationship and if not, what the hell was going on? Tess was not understanding why I was on the telephone arguing with another woman about my whereabouts if we weren't in a relationship. So as best as I could, I decided to let Tess know what kind of friends that Jean and I were, and how it came to be that way. However, it wasn't something easily understood or shall I say easily accepted.

Tess – "Tyra! Tyra! I said you better get your ass up, and don't let me tell you no more!"

Tyra – "I'm up!"

Tess – "You're a lying ass, if you were up you should have been in this damn bathroom by now. Now get your ass up!"

I was in the bed asleep and I woke up to all this yelling and cursing. I sat up in the bed and said in a low voice, "What the hell is going on? Hell no, this is not how I can deal in the mornings. You gotta be kidding me! I better limit myself to Friday and Saturday nights only! School days I will not!" At that moment, I realized that that was how Tess and Tyra communicated on Monday mornings. During the rest of the week, Tess left for work too early to wake Tyra up for school. Maybe I forgot to mention to Tess that I was a very peaceful person who didn't like to argue and I didn't like noise. And on top of that I am not a morning person. Therefore, screaming, yelling and cursing first thing in the morning would drive me away faster than running water. Tess apologized and she laughed at me realizing how serious I was and made a joke. But in my mind, although I laughed at the joke, I was serious as hell.

Nothing ever came out of Vee and Shay other than a friendship. However, Tess and I kept it going. We got along very well, and we enjoyed our time with one another. I had always looked forward to spending time with her and Tyra. However, the relationship was quite different for me because Tess was friends with every one of her ex-girlfriends. I didn't find that to be a problem because I am as well. But, it became a problem with me when I was always faced with one of Tess' ex-girlfriends and sometimes two whenever she would bring me to a function that a friend was having. And with that came attitude from the ex-girlfriend towards me. I mean these women would give me shade, and was slick with the tongue and often times I had to put them in their place.

I knew that I didn't have anything to worry about because I had known how Tess felt about me. And I had never felt threatened about another woman. I had always said to myself, if for any reason while in a relationship and I felt a certain way about something I would back out of it before it blew up in my face. I never wanted to feel uncomfortable in a relationship. Although I knew I was a bad ass, I had to be mindful that I was in New Jersey alone and without help if I needed it. Therefore, I was respectfully, sarcastically nice nasty when I had to be so that the women would back off. Still, they would return like flies.

After a few exchanges with these women, I realized that Tess never opened her mouth to correct any of them. So I started paying attention more towards Tess's actions when these women would show up. Often times all she did was laugh. I didn't find a damn thing funny. I found them to be rather disrespectful. Although later on Tess and I would talk about it, and she would apologize for not saying anything, I didn't know how to deal with that because it continued. Actually, I started to feel something. I felt like I didn't have the backing that I needed. Because Tess was the aggressive one in our relationship, she didn't make me feel secure enough to go forward in it. I dreaded having those interactions with other women because my mind was on some other stuff. And dealing with that sort of drama wasn't in the plans that I had.

Although it wasn't an easy transition to just be friends, I had decided that it was best. Till this day Tess and I remain as friends. I often thought about what it would have been like if I had pushed past the other women, and hung in there. But with my personality, I didn't know how to do that. I had learned how to remove myself whenever I felt uncomfortable. And that situation often times had made me just that. Don't get me wrong, my feelings for Tess were very deep. Like I said, you couldn't help but to love her. But there were certain things such as another woman in the way I just wouldn't allow myself to get past. Although she confirmed with me several times that it was nothing. But for some reason, that nothing always seemed like something when we were in each other's company. The reality of it all was that I never liked drama. And to me that's what it always turned out to be.

Later when I really took the time in my life to think about things, I had realized because Tess and I were both under the astrological sign of Cancer, we had some similar ways. During that time in our lives we were both afraid of each other in our own way and here's why. I was afraid to completely release my heart because of the other women. I wasn't certain what was really going on and Tess didn't help the situation. After what I experienced with Jean regarding her wife, I needed to be reassured that we were fine, and Tess had never given me that assurance.

On the other hand, I believe Tess allowed certain things just in case it didn't work out between her and I. Tess never believed that there was nothing going on with Jean and me because how was that possible? Two women who used to be in a relationship continue to sleep in the same bed. And that Jean continued to take care of me. Really! Yes, Tess was also insecure about our relationship. But I knew that I wasn't going to stop being friends with Jean, and I couldn't leave her house to be with someone unless I felt secure in the relationship. I had uprooted my life once for a woman who wasn't totally honest. I couldn't take that chance again knowing that other women were still hanging around.

Therefore, feeling insecure made the both of us do what we did. But through the years, Tess and I remained great friends. For years Tess and I would make Mondays our hang out day. We would go to the movies and out to eat. Sometimes, we would leave out the movies and just enjoy drinks. Whatever we did, we would laugh and talk through it all. I'd always update her on what's been going on in my life and vice versa. I would look forward to every time we were going to meet up because I just knew that we were going to have a great time. I enjoyed Tess in many ways. What I loved most about Tess was that she listened to me. And she always knew what to say.

# CONGRATULATIONS

ACORN had started to become a normal conversation between Jean and I, and all the business that had came along with it. Jean had been chosen to run meetings with Sylvia. She had also been chosen by Brooklyn's Borough President Marty Markowitz to be on the District Community Board. I was so proud of her. I had given her a card that read, *"Congratulations to my friend. Thank you for a friendship like no other. We share a friendship that is built off of acceptance, challenges, experience and love. It is a friendship that no one can compare to the friendship that we share. Love Wooka."*

I had started a new job working for Boys Town. I was so excited about this job. Not only because I had been out of work for a while, but also because it was to work with the youth. I enjoy working with the young population for many reasons even till this day. Mainly because I wished that someone was there for me in the same way I am willing to be there for another young person. I enjoy encouraging, helping with life skills, and mentoring. My compassion for the youth is a light inside of me that will never go out. Instead, it keeps getting brighter.

However, before working for this company I was required to go away for two weeks to Omaha, Nebraska for training. Going away for two weeks wasn't an issue. I had completed a semester without starting another one. T.J. was no longer in college, and was now living with his Dad on Pacific Street. Therefore, going away was not a problem. But, I had never flown before, and I was scared to fly and doing it by myself.

Jean was amazing, she made me feel as best as she could by reassuring me that plane rides were just as safe as car and train rides. She took me to the airport and stayed with me right up until the last minute. Surprisingly, flying was very exciting, and I found a love for it. Flying was simply an amazing experience, and I look forward to it every time.

Training was great, but I really wanted the two weeks to hurry so that I could get back home. Finally I was back on the plane Friday afternoon. My assignment was to work in the Bronx in a house with eight girls on the overnights starting the following Monday. I had held many positions in my lifetime and I had done many things. But working for Boys Town was the best job by far that I've had. I enjoyed the girls. I enjoyed working with them in every way that I could. I had worked other shifts for overtime, and I just loved what I was doing. I was really making a difference in the lives of young people. I started feeling like I was right where I needed to be in my new career.

# WALK AWAY

In 2001, I was reaching the end of my second year going back and forth to court, fighting for my house. Every time we had a court date, the tenants would come up with a new order. I was fighting four individuals and one family for them to leave my home. I was not only losing my house but I was losing myself. My bank account had depleted, and so had my patience. I was dealing with attitudes and disrespect and it was getting to be too much. I was glad that I had begun a new job because I really needed the funds.

I thought that I was finally on the right track, although it was a very stressful situation. I continued to do what was right, but then I had had enough! My last straw was when I had gone to my house to attempt to pick up my rent, when the people upstairs and downstairs decided to stand in front of me together as if they wanted to hurt me. At that moment I saw blood and I saw me on the count in the same jail that I used to work in. In my mind I had watched how it all was playing out. I had gone to the car and got my bat and I started swinging. And blood was everywhere.

Thankfully, something moved me to walk to my car and sit inside. I sat there for a moment and drove off because my thoughts were taking me straight to jail. I appreciate when my mind allows me to play a situation out. In doing so it gives me time to make a choice that may work in my favor. We all have choices, and for the second time in my life I can truly say that I had made the best one. The first time was when I had decided to have my son.

I couldn't think of anyone to talk to that could give me wise council or any advice, or help, for that matter. I didn't want Jean's advice anymore because I felt that she had gotten me into the situation. Besides, she didn't know what to do other than tell me to continue to go to court. At this time the mortgage was backed up a few months and the lawyer fees were adding up as well. I couldn't take another court day and I couldn't take any more attitudes. I decided if I can walk away from people that I loved then I could walk away from things. I walked away and filed bankruptcy. Tony had given me the $5,000 to pay the Attorney fees and I was done with it all. I allowed myself to feel better knowing that I had the house for the purpose of taking care of my mother till her last days. I believed that God wanted me to do just that so I gave it no more thought.

# SHYNESE

Within two weeks working in the Bronx at the girls' residence, I had to attend my first in-house meeting. It was on a school day, therefore no kids were home. The meeting was mandatory for all staff who worked at the residence to attend. Oh my goodness, I am in love. (I know it doesn't take much, right? Lol!) I didn't know who she was, but I wanted to know everything about her. Oh, she is so cute I said to myself. She was tall, at least 5'10", she had a tan complexion and she had dimples that truly complimented her smile. She had a beautiful smile with white teeth, and she was neatly dressed. I wanted to know what shift she worked, where she lived, did she have children, what she liked. I was instantly in love. Whoever said that you can't fall in love at first sight? I did! I fell in love on that day, within that hour at that very second and I didn't care who knew it!

That following night I had to be at work at midnight. I had found out at the meeting that Shynese worked the 4 – 12 a.m. shift. I purposely came to work at 11 p.m. in a cute summer dress that was long enough to be appropriate for work but short enough to show my sexy. I walked up to the office where I knew she'd be because she was a Supervisor, and I let my sexy chime right on in. To my surprise, she was also under the astrological sign of Cancer, and with sex appeal.

Shynese – "Hi Ms. Harriet, aren't you early."

Joyce – "I know I felt like being early tonight. How was your shift, Ms. Hynes?"

Shynese – "The shift was good I may have to stay for the overnight."

Joyce – "Is that so?"

Shynese – "You look really cute, I like your dress."

Joyce – "I'm glad you like it."

Shynese – "Excuse me Ms. Harriet give me a second. Boys and Girls Town, you owe me one… You got me all night Ms. H, as you can see the other Supervisor just called out for her shift, so I'll be here with you tonight."

Joyce – "Is that so?"

Shynese – "Yes that's so! And, I want you to know that I'm staying on purpose!"

Joyce – "I am so glad to hear that because I am here early on purpose."

Throughout the entire night Shynese and I laughed and talked. There wasn't much to do because the girls were all asleep. However, whatever duties we both had were adhered to without taking away from us communicating. Towards the end of our shift Shynese and I knew that we both had really liked each other and wanted to be in a relationship. Shynese made it perfectly clear to me when she said. "So, now that we will be dating each other, you gotta know that I go to church, and I also date men!" At that moment I didn't care if she said she had an infectious disease, I felt like the happiest woman on earth. I never dated bisexual females before, at least not knowingly, but it didn't matter to me. This woman had my heart. Besides, what did going to church have to do with me?

Ever since that night Shynese and I couldn't stay apart. Shynese had switched her shift to the overnights with the same Supervisor who had called out the other night. Apparently, that Supervisor was having issues and the overnights had become too much for her. That worked well for Shynese and me because with the exception of one night we had the same schedule. The funny thing was when Shynese would drive me to work on the night she was off, she would tell me to tuck and roll so that nobody would see her dropping me off. Still, I didn't care nor think about it. Besides, I was just glad that I was getting a ride all the way to the Bronx.

For the next six months Shynese and I had been enjoying each other in every way. I enjoyed her cooking, but we both were enjoying our family and friends. I couldn't introduce Shynese as my girlfriend, as in lover, because she never wanted anyone to know. Therefore, I had lied to Jean as well as anyone else when they asked. Later on Jean had figured it out for herself, because it had become rather obvious. It wasn't that I wanted to keep secrets from her it's just that I wanted to honor Shynese's wishes. As long as I had her I didn't have a problem going along with the lie, and if I had to defend it I would have.

Working at Boys Town required mandatory meetings at other residences as well. Everyone who worked overnights in all residences had to attend a 10 a.m. meeting in Brooklyn at one of the boys' residences. The 8 - 4 p.m. staff from that residence also attended because their children were in school. During one of the Brooklyn meetings there was this very attractive dark-skinned, handsome, well-dressed brother that kept watching me. Shynese noticed that he was watching me too and told me. I turned and smiled and continued to focus on the meeting.

During a break, the gentleman approached me and Shynese and said hello to Shynese and introduced himself to me as Avery. Obviously he and Shynese had met before because they both worked for Boys Town prior to me coming aboard. At that very moment, I wanted to let him know that Shynese and I were a couple but I was forbidden by Shynese to let anyone know. Then I felt like maybe her way of thinking would change when she saw me get his number, because he was refusing to let me out of his sight without giving it to me. I even wanted to have fun by giving her the number right in front of him, letting him know that Shynese was my lady, but I couldn't do that either.

Now that the meeting had resumed, I sat there thinking to myself what if Shynese meets a man and she decides to walk away since she was bisexual. I immediately dismissed the idea because I didn't ever want to think of her walking away from me. After the meeting was over, Avery approached me again asking would I be attending the Christmas party that was coming up, and that he would love to see me there. I told him that I would be attending and I guess we will be seeing each other soon.

The music was right and I enjoyed dancing. However, Shynese and I couldn't dance together unless there was a group of woman dancing. I decided that I didn't come to the party looking as good as I'd looked to sit down, so Avery and I danced and enjoyed ourselves. At the end of every dance, I went and sat down next to Shynese trying to encourage her to have some fun and dance with me. Instead, Avery and I continued to do so. At the end of the party, Avery wanted to continue to hang out with me, but I turned him down by saying that I couldn't. I wanted to tell him that I was Gay, but that would have probably made him question Shynese and my relationship and I didn't want to involve her in any way.

That night, I had really enjoyed myself with Avery. He was the funniest guy that I had met in a very long time, and we were sweeping the dance floor. Later that night, I talked to Shynese regarding her feelings about me dancing with Avery. Shynese said that she didn't mind and she reminded me that we were only temporary. Although that didn't set well with me, I continued to enjoy what Shynese and I had, while Avery and I kept in touch.

I had only been working for Boys Town for six months when Shynese said that a friend of hers wanted her to be the Program Director of a new Pilot Program that she had started in Queens working for the Salvation Army. She wanted Shynese to hire a Supervisor to come along with her. And to bring along a few people that would like to work as an Outreach Worker to come the day of the Meet & Greet. Shynese asked me would I leave Boys and Girls Town knowing that I really liked it, to be a Supervisor working under her? That was a no brainer, and of course, without thought, I accepted the offer. I didn't even think about my job at that point. All I knew was that I was going wherever Shynese was going. Oh yeah, and of course a better position with more money.

Joy – "Babe, I'm changing jobs. I gotta type up a resignation letter."

Jean – "What, What do you mean you're changing jobs you love that job!"

Joy- "Shynese was offered a position as a Program Director, and she offered me the Supervisor position over thirteen Outreach Workers from 8-4 p.m."

Jean – "Joy, are you sure about that? You love your job. You yourself said that out of your 15 other jobs you have held, that you finally have your dream job. Are you sure about this?"

Joy – "Yeah, I get to be a Supervisor and I'll have a salary increase. Isn't that's what it's about moving up in life? Oh, and guess what, I get to hire Tony as an Outreach Worker. He will be excited about that because I'm sure he'll be great at it."

Jean – "So now you and Shynese will really be spending time together. Wooka, that girl say she's not Gay but I know different. Wooka, can we get away for the weekend? Let's hang out in the Poconos at your Time Share."

Joy – "Ok, that sounds cool. Is it okay if I ask Shynese to come along with us?"

Jean – "Sure"

At this point I already knew that Jean was not happy about Shynese and my relationship. Shynese was taking up all of my time. We were together at work and after work. The only time that we weren't together was Sundays because Shynese was at church all day. I knew Jean and I weren't spending much time together, but I was so opened by this woman, my whole world revolved around her. T.J. was trying to find his way, and seemed okay living with his Dad. I took care of what I needed to take care of in the house. And from time to time Jean and I did hang out, especially on Sundays. I also knew that Jean had rather taken the trip to the Poconos to be like it's always been, just the three of us. Me, her, and Frenchie! Frenchie was Jeans' poodle.

Shynese didn't only come with Jean and me to the Poconos she went with us everywhere. This is how the conversation would go, "Wooka, it's apple picking time again. It's time to gather up the kids." Every year since Jean and I became friends I would get my niece and nephew or Cathy's boys to go Apple or Pumpkin Picking with us. We'd always looked forward to it, because Jean and I would enjoy making fresh Apple or Pumpkin Pies together.

Joy – "That's right! Are we going this weekend?"

Jean – "Yep"

Joy – "I'll call my sister and let her know we'll be picking them up Saturday morning at 10. Babe, do you mind if Shynese and her niece come along?"

Jean – "Sure"

I knew she didn't like the idea, but I couldn't go without Shynese. We had become inseparable. Besides, I enjoyed our hanging out together. I never paid much mind to how they would be uncomfortable or envious of one another.

The funny thing was whenever all of us would go someplace together Jean and my behavior wouldn't change. We looked out for each other so much people would think that we were a couple. This was our behavior since we met. It was all in the way we spoke to each other, and showed concern for one another. No one understood that! It was like we were the protector over one another. We protected one another from simple things like stopping the other person from walking into a puddle of water. And Shynese hated it! She just didn't know how or where to place it, being our relationship was a "secret." So here on one hand Jean hated the fact that Shynese came on every trip we would take, and Shynese hated the fact that Jean and I were so close and took care of each other. Me, I'm enjoying my life not focusing on either one of their feelings. I just thought that as long as I made everyone happy and was attentive to everyone that was all that mattered.

Working together with Shynese in my new position was awesome. I had not only taken the role as a Supervisor, but I also was working directly under her. I was learning so many new things and loving it. What I didn't know was that the Director didn't like the fact that Shynese and I were as close as we were. The Director started requesting things from Shynese that she knew nothing about, nor was she willing to assist Shynese in any way because she had ill intentions. She would have Shynese work extra hours so that it would just be the two of them in the office. At least she thought it was going to be just the two of them until the Director realized that I would stay late without pay inside my office. I would stay simply because Shynese would ask me to stay and help her, and I would. But then the Director would have Shynese come to her house to work on some things just to be alone with her. Shynese didn't like it and she would have her cell phone on communicating with me and allowing me to hear how she would talk to her. My only response was for Shynese to leave her house, and whatever work needed to be done, do it in the office only.

The Director wasn't a nice person at all. It seemed as If she would dream about how to make someone's life miserable if they ignored her. She was like this spoiled little girl who wanted things her way. When I first met her I thought she was a beautiful woman appearance wise. But inside she was as ugly as an old potato and no longer was beautiful to me. She had given Shynese an ultimatum and Shynese decided to walk away from it all. Before doing so, Shynese tried to encourage me to stay on and I tried. However, once again, the Director's control wasn't worth my sanity, so I too walked away from my position. However, I didn't walk away silently. I said to the Director, that she shouldn't be so wicked because when she gets older she will be haunted by her own wickedness, and then die alone.

Tony had stayed on because he was very good at what he was doing, and he enjoyed it. As a matter of fact, Tony stayed on until the program eventually ended, and he picked up the same position with another agency. Luckily no one knew that Tony was my son's father unless he too would have become the Directors target. Although Shynese and I were unemployed we utilized our time with decorating her Two Family home that she had just purchased. And Jean utilized my free time as well and wanted to get a way, but not to the Pocono's.

Jean wanted to go to Puerto Rico. I had never been to Puerto Rico and I would have loved to have visited Abby who had been living there for a few years now. But I also realized what Jean was doing. Jean wanted to be away with me alone. She knew that Shynese was not traveling to Puerto Rico, especially now that she was unemployed and had just purchased a home. She needed to hold on to whatever funds she had for other uses. Jean had a plan and she was in execution mode. I had told Shynese that Jean and I were going to Puerto Rico and when we were leaving. At that moment all Shynese said was, "Okay."

Afterwards, Shynese and I started to get into little arguments. The arguments didn't even have a cause. It was the night before Jean and I would leave to go to Puerto Rico, Shynese and I would say goodbye and not see each other for seven days. She dropped me off in front of Jean's house and while I'm getting out of the car she said to me, "When you come back from your trip, I don't want to see you again."

Joy – "Why are you saying that to me? You knew Jean and I were going to Puerto Rico together. Why are you so mad with me?"

Shynese –"I'm not mad. We're just breaking up!"

Joy – "What happened, why are you all of a sudden treating me like that?"

Shynese – "I just don't want to be with you anymore that's all."

Joy – "You're mad at me because I'm going away? Or because I'm going away with Jean?"

Shynese – "I'm not mad, we are just breaking up."

Joy- "You can't be serious with me right now. Shynese, this is coming from out of the blue."

Shynese- "You need to go in the house, and stop standing out here crying."

Joy – "I won't go! I won't go to Puerto Rico then. Please don't break up with me."

Shynese – "You need to get out of the street and stop crying. People can see you, you know!"

Joy – "You think I give a damn about people? My heart is hurting, and I don't want to leave you, I'm not going."

Shynese – "I'm about to pull off, you should really go in the house. I'm pulling off, Joyce! Bye Joyce, enjoy your trip!"

Shynese had pulled off and I was literally standing where she left me crying. Jean's mother had lived around the corner so Jean decided to walk around the block to take Frenchie so that her mother can dog sit while we went away. When Jean was returning home, Shynese had seen Jean in her passing. Shynese had offered Jean a lift back home and upon their return I was still standing there. My face was soaked with tears. Jean's voice had gotten me out of my trance. "Joy, why are you standing out here in the streets crying? What the hell is going on? If this is about us going to Puerto Rico tomorrow, then I'll give y'all the tickets and you two go!"

Jean walked away into the house. For a minute that had sounded like a plan, but I dismissed the thought immediately because I did look forward to the trip with Jean. I felt like I had to choose at that moment between Jean and Shynese. This girl had me whipped! It seemed like Shynese was enjoying the scene because deep down she was the one who was miserable because I was leaving.

Then without dragging it out any longer, Shynese told me to go in the house. Go to Puerto Rico with Jean, and enjoy myself. She said that she would be there waiting for me when I got back, and that she wasn't going to break up with me. I asked Shynese were we okay, because I had loved her so much I wanted and needed for us to be. Shynese had never apologized for the way she treated me, but I dismissed it. She reassured me that we were okay! I had realized that was Shynese's sick way of testing my love for her, or maybe showing Jean what she could do. I went in the house, apologized to Jean for my behavior, and told her how much I have and was still looking forward to our trip. Thus, I had realized that Jean and Shynese both were flexing their control over me while proving themselves to one another in different ways.

The resort was beautiful. Jean and I had a relaxing fun-filled trip. We visited Abby, and my nephew Jamel, and we simply enjoyed our time together. When Jean and I returned from Puerto Rico I couldn't put my bags down fast enough before I would go see Shynese. She had missed me just as much. She had prepared my favorite Trinidadian dish called Pealow which is made with chicken and rice and all of her spices. Oh how I loved her cooking! Till this day, I crave her food. Shortly after, Jean and I decided to have a BBQ, which we did often. Everyone had left except Shynese because she was waiting for me. Jean and I were cleaning the kitchen when Shynese started asking questions. Shynese asked Jean did she think that people were born Gay?

Jean – "Yes, I believe that!"

Shynese – "Do y'all think being Gay is a sin?"

Jean – "How can loving someone else be a sin?"

Joy – "Exactly, because God says He loves everybody. He didn't separate us. He said I love you, meaning Gay people too. I love Him and He loves me!"

Jean – "What, you having some Gay issues?"

I knew at that moment Jean wanted to say, "Because everybody already know that you're Gay. You just have issues." Instead, Jean and I just continued cleaning up while Shynese waited for me patiently, and we left. Oftentimes Shynese would tell me about programs they were having at her church, and the roles she was assigned to play. She seemed to have been enjoying it but yet she wasn't. I couldn't figure out the personality changes.

Then one day out of the blue she came to my house in a rage and said, "We can't be together anymore! This relationship is over Joyce!"

Joyce – "What, What are you talking about? Everything is going so well between us."

Shynese –"Like I said, this relationship is over! It's not right, and I can't do this anymore!"

Joyce – "You don't mean what you're saying, you love me and I love you, and our relationship is doing just fine. What is wrong with you, and why are you yelling?"

Shynese – "Joyce, I am telling you that this relationship is over! I can no longer be a part of something that God is against. I love you so much, but I love God more. And, I'm inviting you to come to church so that you can learn all about Him and Salvation."

Joyce – "Stop crying, please, stop crying. Baby, you want me to come to church then I'll come to church. I will go wherever you want me to go. Please stop crying, I love you so much!"

At that moment all I could do was hold her. We stood there in my kitchen holding each other crying, and Shynese kept saying that she couldn't do this anymore and that it was killing her inside.

Now that I was going to attend church with her, Shynese did the unthinkable. She bought me "church" clothes and a Bible. I went to the church with Shynese that following Sunday. And to my surprise, Shynese was an Usher. I'm sure she told me but I guess I didn't give it a thought. What I did know was that Shynese had looked fabulous. All I could do for three Sundays in a row was simply stare at her while she Ushered. She was even more beautiful! Her Sunday gear was far different from her everyday gear. Shynese had transformed completely! She wore a nice skirt suit with a matching hat. She wore heels that complemented her long legs, and makeup, with fancy cosmetic jewelry that completed her look. She went from looking like an aggressive Gay woman to a straight feminine beautiful woman with a purse and lipstick. The transformation was simply awesome. I couldn't keep my eyes off of her.

"Don't you realize that those who do wrong will not inherit the Kingdom of God? Don't fool yourselves. Those who indulge in sexual sin, or who worship idols, or commit adultery, or are male prostitutes, or practice homosexuality, or are thieves, or greedy people, or drunkards, or are abusive, or cheat people none of these will inherit the Kingdom of God. Some of you were once like that. But you were cleansed; you were made holy; you were made right with God by calling on the name of the Lord Jesus Christ and by the Spirit of our God.

You say, 'I am allowed to do anything' but not everything is good for you. And even though 'I am allowed to do anything' I must not become a slave to anything. I must not become a slave to anything. You say. 'Food was made for the stomach, and the stomach for food.' (This is true, though someday God will do away with both of them.) But you can't say that our bodies were made for sexual immorality. They were made for the Lord, and the Lord cares about our bodies.

Don't you realize that your bodies are actually parts of Christ? Should a man take his body, which is part of Christ, and join it to a prostitute? Never! And don't you realize that if a man joins himself to a prostitute, he becomes one body with her? For Scriptures say, The two are united into one. But the person who is joined to the Lord is one spirit with him.

Run from sexual sin! No other sin so clearly affects the body as this one does. For sexual immorality is a sin against your own body. Don't you realize that your body is the temple of the Holy Spirit, who lives in you and was given to you by God? You do not belong to yourself, for God bought you with a high price. So you must honor God with your body." 1 Corinthians 6: 9-20.

Tears were falling from my eyes I'm battling with the words in my mind saying "Why won't I inherit the Kingdom of God? Is it my fault that my cousin raped me in my sleep all those nights? What is the Kingdom of God? Homosexuality isn't the same thing as me being Gay. So what I drink, that doesn't make me a drunkard. Am I committing sexual immorality? If my body is a part of Christ's body then why don't I care about my body? I have sex with who I want to have sex with, and when I want too! So am I one with all the people that I slept with and they are one with me? If so, I feel so dirty right now! Run from sexual sin. What does he mean? When I went to my mother telling her what my cousin had been doing, nothing happened. So who am I supposed to run to? My body can't possibly be a temple of a Holy Spirit. What Holy Spirit, and what price did God pay for me? Why do I feel like my breath is leaving me? I feel like my disgusting life is flashing before me. What is happening to me? Somebody help me please." The tears would not stop.

After the Pastor read the verses from the Bible I started listening to him speak still as the tears continued to fall. He reminded us of the topic saying: "My body is not my own" It says in the book of John 3:16-17 "For God so loved the world that he gave his one and only Son, so that everyone who believes in him will not perish but have eternal life. God sent his Son into the world not to judge the world, but to save the world through him." Some of us think that it is okay to have sex before marriage. We say we can do anything with our body because it is our body. We say that we can sleep with whomever we choose because it is our body. Some of us decided that it is ok for woman to sleep with woman, and man to sleep with man because it is our body. Well I come to let you know that not I, but the word of God says that it is not okay! It is not all right! God says that it's not all right to live immoral lives. The word immoral means: morally wrong, wicked, evil, unprincipled, dishonest, unethical, sinful, corrupt, vile, indecent, degenerate, debauched and lewd.

But because God is aware of our sinful nature, He loves us so much that He is a merciful God. He sent His son so that through Him all sins are forgiven. It's through the blood of Jesus Christ our Lord and Savior we can all be forgiven of our sins. He said in the book of Romans 10:9-10, "If you confess with your mouth that Jesus is Lord and believe in your heart that God raised him from the dead, you will be saved." For it is by believing in your heart that you are made right with God, and it is by confessing with your mouth that you are saved. It doesn't matter if you're rich or poor, a prostitute, a beggar, a teacher, or a thief. If you are black, white, Jew or mixed. If you were raped, beaten or ridiculed. If you were forgotten, neglected or disrespected. Just come! This Salvation is for everybody. And it is free. Your sins can be forgiven at this very moment if you come. Just walk out of your seats and receive this free gift....

Before I knew it, I was at the Altar. I didn't know how I got there because I didn't remember moving my legs. Then I felt the Pastor take hold of my right hand that had been paining me for so long, and began praying for me. Then he said, "If you confess with your mouth the Lord Jesus, and believe in your heart that God has raised Him from the dead, you will be saved." At that moment I had accepted Christ in my life. Immediately my hand had stopped hurting me and I was amazed because it had been hurting me for a very long time. I felt something inside of me that I couldn't explain. I became thirsty for God. I wanted to know everything about Him. Who was this Jesus? I sat in church for the remainder of service feeling like a new person. Why hadn't anybody told me about God before to this magnitude and not just to pray over my food? I wasn't the same person. My thoughts weren't on Shynese anymore. All I wanted to do was go home and read about this God. And after church that night, that was exactly what I did.

I was home sitting at the kitchen table reading the Bible out loud, yet in a low voice. Jean seemed to have been a little disturbed. "Do not practice homosexuality, having sex with another man as a woman. It is a detestable sin." Leviticus 19:22. "If a man practices homosexuality, having sex with another man as with a woman, both men have committed a detestable act." Leviticus 20:13. "So God abandoned them to do whatever shameful things their hearts desired. As a result, they did vile and degrading things with each other's bodies. They traded the truth about God for a lie. So they worshiped and served the things God created instead of the Creator Himself, who is worthy of eternal praise! Amen. That is why God abandoned them to their shameful desires. Even the women turned against the natural way to have sex and instead indulged in sex with each other. And the men, instead of having normal sexual relations with women, burned with lust for each other. Men did shameful things with other men, and as a result of this sin, they suffered within themselves the penalty they deserved." Romans 1:24-27.

I stopped reading and placed my hand on my forehead and shook my head, and continued reading. "So I say, let the Holy Spirit guide your lives. Then you won't be doing what your sinful nature craves. The sinful nature wants to do evil, which is just the opposite of what the Spirit wants. And the Spirit gives us desires that are the opposite of what the sinful nature desires. These two forces are constantly fighting each other, so you are not free to carry out your good intentions. But when you are directed by the Spirit, you are not under obligation to the Law of Moses. When you follow the desires of your sinful nature, the results are very clear: sexual immorality, impurity, lustful pleasures, idolatry, sorcery, hostility, quarreling, jealousy, outbursts of anger, selfish ambition, dissension, division, envy, drunkenness, wild parties, and other sins like these. Let me tell you again, as I have before, that anyone living that sort of life will not inherit the Kingdom of God." Galatians 5:17-21.

Again, I stopped reading. This time I placed my hand on my cheek and the other hand across my chest and sat there. Shortly after, Jean came out of the room and broke my concentration. "Jean, didn't you say that your father was a Deacon in the church and that you were raised in the church?"

Jean – "Yeah"

Joy - "How did you feel growing up and living a Gay lifestyle knowing that God said that being Gay is an abomination?"

Jean – "What I know about God is that He loves everybody the same. Now what, because you go to church you're going to start judging me. Isn't that in the Bible we shouldn't judge each other?"

Joy – "Jean look, I'm not judging you. I'm trying to understand! Since you were raised in the church the stuff that I'm reading should be known to you. So how is it that you know this and still decided to be Gay? Please just help me understand? The stuff that I've been reading is blowing my mind."

Jean – "First of all, the Bible is a book that has been written over and over again and translated by too many people. You cannot believe what you read at face value. And on that note, I'm going to bed!"

Joy – "Wait a minute! Then why was it so easy to believe all the books you read in school that helped you get your Degree? I'm sure those books have been revised as well. Also, we have Professors, Presidents, etc., who would quote passages from books for teaching purposes, and use it as their life model as if it were law. But yet you question the Bible's truth. If I don't know anything else about God, I do know that the Holy Bible is a Sacred Book. And, why does it seem like you have an attitude with me because I'm asking you questions about God?"

I was thirsty to learn more. And the more I read the more I would understand. It was like something was teaching me as I was reading. Something was encouraging me, and pushing me further and further into the Bible. I would stay up all night reading and sleep all day. I couldn't wait to return to church. Shynese was no longer on my mind other than to help me with questions I needed answered. Shynese seemed happy that I was now attending church.

We started talking about getting into Real Estate. I went to Real Estate School and passed the test for my license. Shynese was fortunate enough to work for her sister-in-law without going for her license. It didn't matter that Shynese and I both sucked at Real Estate because we both found it to be a real cutthroat business. Then Shynese decided to turn her basement into a Daycare and we both loved the idea. So we started doing research on opening a Home Daycare.

Shynese said "Now that you are saved, it is not right for you to still be sleeping in the same bed with Jean. You are no longer in that lifestyle, so you need to be mindful of what you are doing. So, I am making you an offer. You know my computer room is a spare bedroom, you can come live with me until you get your own place." I was actually excited about that because based on what I had read and understood, my life had to change, and I had to make some changes. Shynese told me not to worry about anything because she knew that I wasn't working. However, she did know that I would begin work soon to help her out during my stay. So, I accepted the offer.

Joy – "Jean, I'm moving out, I'm going to stay at Shynese's house in her spare room until I'm able to get an apartment."

Jean – "But why are you moving out? You can stay here until you get an apartment."

Joy – "It's different because it's not right that we sleep together, and I am no longer in the same lifestyle as you. I love you, but being Gay is wrong."

Jean – "What, now that you go to church you think you're better than me? Now you all high and mighty you can't be around us 'Gay' folks?"

Joy – "I'm just saying that I know different now, and there are certain things that are changing within me, and this lifestyle is not right. That's all I'm saying. I'm not saying we are going to stop being friends. I love you!"

Jean – "So why would you want to be friends with somebody who is Gay if it's so wrong?"

Joy – "I'll figure that out as I go along, right now I just know that I can't live here with you. But, I will still be here if that makes any sense."

Jean was not pleased with my decision. However, I felt good knowing that Jean was involved with other things that would now keep her busy. And that she had gotten more actively involved with friends. Because in my mind, I had no one to keep me back from what I wanted to do. I did what I wanted to do all my life thus far. I admit I act on impulse. I can also admit that acting on impulse is not good. My spiritual life was moving fast. I had become a member of my church and Baptized in the name of Jesus.

I had landed a job at Macy's on Atlantic Avenue as a Store Detective. I had to start making my own money again so that I can support myself and help Shynese since I was now living with her. I had realized that finding a job was never a problem for me, but deep down inside I wish I had never left Boys Town. Over the years I would come to realize that Boys Town was the only agency that I had worked for that actually helped the youth. The other places simply just provided shelter, food and medication.

At the beginning of my stay at Shynese's house, things were going fine. We were going to Church together on Sundays, Tuesday night Bible Study, and Friday was youth night. I had come to realize that there was something going on at the Church that I tried not to associate myself with. I wanted to focus on learning more and more about God. I had appreciated Shynese making it a point not to share anything negative with me regarding what was going on. She made certain that her experiences were not going to be mine, and for that and other things I had a great respect for her.

Actually I was surprised at myself for attending the Church, being that I was the only African American. The small Pentecostal Church was filled with Islanders mainly from Jamaica. Growing up I never really had gotten along with Islanders because in my opinion they thought that they were better than American born African Americans. And in the past I had some run-ins with quite a few of them because of the way they had spoken to me. I thought that they were rude and very disrespectful to African Americans. Even with that, I didn't hold onto it. I had never met any of these people before, and they had welcomed me into their Church.

However, my decision to stay regardless of what had been going on was immediate. From the moment the Pastor of the Church held my hand and prayed for me, I had already made the decision to stay. I had experienced a miracle, a miracle that even today makes me believe. From that moment I had a love for the Pastor. Not the kind of love that's wrong, but the kind of love that was healthy and felt safe. The kind of love that let me know that it was good to be there, a love that let me know that I was going to be under great leadership. I felt that he was a very sincere man. A man that I believed God was using because of what had already happened to me. To love the Pastor felt right and natural.

I had also had a love for a mother at the church that also seemed sincere and genuine. I watched how she mingled with her grandchildren and the youth in the church, and how they all simply loved her. Mother Love was a very sweet woman who showed everyone love simply by being herself. I can still hear her voice when she would greet people by saying, "Hello my Darlin'." Often times I would go to her house and bring a plant or flowers and listen to her speak and sing. I just loved her. However, after the first year of knowing her, she would move to Kansas City to be with her daughter and grandchildren. That was a very sad moment for me, especially not seeing her in the Church praising God and hearing her voice.

The Pastor would have testimony services on certain nights, and I would share mine. Often times a basic testimony would be given by others who were thankful that God woke them up that morning and sent them on their way. To God be the Glory! So now here comes this American girl sharing some stuff that most people would have kept to themselves especially among strangers.

I would testify and share my experiences, my screw ups, my hurts, pains, and temptations. I didn't hold anything back because inside I knew I needed to heal. And I thought if my hand was able to heal then so could my heart, and the rest of my life moving forward would get better. I just didn't want to waste my time by holding back. The good thing was I never cared what anyone ever thought of me because I didn't think that I was a bad person. And I had never sought to hurt anyone.

I think the members were getting a kick out me in the church. I think my boldness may have given some of the members mixed feelings about me. On the other hand I knew for certain that my Pastor and Mother Love were very genuine with their feelings towards me and I felt it, as mine were with them. They made me feel safe and welcome, and both of them gave me what I had needed to stay in a church that was filled with Jamaicans.

However, I realized that Shynese didn't seem to like the attention that I was getting, so she and I would start to argue more about silly things. Things that made absolutely no sense, but it was happening. She seemed bothered when people would talk to me in Church, and speak well of me to her. A jealousy was coming about and I thought the best thing to do was stop going to the Church so that she would stop being upset and we would stop arguing.

The way things started going between Shynese and me was hurting me really bad. I really needed to talk to somebody. I opted for Godly advice so I thought it was best to sit down with the Pastor and talk about it. He had already understood much about my past as I had willingly shared during testimony services. I also went and spoke with Mother Love and the advice from the two of them allowed me to remain at the Church while things at home had started to get worse.

Things weren't only getting bad with Shynese and me. I had started changing. I was invited to one of my friend's Bridal Shower and it was inside of a club. When I sat at a table with a few of my friends I was annoyed with their language. They kept cursing and it was bothering the heck out of me. Prior to me giving my life to the Lord, I laughed and did the same things that they were doing. I was used to the conversations because I often held them. But I couldn't sit there and listen. So I had changed my seat and sat with another friend who had been going to Church for a period of time.

Changing my seat didn't help matters because as soon as I sat down a stripper came straight at me as the crowd cheered on. I repositioned myself letting him know that I wasn't interested. He didn't get the hint so I removed myself. Normally, that wouldn't have been a problem for me either. I would have had some fun with him along with everyone else. Instead, I felt disgusted. Well changing my seat didn't matter, because another one came and did the exact same thing. All I could do at that point was leave because I had felt very uncomfortable.

# GOOD 4 U GOOD 4 ME

Shynese started dating, and at first it affected me but I said nothing because we were not at that place anymore. So when she started dating and having company, I pulled out my Avery card and decided to give him a call. Avery and I had always stayed in touch because we enjoyed each other's conversation over time. But now that I felt it was okay to date him I did. I had already come to the understanding that I couldn't be in a relationship with another woman so dating Avery felt good especially since he also went to church.

Sometimes he would come with me. Although Avery didn't care too much about the Pentecostal way of doing things, he enjoyed being with me and vice versa. Avery and I started spending a lot of time together inside and outside of the house. I was working 10-6 p.m. at Macy's in Brooklyn on Atlantic Avenue as a Store Detective, while Avery had still been working his 3-11p.m. shift at Boys Town. At the end of Avery's shift he would always come to Shynese's house so that we would be together. Without realizing it, Avery had spent every night with me inside my room. The first time he had ever spent the night we had just fallen asleep while watching TV. I was so afraid because he had spent the night without me asking Shynese's permission. To my surprise, when I did ask she responded by saying, "I don't care!"

Things were fine as long as Shynese and I both were dating. But when she no longer was dating, she would talk about moving to Philadelphia where her colleagues were, despite all the work we were putting into getting the Day Care started. I didn't think twice about what she was saying because she had just purchased her house, and to me she was talking crazy. So I didn't listen to her although she constantly said she was thinking about moving. Arguments between Shynese and I picked up to higher levels, and whenever

I was home, I would isolate myself in my room to avoid seeing her because it had started to get really uncomfortable for the both of us.

One night Avery had come over and I had been feeling bad all day. Shynese and I had gotten into a terrible argument and I wanted Avery just to comfort me. I wanted to tell him how I was feeling and why. When he finally came over after he had gotten off of work, I told Avery everything. I told him that Shynese and I used to date but when I moved in we were no longer dating. Avery already knew about my old lifestyle because I shared my past with him during one of our conversations. But now I was telling him the truth about Shynese and what had really went on between us. Avery shed some light on what was going on, being a person looking in.

He made lots of sense stating that I had to leave her home because it wasn't right for me to have been dating her and now that we were just friends I shouldn't bring men into her home. Although she had given me permission, it still wasn't okay. Avery made a lot of sense because I wondered at that moment how would I have handled that. And honestly, I don't think that it would have set right with me. I said to Avery that I was wrong for what I was doing, but it wasn't intentional and I realize that I had to leave.

Then things had gotten very quiet between Avery and I and I wanted to know was he saddened by me not telling him, or was it something else on his mind. He assured me that he was glad that I was honest with him, and that he thought that between Shynese and I anyway he was just waiting for me to tell him the truth.

Still as the night went on I sensed something else going on and it had nothing to do with me. I asked Avery to tell me whatever it was because I didn't want to spend any more time wondering. Finally, Avery let me know that during that brief intermission from the time that he and I met, he had met someone else. And now the person was saying that she was pregnant with his child. My heart skipped a beat.

He said that he didn't want to be with the woman and that he wanted to be with me. Then he said that he was sorry and he really wanted it to work with us. I was speechless for about ten minutes. When I finally spoke, all I could say to him was that he owed me no explanation. I said that I didn't even think that people had unprotected sex anymore. Finally, my heart spoke and said, "You need to go and make it work with her so the child can grow up with a father." He insisted that he didn't love her and that he didn't want to be with the woman. I told him that I might sound selfish but I refuse to go through any baby momma drama. I told Avery that I didn't have the time or the energy. I said that I wish him the best and hoped that it all work out for the child's sake but as for Avery and me, we were through.

That night after Avery and I had spoken, I laid on his chest, he hugged me, and the both of us laid in the bed crying without sound simply feeling each other's tears. The music was on low and we both knew that that would be our last time together. Before we knew it, we had fallen to sleep in our tears. When morning came, Avery asked if he could wait for me while I got ready for work and he did. We didn't say a word to one another, but still the sadness in our eyes had spoken.

Later on that day while I was at work, Avery had arrived at my job with a gift. He kissed me on my cheek and whispered in my ear saying "I love you" and departed. I stood there while my eyes watered realizing that I was at work and that I needed to get it together quickly, so I did. When I went into my office I opened the gift and it was a Woman's Devotional Bible with the inscription, "Trust in the Lord with all your heart and lean not on your own understanding." Proverbs 3:5

Avery and I remained friends over the years. You might even say that he is one of my best male friends till this day. We continue to talk about everything as often as we can and we look out for one another in ways that reassures a friendship. His son is growing up to be a very handsome respectable fella of which Avery has had custody of basically since birth.

After Avery and I separation, I too had picked up an attitude and I'm certain that it had a lot to do with missing him. I had enjoyed Avery in every way and I had always looked forward to spending time with him. The way he and I communicated with each other was like no other experience I'd had and I loved it. Shynese and I had become two miserable women, and both of us being under the horoscope of Cancer didn't make matters easier. We would argue over a conversation starting this way:

Woman – "ello, me wan speak to shynese."

Joy – "Sure, who's calling?"

Woman – "Me just wan speak to Shynese, why ya ask who callin fa?"

Joy – "It's for you."

Shynese – "What…hold on, let me call you back! Joyce don't be asking know damn body who it is when they call my damn house. It's not any of your business, you too damn nosy."

Joy – "I'm being nosy because I ask the other person on the line who's calling? I always asked who was calling when I answered your phone, and sometimes you would signal me to say that you weren't home, or you were asleep! Now it's a problem for me to ask who's calling?"

Shynese – "Like I said don't be asking no damn body who's callin' my house mind ya damn business!"

At that moment I was furious with her, because I didn't appreciate or deserve to have been treated and or spoken to in that way. Long end of the story, Shynese and I started arguing so much that eventually I had to move out. And yes, I moved back to Jean and she welcomed me with open arms.

# THANK GOD FOR JESUS

Everyone turn with me to Colossians 3:12-15 "Since God chose you to be the holy people, you must clothe yourselves with tenderhearted mercy, kindness, humility, gentleness, and patience. Make allowance for each other's faults, and forgive anyone who offends you. Remember, the Lord forgave you, so you must forgive others. Above all, clothe yourselves with love, which binds us all together in perfect harmony. And let the peace that comes from Christ rule in your hearts. For as members of one body you are called to live in peace. And always be thankful."

"And forgive us our debts, as we forgive our debtors. For if we forgive men their trespasses, your heavenly Father will also forgive you: But if ye forgive not men their trespasses, neither will your Father forgive your trespasses." Mathew 6:14-15.

As you all think on these verses, just know that we are not here to play Church. We are here to be obedient to the word of God and live Christ-like lives. Know that if God didn't forgive us, none of us would be here. So who are we not to forgive our brother and sisters whom we see; let the Church say Amen! Hug some necks, and let them know you love them. Is what the Pastor said.

Clearly Shynese and I received the message. We had become friends again. After service I listened to some of the Ushers say that they wanted to put on a play because the Usher Department hadn't been doing much lately besides Ushering. I joined into their conversation and asked, "If you were to put a play on what would it be about?" One Usher said about three friends, and the other one said she didn't care what it was about she just wanted to put one on. I smiled and said "Humm."

At that moment the Pastor was coming towards us to shake our hands as it was custom after every service. Then I asked my first question. I said, "Pastor, who was the Bible written by, and does the meaning of God's words change when it's revised?" He smiled and said "Sister Joy, what good questions you ask my Dear. Hold on one minute while I finish greeting everyone."

When the Pastor came over to me he grabbed hold of a New Living Translation Bible and he told me to go to 2 Timothy 3:16 and said read it out loud and I did. "All scripture is inspired by God and is useful to teach us what is true and to make us realize what is wrong in our lives. It corrects us when we are wrong and teaches us to what is right." Then the Pastor asked someone to pass him a King James Bible.

The Pastor again said to me to go to 2 Timothy 3:16 and read it out loud and I did. "All scripture is given by inspiration of God, and is profitable for doctrine, reproof, for correction, for instruction in righteousness." Then the Pastor asked me what I thought since I had just read the same verse in two different Bibles. I clearly said the difference was like when one person says tomato and the other says tamato. They are saying the same thing but in a different way.

The Pastor said that oftentimes people would say that they don't believe in the Bible because it has been revised and that it was written by man. He said yes, it was written by man, but first it was God that had given man the words to write. Then later on people revised it for a better way of understanding. We continued talking and I remember Pastor closing that conversation out with, "Regardless to whatever version you read, one must "study to show yourself approved unto God, a workman that need not to be ashamed, rightly dividing the word of truth." 2 Timothy 2: 15. Pastor walked away smiling, saying "Study for yourself Sis Joy, and be encouraged!"

From that moment on I had realized that the Pastor referred to the Bible for everything. He didn't give me an answer based on head knowledge. He specifically would tell me where to go for my answers, and that's how I learned. For me that was a quick but effective one-on-one lesson. And sense

# HANDLE IT

I was taught from the Kings James Holy Bible, that's what I always refer too because "nothing" seems to be missing.

After Church Shynese asked if I wanted a ride home and I said yes. We sat in her car and we apologized to each other for our recent behavior. We decided to continue to work on getting the Daycare started as we had been planning before things were getting crazy between us.

That night while I was asleep I was awakened by something unknown to me. I grabbed something from the night stand to write on and I didn't stop writing for a long period of time. Eventually I fell back into a deep sleep. This went on for five consecutive nights. On the sixth night I was awakened again, but this time I was instructed by that same something to go into the den and turn on the computer. I started typing what I had written the past few nights from scraps of paper. I stayed up throughout the night until I had completed a script titled, "THANK GOD FOR JESUS." I was amazed at what had happened. I printed it out, and showed it to Jean without letting her know the content. Jean was very excited for me and said, "I was wondering what you were up to when you would be up in the middle of the night."

The following Sunday, I went to Church with a full 12 character, 2 hours and 20 minute script. I went to the Ushers and told them what had happened and presented it to them. They were excited and together we went to the Pastor to ask if we could put it on. After getting the go ahead, I immediately asked the members who wanted to participate and rehearsals began.

During the rehearsals I had realized that the play was about me; A Gay girl who I "was," a promiscuous girl who I "was," and the girl who had given her life to Christ. The girl who had given her life to Christ was struggling to try to get her friends to understand that she was not that same person anymore. She was trying to convince them that they too should stop living the way that they were living.

I thought that I had all the answers. I was learning what was right and what was wrong. I decided not to be around certain people and go to certain places. I would get upset when people cursed around me. I would say to the person that would curse around me to please stop because it did something to my spirit and I didn't like it. Or I would simply remove myself without saying a word. I had completely changed without thinking. All I knew was that I was learning about God, Jesus Christ and The Holy Spirit, and that no matter who did what to me or what I did, I was loved and that my pass had been forgiven.

---

The members who were in the play had assisted with decorating, sound effects, music, and scenery. Everyone was willing and helped pull everything all together. Shynese played one of the main characters and was very excited. The day had come to perform. Saturday, April 24, 2004. The church was packed! Most of my friends and some family members had come to see the first play that I had ever written.

Everyone had seemed to have enjoyed themselves. Tony said that I would be the next Tyler Perry. I felt good about what I had done, but realizing that it was God who had allowed me to do it. That night Jean had prepared a small gathering at the house for those who wanted to celebrate with me. Shynese didn't come but most of my friends did.

The next day was Sunday and the service was filled with everyone simply praising God. Pastor had allowed the Holy Spirit to have His way so he didn't preach his prepared lesson. He was thanking God for a wonderful play that was put on last night by the members. Everyone was simply filled with praise.

"Praise the Lord, Praise the Lord." said the Pastor. "Give God the praise. Before our Secretary comes up and gives the church announcements, I would like to inform everybody, as I was just informed today, that this will be Sis. Shynese's last day with us as she is moving to Philadelphia on Friday."

What! Did he just say that Shynese was leaving to go where? I was furious! I started crying. I couldn't contain myself. Why didn't she tell me? Why did I have to find out this way? We were just talking about the Daycare she wanted in her basement. Couldn't she have told me so that I could have cried in secret? What was that about? I could not stop crying. I ran downstairs in the basement of the church and continued to cry. My tears felt like drops of blood coming out of my eyes. I had gotten so angry. I was so hurt I could barely breathe. I thought that if somebody didn't come and help me at that moment I was about to lose my new religion and cuss her out.

Instead, in the nick of time, the Pastor's wife had come downstairs to check on me. I told her that I was so angry and why. She spoke to me and immediately she wrote down the scriptures on anger, Psalm 37:8 "Stop being angry! Turn from your rage! Do not lose your temper, it only leads to harm." Proverbs 15:1 "A gentle answer deflects anger, but harsh words make tempers flare." Proverbs 19:11 "Sensible people control their temper; they earn respect by overlooking wrongs." Ecclesiastes 7:9 "Control your temper, for anger labels you a fool." And Philippians 4:6-7 "Don't worry about anything; instead, pray about everything. Tell God what you need, and thank Him for all He has done. Then you will experience God's peace, which exceeds anything we can understand. His peace will guard your hearts and minds as you live in Christ Jesus."

I sat there and read the scriptures over and over and over and over again. Then there was one particular scripture that was resting in my heart. Philippians 4:6-7 "Don't worry about anything; instead, pray about everything. Tell God what you need, and thank Him for all He has done. Then you will experience God's peace, which exceeds anything we can understand. His peace will guard your hearts and minds as you live in Christ Jesus." That's when I realized for myself the power in the scriptures. And at that moment I was able to calm down. I knew that whenever or whatever I would go through I will pick up my Bible and read! Just like her husband she knew that whatever it was that I needed to always refer to God's word. Since then, I never forgot what the Pastor's wife did for me that day. I kept that piece of paper that she had written down the verses for many years to follow inside of my Bible. And today I too pass the same verses on when I'm aware of someone who is going through a challenge that they may be applied.

I wiped my tears and I began to pray and give God all that I had felt at that moment and I thanked Him for the peace that He had given me. I thought if Jesus had to use God's Words for the Devil to flee, then so should I. I believed in God and I believed in His words. I went upstairs and wished Shynese well. She smiled at me and then had the audacity to ask would I come and help her pack. I smiled and walked away. "Touche!"

# TRUST

Macy's at Atlantic Terminal was closing down and they were sending people to work at the Downtown Brooklyn Macy's on Fulton Street. I didn't want to be a Store Detective anymore due to them stereotyping every African American that walked into the store, not realizing that a thief comes in all shapes sizes and colors. So I had been planning a backup and was called for it at the right time. I had gotten hired to be a Transportation Security Agent which is known as TSA at JFK airport.

I had really enjoyed having conversations with my Pastor. I had never met a man quite like him before. He was my Pastor and now my friend. I felt comfortable sharing my past, my struggles, and my present situation with him. It was obvious to me that although he was a Pastor he was also still learning, growing and willing because we all have flaws. And because of his flaws he was eager to grow and do better. I had really respected and appreciated him being a man of God being God's hand extended. He was not just pasturing the church on Sunday's. He was a full time Pastor on Sunday morning and evening. He taught Bible Study every Tuesday evening, often times coming in on Wednesday evenings for prayer nights, and participating with the youth every Friday evening. Not to mention having a full time job as an Electrician Monday thru Friday.

Over the years I've had several great conversations with people and enjoyed them all. However my Pastor was the only person that I had ever spoken to who had some of the same interests as I did. Therefore, talking about our interest were often our conversational topics. We had shared a passion for helping the youth in a similar way. I had expressed that I had admired what Mother Hale had done. Mother Clara Hale founded an orphanage for AIDS-infected and drug-addicted newborns in 1969 and took care of them as her own. She was hailed by President Ronald Reagan as an "American Hero."

One of the ideas that I had shared with the Pastor was to have a home and get foster children who were aging out of Group Homes and raise them like my own. In the same way Pastor spoke passionately about opening a home for boys. I had told him that Shynese and I had taken classes together to become Foster Parents on our own from a program called "You Gotta Believe." When I said that, he offered his home. He said that he and his wife had just moved to Long Island to their new home. He said that the home they had been living in for years was empty, and if I would like to see it I could. I was flabbergasted!

I thought to myself, this man doesn't really know me, and yet he's willing to allow me the opportunity of a lifetime. No credit check, no upfront money, just my word. Really! I was praising God out loud and saying thank you to the Pastor. We didn't discuss money because I hadn't seen the house. However, based on the way the conversation was going, it appeared that I had no worries.

Shynese and I were still talking although she had moved to Philadelphia. I couldn't stay mad at her, I still loved the girl just in a different way. Besides, I never stayed upset at anyone. I couldn't wait to tell her what the Pastor was willing to do for me. I couldn't wait to tell Jean how excited I was and the reason I went to see the house in Bushwick. Although the house needed a lot of work, I had looked past it and saw the vision flash before my eyes. It was a two story one family semi-attached house with three bedrooms. A dining area and laundry room, with a back yard. And I loved it. He asked me was the house a place I can have the children and I said yes.

I moved into the house and realized that there was a tremendous amount of work that needed to be done before any child could be approved to live there. It wasn't a problem, I pulled out my handy hands and called in some friends, and my cousin Timothy and the work began. I was making more and more trips to Home Depot. Sheet rock was being delivered every day. Money was being spent before I could make it. I was determined to get the work done. Little by little, accomplishments in the house were being made.

Meanwhile, Shynese was making trips to the house quite often and with that came our old passions for one another. We were at it again! It didn't take long for me to start feeling convicted in my Spirit about what we were doing. I would say "Joy, how dare you have sex in the Pastor's house." I had really starting feeling bad about what we were doing. The strange thing was, my conviction was not about being right or wrong, but more of having sex with Shynese inside the Pastor's house. My brain was going through it. I started feeling like the Pastor and that God was watching us. Either way, I knew we had to stop!

Still, I was feeling good about some of the work that was being done inside the house. More work was being done on the inner parts of the house opposed to the outer parts. Basically, you couldn't tell when you walked in because the work was being done to the roof, inside the closets, inside cabinets and sheet rocking the walls. I had purchased a brand new toilet and I scrubbed the tub pearly white. I had fallen in love with the upstairs bathroom. It was large with an old fashioned tub. Actually the bathroom was my favorite room in the entire house after the work that was completed. I had kept it totally white and it was beautiful.

Jean had never come by. Shynese continued coming almost every weekend. And we continued our behavior. But when she would leave, I would cry. My tears weren't for her they were because I was feeling shameful. One day while Shynese was at the house with me, the doorbell rang and I peeked through the window and it was the Pastor. I panicked like a little girl who had just done something terrible. I told Shynese that I was glad she had gotten a new truck because he would have known that she was there. I never answered the bell.

The Pastor had come by the house another time shortly after and I showed him what I had been doing with the house. He smiled and asked how were things going? He seemed as if he knew something that I didn't know and that made me feel uneasy. He wanted to know the progress on the children coming and I said that process had not even begun because there was still much work in the house to be done. He seemed to be perturbed at that point and reminded me that I said the house was good. I tried to explain that I didn't know the seriousness about all that had to be fixed just by looking in. I told him that I was so excited that I didn't think to check the areas that needed much fixing.

Meanwhile, I thought that the money that I was giving him was understood until things progressed. Apparently it wasn't and that's when I realized that I had gone a little over my head. So I opted out and was blessed with a two bedroom apartment in Flatbush thanks to Tony. Once again, money and time was wasted. But I didn't want to lose respect for him as a person, yet alone a Pastor.

I wasn't upset at the Pastor. I am becoming aware of some of my actions. I am hasty when making decisions. I come up with a plan or an idea and I move on it. I spend no time in thought, in planning, nor do I seek council. I allow my excitement to get the best of me and it often gets me in trouble. And I know that way of doing things needs to stop as well before I find myself in a situation that's not so easy to opt out of.

On the other hand, I felt that I had desecrated the Pastor's house, and I didn't deserve to be there. The house was blessed and it was given as a blessing to be a blessing. I truly believe that God shifted some things because of my behavior. Therefore, I no longer felt right. I spent a lot of money on that house, but I blamed no one but myself. There are still some things that are a mystery to me regarding how it had all gone down, but for the most part moving had once again solved my concerns.

I had gotten all settled into my new apartment. Within the same month the church would have its annual fast. We would fast for 21 days praying and expecting to hear from God. We would come into church throughout the week coming together in prayer to pray for one another's situations. Part of the beauty was that the entire church participated in the fasting. We would not eat anything from sun up to sundown. However, a peppermint would be good to maintain our breath. At 6 p.m. we were able to eat a light dinner. Even through fasting a person had to use wisdom if they were on medication. In that case, they had to determine how to fast throughout the day without causing any health issues.

We were all reminded that during this time of fasting that we must continuously pray throughout the day. At school, work, walking, sitting wherever and whenever we were able. It was stressed that it was very important to keep communicating with God during that time. In addition we had to refrain from having sex. Married couples worked it out as best as they could, however, not having sex was the objective.

# HANDLE IT

I had purchased different kinds of beans in order to prepare soup throughout the fasting period. Split Pea Soup had been my favorite, so I would eat Split Pea Soup for the first three nights of the fast. I also thought it would be a great idea to schedule all of my medical appointments during this time so I did. The Mammogram specifically was scheduled because I had a concern about a discomfort in my left breast. On the fourth night of the fast, I had just finished my prayer to break my fast before eating dinner and my telephone rang. It was my Doctor letting me know that I had to repeat my Mammogram test because something was seen and he wanted to be clear as to what it was.

I said to my Doctor without worry or concern, no problem. I told my Doctor that I will schedule another appointment tomorrow. I was amazed that I didn't feel afraid or concerned. I had such a peaceful feeling all over me. After I finished my dinner, I went in my bedroom and got on my knees and I prayed that whatever the Doctor may have thought he saw he would no longer see.

"Ms. Harriet, please do not put your clothes on yet. The Doctor would like to review the film." I said to the Technician. "No problem." I sat and waited and sang softly to myself. I was giving God praises while I waited. The Technician returned and asked that I come and retake the Mammogram for the 3$^{rd}$ time. This time the Technician came in with the film in her hand showing me what the Doctor had circled. I looked at it and said, "Not a problem." When she was done, I asked the Technician again can I get dressed and she said, "Not yet." I sat down and continued singing "I just want to thank you, I just want to thank you, I just want to thank you Lord!" It was a gospel song that stayed in my head during the entire stay at the Doctor's office.

Next thing I knew the Doctor himself came running inside to speak with me. He started talking really fast until he caught himself and slowed down. The Doctor said "Ms. Harriet, I must first tell you that there is nothing there. I thought I had seen something but then I didn't. The bottom line Ms. Harriet, is everything is okay. I'm sorry that you had to take the test more than once. Sorry! Sorry!" I looked up and said, "Thank you God," and continued singing, put my clothes on and went to church for prayer.

In the past, whenever I went to take a Mammogram or any other special test, it was always done by a Technician who would then tell me that my Primary Doctor would give me the results. I had never received results at the sites where test were taken. Although I've tried to get an answer I never would get one. Clearly that was a miracle from God. And I had received it. Strangely, while writing *"Handle It"* that same pain in my left breast arose and it was quite annoying. *Still*, trusting God will be my plan of action.

Each time we would come together at church we would share a testimony that we were giving God thanks about throughout our fast. The testimonies were awesome. Everyone was experiencing God's hand at best. The testimonies were bringing tears of joy to our eyes for one another. I had learned the importance of fasting and that it is a major part of a Christian's life. Jesus Himself had gone into a fast and by doing so He was also letting us know the importance of fasting. "It is written, man shall not live by bread alone, but by every word that proceed out of the mouth of God." Mathew 4:2

My doorbell rang, and to my surprise it was Shynese. I had no idea that she was coming over. At that time I wasn't sure if I was happy or not. She stayed with me that night and we didn't talk much. I did what I'd been doing since we began the fast and she watched. I read my Bible, I prayed and I meditated. She tried to get me to talk about what was going on in church but all I would say was we were fasting. I figured that should be enough because she knew what fasting was like in the church as she was once a member.

Shynese seemed to have been getting an attitude because I wasn't saying anything about what had been going on, or who's there or not there anymore. But I also knew that she had people there who informed her of everything. I wasn't sure what she wanted. But what I did know was that I wasn't about to discuss anybody in the church, or anything pertaining to the church. I felt if it were important to her she wouldn't have left. Therefore, I had nothing.

That night while Shynese and I slept together in the same bed, the attempt was made by her to have sex but I had denied her and said that I couldn't anymore. She asked me was it because I was fasting or because I really didn't want too, I responded by saying both. At that moment I realized what I had said had felt really good, and I knew that fasting had played a large part in my choice.

The next day Shynese left to return to Philadelphia. A week later I received a telephone call from Shynese. She was angry as hell. She was demanding the money that I owed her that she had given me to help get my apartment. She was talking to me as if I had committed the worst crime and it was unforgivable. When I asked Shynese why was she talking to me in that way, she said that I had better give her the money that I owed her and never ever speak to her again in my life. I asked her again what had I done, and all she would say was that she didn't want to speak to me, the Pastor, nor his wife ever again. Before slamming the phone down she demanded the money that I owed her to be paid and it was immediately after.

I was very, very hurt after speaking with Shynese. I didn't know what had happen or who had told her what. I wracked my brain up until a year ago wanting to know what I had "supposedly" done. I had never talked about her to anyone other than my Pastor. Even then, it wasn't in a bad way. I had a great respect for Shynese and a love that can never be forgotten. I knew that not for nothing Shynese was a beautiful person inside and out, and she would give you her heart if she could.

Although she and I were no longer together, I had still loved Shynese deeply. Every prayer I pray till this day, she is always in it. I am still thanking God for allowing her to bring me to Him. I often thought about the "godly" person that would say something that would make her feel so much anger towards me. For that reason, I had at that moment decided that people regardless of their faith wouldn't make them trustworthy. Instead I went to Gods words for understanding. "Better to trust in the Lord than to put confidence in man. Psalms 118:8

A year or so later I had found out that Shynese had gotten married and had a son. I had run into her sister and she had told me the good news. I was actually happy for her. I felt that she had already done what God wanted her to do and that was lead me to church. The funny thing is that sometimes people can be so mean spirited inside or outside of the church. While at church one evening I was twisting one of the sister's hair and she said to me, "Oh by the way, do you know that Shynese got married and that she had a son?" I said, "I sure do, and I wish her well." Here I was doing this chick's hair and she wanted to be mean-spirited. I'm sure she expected a different reaction out of me, that I would appear distraught. I knew her purpose for saying what she said wasn't out of kindness or love because of the way she said it. Mind you, I was doing her hair for free!

I had already come to the understanding that Shynese had served her purpose in my life. Ecclesiastes 3:1 "To everything there is a season, and a time to every purpose under the heaven." And her having a new life had set well with me. The only difference was the way I had prayed for her. I don't only keep her in my prayers, I continuously pray for her, and her family. And I will never stop praying God's blessings over their lives. I also pray that someday the Lord will touch her heart to forgive me for whatever I may have unknowingly done.

Our 21 day fast ended well. We were thanking and praising God for all the answered and unanswered prayers. We had come to an understanding that God answers prayers at His will and time. We had all received the blessings and were encouraged to continue in our faith.

The Lord remembered that I missed Mother Love's presence because He opened my eyes to another beautiful, wonderful mother of God named Mother B. My spirit had connected with her in such an awesome way. She and T.J. had the same birthday and I thought that was really groovy. She became my unspoken mother of love. I enjoyed seeing her smile, and watching her praise God. I even made sure that I sat next to her every Sunday. She didn't speak much, but when she did, I welcomed her every word. I enjoyed going to her house as well just to sit with her for no reason at all.

# BABE AND WOOKA

Throughout my move in and outs Jean and I remained very close. I still had the keys to her house as if it were home number one. I couldn't stay away if I wanted to. Jean and I were entwined with one another. I think we had established that bond the night when she broke down in my arms. Even though I had made decisions to move out, return, come around often or come around less. Jean and I were friends. It remained Babe and Wooka and nothing or no one was able to come between that. Me living there wasn't what kept us close, it was simply love and understanding. We had a relationship. It was like supplying the need to the other person means. Friendship is not only through words calling someone your "Bestie." Friendship is part of a sacrifice of oneself. Neither one of us were selfish in any part of what the other person needed. We gave and we gave out of love without making the other feel bad about it in return. It was who we were and I wouldn't have changed it for the world.

The awesome part in having a friendship in the way we shared one was to allow ourselves the freedom in being so transparent that you can allow that unspoken and often hidden child in you to be explored in other ways. We would talk like children and act it out. Yes we did! One of the ways that I enjoyed our childish behaviors is when I would watch how Jean would enjoy her favorite candy. It was the little chewy red fish. Whenever I would walk into a grocery store that sold little candy fish I would get excited. I would buy a bag full and keep some in my purse for the appointed time. The conversation would go like this:

Babe – "Wooka"
Wooka – "What"
Babe – "Ya got suffin' fa me"

Wooka – "I ain't got nuffin"
Babe – "You ain't got no canny or nufffin"
Wooka – "Nope I ain't got nuffin"
Babe would pretend to cry.

Wooka – "Kkkkk! Let me see wad I got!"

I would then peek in my purse and pull out four goldfish hold my hand open and say,

Wooka – "Look wad I got!"

Babe would give me the cutest child-like smile and chew the candy just like a little child who put to much bubble gum in their mouth. That was a moment of fun for us. That made her happy and I enjoyed seeing her smile. I couldn't believe that the simple things in life can really put a smile on someone's face and I would as often as I could.

But, if I didn't have any fish the conversation would go this way,

Babe – "Wooka"
Wooka – "What"
Babe – "Wooka"
Wooka – "What"

At that moment I knew I was in trouble! I would say to myself, darnit! I switched pocketbooks and forgot to put candy inside my bag.

Babe – "Ah…Wooka Ya got suffin for me"
Wooka – "Ah…Babe, pull over at the next Rite Aide or Duane Reed please, gotta get suffinnnnn!"

Babe – "You better get my damn candy, woman!"

Babe would pull over and say, "Go handle yo binnis!" When I would get back inside the car, I would say to Babe, "Look wad I got." I would open my hand and to give her four fish. Babe would say, "Oh hell no, now I deserve six. So you better go back into that purse of yours and pull out two mo. And, the next time you don't have my canny, girrrrrl!"

Our childish behavior was also in the house. We loved snow days. Babe and I would wear our matching footsie or onesie pajamas. We had different ones, red was for snow days, and black was for movie nights with ice cream, which we called cream. T.J. and anyone else who had seen us would just shake their heads and smile. I believed that Jean and I were to each other what the both of us had lacked in our childhood, because we really enjoyed our childish moments.

Most memorable moments between us would be when I would buy loons. Loons were short for balloons. Normally people surprised their loved ones on certain occasions with flowers, chocolate, jewelry etc. I'd always surprise Jean by filling her room with loons in multiple colors. Man, the look on her face would make my heart smile. Her smile would light up the world and she would shout, "Loons! Wooka got Babe loons!" Jean would stand there and pull the strings and watch them wiggle going back to the ceiling. She actually got a kick out of watching the loons wiggle their way back up. You had to see it for yourself. Watching Jean with that childlike smile was absolutely without a doubt priceless.

It didn't take much to please Jean at all. At Christmas time she would be excited because T.J. and I along with other gifts would buy her toys like Legos, and she loved it. Jean had a large plastic bin with just her toys. Hey, some adults like to play video games. Babe enjoyed candy fish, loons, Legos, and Wooka's love. And I enjoyed good food, a new pair of shoes, and watching Babe smile.

I was hardly ever in my apartment because Jean started to get sick more often. I had quit my job at TSA because I didn't want to get fired for calling out. Honestly, there was no job in hell that was going to make me choose it over her. Besides, I didn't care for what I was doing anyway. Checking bags all day was not my idea of a career.

Jean had taken off work due to having a Doctor's appointment with her Pulmonary Specialist. Most times I would go with her so that Jean would be honest when answering the Doctor's questions. Or just in case she forgot something, I would always have the answer. Her Doctor had decided to do a Sleep Study with her to help determine any problems during her sleep. Afterwards Jean and I ran a few more errands before heading home. All of a sudden Jean stopped dead in her tracks saying that she couldn't move. We stood there wondering what was going on, but didn't understand what was happening. When we reached home Jean didn't seem like herself so I called the ambulance. After she was checked, the Doctor decided to admit her for Pulmonary reasons.

Jean was still in the hospital on the day that I had an interview for another job. It was a rainy day, and I really wanted to stay at home. But the job was promising and I had wanted it. Before I went on my interview I decided to go and check on her. She had gotten upset at me because she said that I wasn't dressed warm enough, and I didn't have on my rain boots. Jean always reminded me to wear scarves and I would often forget. Actually, Jean was the one who started me wearing T-shirts because I never would wear them either. For those reasons along with many others were reasons why I had loved my Jeanie as much as I did. In so many ways she let me know that she genuinely cared about my well-being.

I couldn't wait to call Jean to tell her that I had gotten the Supervisor's position working with the Mentally Ill. I didn't like the fact that it was all the way in the Bronx, but the salary was decent. But first, I wanted to go home to my Flatbush apartment and get out of my interview clothing and change into clothing that was appropriate for the rain. Then the unexpected happened. I was getting ready to walk up the steps in the train station and couldn't. My right leg wouldn't move and I was in excruciating pain. I was so scared at that moment I didn't know what to do. Luckily I did carry that big umbrella that Jean had just bought me because I had used it as a cane to get upstairs and to walk with. I had pulled over to the side and prayed that God just get me home. And He did! When I reached home I thought maybe taking a bath in Epsom Salt would help. I was so afraid. I had never felt that kind of pain before, and I had no idea what was happening to me.

Soaking in the tub did absolutely nothing. I was literally crawling around inside my apartment. I called my friend who worked nearby and asked him to take me to the hospital. When the doorbell rang I crawled to the door to open it. My friend had to help me finish getting dressed and basically he carried me to the car and into Interfaith Hospital. I still had not called Jean because I didn't want to worry her. I needed to at least hear what the Doctors had to tell me.

I was admitted at Interfaith Hospital while Jean was still at Downstate. The Doctor decided that I should stay because my blood test had returned

## HANDLE IT

with concerns. Later it was clarified as a Rare Blood Disease. I said to myself, "Wait a minute. My mother had a Rare Lung Disease, and now I have a Rare Blood Disease." During that time being diagnosed with a Rare Blood Disease was a grave concern because people were dying from it. It was described on the news as some sort of Bacterial Infection going into the bloodstream that caused death. At that moment, I knew that I had to pray and read my Bible.

When I called Jean she started crying saying, "What's wrong with my Wooka?" I told her what the Doctor said and that they had to run more tests on me. I asked Jean how was she feeling and had the Doctor spoken to her. She said that they had to keep her another day for observation. I heard the sadness and concern in Jean's voice for me that I too started to get sad. I told her that I had to call T.J. and let him know that I was in the hospital. Jean shared words of comfort saying that the both of us were going to be okay.

The next day I was put in my own room. Still uncertain what was going on with me, I was so afraid. The good thing was that ever since I had given my life to Christ I would carry my Bible everywhere. I began reading my Bible and enjoying God's words. When I looked up I saw my Doctor and the crew. I say crew because every time my Doctor would come in to see me he would be traveling with an entire entourage. My room would be filled with Doctors as if I were a science project. They wanted to see me. They wanted to hear what I sound like. They wanted to know my history, and did I travel outside of the US? They wanted to know EVERYTHING so they can figure out what was going on with me.

All I could do was continue reading the Bible because if I didn't I would have freaked out because I was scared to death! The pain medication was wearing off and I started crying, trying to get the Nurse's attention. To my surprise I looked up and there was Babe. I just started crying even more. I was crying more because I was glad to see her. But, she shouldn't have been there when she was sick herself. Without words, Jean just looked at me held me and I continued to cry.

After she held me for a moment she wanted to make sure that I was okay, and I told her that I was in pain. Jean went and got the Nurse to give me more pain medication. Before I knew it I was knocked out. When I opened my eyes I was greeted by the entourage of Doctors again letting me know that I was being treated as if it were a Blood Infection, and that I will be staying at the hospital for a few more days.

I still didn't understand why I was in so much pain from a Blood Infection or Blood Disorder or whatever was going on. I wanted to know why was I only feeling the pain in my right leg. And why I couldn't walk. I really wanted some answers, but the Doctor's didn't seem to have any. My case seemed to have been some bizarre situation that they came across for the very first time.

Jean was there with me still. She wanted me to eat but I didn't have an appetite. The only thing that I wanted and craved was Jell-O. Jean decided to leave because she wanted to bring me some personal items and pajamas to the hospital. I tried to convince her to stay home and let T.J. bring them but she wouldn't have it. When Jean would leave I would get sad because the Nurses weren't very nice and I didn't want to deal with them. I received more drugs and went to sleep.

Once again when I woke up, there was a different team of Doctors looking at me as if I were another research problem. Do you feel this? Can you do that? Does this or that hurt? But then I smiled because I had seen T.J.'s face. Looking at T.J., I can tell that he was concerned about me as he watched the Doctors that were around me. When I told T.J. that I really didn't have any answers due to the Doctors being unsure themselves, he seemed worried. Still, I said that God was going to take care of me and not to worry.

I really was blessed to have Jean as a friend. I felt myself feeling other than myself but I couldn't do anything about it. When Jean came to see me she said that I was talking very strange as if I was delirious. She touched my forehead and said that I was burning up. She had told the Nurse but she didn't wait for them to do anything, she started taking care of me. She wiped me down constantly with a cool cloth until my fever disappeared. Finally the Nurse had come in and Jean and I looked at her and didn't say a word. My friend showed up and she had showed up on time.

Five days had passed and I still could not walk. And I still had no answers. Test after test were being done and still I had no appetite. Whenever I was alone, all I could do was read my Bible and sleep. This one particular day I wanted to get out of my bed and strangle the Nurse. I really did. The

Nurse was beyond rude and nasty towards me. I grabbed my Bible and I cried asking God to help me remain calm and to give me the strength to get through the moment. When I looked up, standing in front of me was my Pastor and his wife. The Good Lord had sent them to pray for me. That's when I knew that God was an on-time God!

I was really glad to see them. They wanted to know what was going on with me, but I didn't have any answers. I told them what I knew and they insisted that they will keep me in prayer. My Pastor prayed for me before leaving, and I thanked God for sending them and continued with reading the Bible.

Jean came up to the hospital every day, and she had taken good care of me. Sherlene, my friend Tess and others had visited me during my stay but yet I had no answers to give to them. Christmas was coming around and I was still in the hospital. Overall, I stayed in the hospital for 17 days. The Doctor had cleared up the Blood Infection but still, I was unable to walk. He said that it was a really bad infection and that I would heal in time. His advice was to continue to take the medication.

I was finally being discharged January 9, 2006. Jean insisted that I stay at her house until I got better so that she could continue to take care of me, and the reality was who else would have? T.J. couldn't handle all that I needed done, nor would I have wanted to put it all on him. I figured together the four of us would get through it just like we got through everything else. Tony always made the fourth person because the four of us were just there for each other. All we had to do was let Tony know what was going on and he would be there, and vice versa.

Tony continued to be the best father that he knew how to be, and T.J. continued to be the best son that he knew how to be to his father. They would have their moments and would sometimes share it with me. And after hearing what had happen between them it was understood when I would hear Tony's version, T.J. reminded me of myself. When I would hear T.J.'s version, he reminded me of his Dad. I would shout out to the Lord later on and pray for T.J. even more because he had both our ways and I knew that it would take prayer and a desire on his part for change. Tony, on the other hand, remained faithful with his recovery and was making things work for himself. In all honesty, I am very proud of Tony. He remains drug and alcohol free 27 years later and still. I have watched his journey as he remains faithful towards his recovery. He has two beautiful little girls that he takes care of faithfully being a different Dad than he was when he was on the narcotic.

That was a hell of a Blood Infection because when I got home I could hardly sleep at night. My leg was in so much pain that I would cry every night for the first month and a half. At night Jean would massage my leg with alcohol, she would elevate my leg until I was comfortable. She did the laundry, helped me bathe. I was miserable and still only wanted to eat Jell-O. She took care of me without fuss or hassle.

After two months I was getting really restless and started forcing myself to get around, and get better. I started doing most things myself, just doing them very slowly. I was still in a lot of pain and walking around with a cane. I wasn't receiving any income and I had already missed the opportunity for the Supervisor's position in the Bronx, but I still had to pay rent. The reality of it was that I couldn't, so I had to let the apartment go. I was so sad and disappointed that I had to let my apartment go but I had no choice. I didn't know how long my recovery was going to be and I didn't want to fall too much behind in paying my rent. T.J. and Tony had taken care of the moving and everything because I wasn't able to. Now I was back to totally relying on Jean once again.

I had really needed some answers regarding my leg. Now that I was able to get around much better I thought it wise to pay my Primary Doctor a visit. I felt very comfortable with my Doctor since T.J. and I both had been going there for almost 20 years. I had told him everything that had happened to me and what was currently wrong with my body. He thoroughly examined me and sent me to get a Hip X-Ray. After all the test came back I was told that I had Arthritis in my Hip. The Doctor showed me my X-Ray and showed me why I was always in excruciating pain. My bone was corroding and it was rubbing on the nerve. He said that I would need a Total Hip Replacement very soon if I could not tolerate the pain. I looked at the Doctor and couldn't utter a word.

# OPEN AND OUT

I had missed going to church so much till I was miserable. Meanwhile, during my recovery period I thought about putting on **"Thank God for Jesus"** again making a few adjustments and having new actors. I had also put together a fundraising idea for the church. I just got into a creative mode. My friend Avery had told me about a small theatre company that rents its space for cheap for rehearsals. I held on to some numbers from people who said they were interested in performing in my next production. My Pastor had introduced me to a young lady who was willing to come aboard. I had taken my cousin Dana up on her offer to be a part of my next production. She knew a few people from her church and got them involved. So I had a team of people that I was communicating with until the appointed time.

For the next three months, while I was healing and learning how to walk again, I would work on my script and create the plan for the fundraising event. On paper I had put who's who and who was going to be good in which area of the fundraiser. The fundraiser event was planned in such a way that a lot was going on. I wanted to put it all on paper so that when I presented it to the Pastor he would see the plan opposed to me just telling him about it, while asking can we put it on. I thought by the time I had returned to church I could get the ball rolling on a few things.

Everything was in place for rehearsals to begin. The venue was in a good location. The dates were set. The actors were ready. The only two missing links were my Pastor and his son, who I wanted to come aboard. With everything in place I had decided also that it was time for me to return to church. Jean insisted that I wait a little longer, but I decided it was time. I had lost some weight so my dress was kind of falling off of me, but I didn't let that stop me. I got my cane and I was ready to go to church! Jean drove me to church and when I arrived I was welcomed with open arms. It felt so good to be in the house of the Lord. I felt wonderful. I didn't stand up much, but I sat in my seat giving God praises with my mouth, hands and with my heart.

"Teacher, this woman was caught in the very act of adultery." Go down to verse 10 the Pastor said to the congregation. "Jesus stood up straight and said to her, woman, where are they? Did no one condemn you? She replied, No one, Lord. And Jesus said I do not condemn you either. Go, and from now on do not sin anymore."

They wanted to stone a woman who was caught in the act of adultery. Now the accusers brought the woman but nobody brought the man. Was she caught in adultery by herself? In order to commit adultery, you would have had to have somebody to commit adultery with. Although there are many points to bring out in this scripture I will bring out "The One Who Forgives Sin."

You see we already know that we were all born in sin. We already know that Jesus died once and for all for all of our sins. But do we know that Jesus didn't die for us to continue in our sins? So I ask should we stay in our sin? Jesus said to this woman "From now on" He said, "From now on do not" He said, "From now on do not sin no more" I didn't say it, Jesus said it. He said that we are already forgiven. He can't take that back because He already died for our every sin. He said forgiveness is already ours. But, He reminded the woman "Do not sin no more" He said stop doing what you're doing, I have forgiven you but stop! He said, "For now on do not sin no more."

If you turn with me to the book of John 1: 9 it reads, "If we confess our sins, he is faithful and just to forgive us our sins, and to cleanse us of all unrighteousness." That includes the rapist, the drunkard, the murderer, the Lesbian, the Homosexual, the pimp, the prostitute, the liar, the thief, the corrupt Politician, the prejudice person, the Pastor, the marijuana smoker, the gambler, the list goes on, and on, because it includes all of us. Depending on where we are and who we are, know that God has already forgiven you. He forgives and He says "For now on do not sin no more." In the book of Romans 6:23 He says, "For the wages of sin is death: but the gift of God is eternal life through Jesus Christ our Lord."

# HANDLE IT

Often times a parent will chastise their child for something with the expectation of that child not doing the "same" thing again. That child has now become aware that what he or she had been doing was wrong. Most times that child will stop doing what he or she was chastised for because the child oftentimes wants to please his or her parents. In the same way God wants us to please Him, but voluntarily. He gives us free will.

Pastor was very passionate about this message because he wanted the congregation to know that although we were born in sin, we are not supposed to stay in our daily sins. At the end of service I was feeling so good about myself. I felt like God was happy with me because I was finally on the right track doing what I can do to be right with God. I had gotten a new understanding. And I was getting it all together. I, I, I, I, I, I, AND I !

As always, the Pastor had given me a yes allowing me to have the fundraiser. He had also said yes in taking part in the play as well as his son. I had sketched out the entire plan for our fundraiser, and prepared the flyers. All I had to do now was make it all happen and I did with the help of the members.

Ever since I was released from the hospital my body was never the same. Although I had stopped walking with a cane, I remained in constant pain from my Hip on down my leg every day and all day. The pain was nonstop. I did at first try some of the pain medication, but after reading what the side effects were, I decided to *handle it!*

Food was being sold downstairs. And throughout the church donated clothes, shoes and other accessories were being sold throughout parts of the church. Prior to the fundraiser, I had asked that everyone including myself donate items that were in great condition to sell for very little price. Nothing was priced for more than $5.00 and for that price it was a brand new item.

The fundraiser was going great. People were coming and going and it was going smooth. When they would leave another group would come. It was going as planned. He was about 5'9", my height, stocky muscular build, dark skin with a bald head and although not handsome, he was attractive with his style and personality. He was going straight for Sister Trudy.

Guy – "Excuse me, can you tell me exactly what it is that you're celebrating?"

Sis Trudy – "We're not celebrating, we're having a fundraiser. Food is being sold downstairs if you're hungry. Come inside."

Guy – "Well then, can I ask you another question? Can you tell me who that young lady is?"

Sis Trudy – "That's Sis. Joy, Sis Joy, this gentleman wants to speak to you!"

Guy – "Hello Joy, my name is Spin. I heard that you all are selling food. I was on my way next door to the Tailor's when I saw you, and then you went another way. You're not running from me are you?"

Joy – "Of course not! And yes food is being sold downstairs among other things. We are having a fundraiser today."

Spin – "Can you tell me what kind of food is being served?"

Joy – "Fish, rice, dumplins', mac and cheese, there is a menu that you can look over."

Spin – "Ok, that sounds good but, can you take me downstairs?"

Joy – "Sure, I'll walk you down but I can't stay with you."

Spin – "You're so kind"

Spin – "The food was delicious. Did you have anything to do with any of it?"

Joy – "Yes, I cooked a few things. But I am glad you enjoyed it! The sisters here can cook!"

Spin – "Did you create the flyer too since your name and number is on it?"

Joy – "Yes I did!"

Spin – "I see you have some skills. Well, thank you and I would really like to see you again. This is for you. It was a pleasure to meet you. Ms. Joy. Oh, and by the way, I think you're beautiful!"

    How nice, he gave me $50.00 bill and his business card. I know the $50.00 should be for donation, but he paid for his food downstairs. Those sisters would not have let him leave otherwise. This $50.00 is going to the "Joy broke foundation, cause she ain't got a job!" Besides, the Good Lord probably sent him to give it to me anyway. I started laughing and then I said, "I want to see that brother again. He looks and smells delicious! He spoke

# HANDLE IT

well, he's very charming and girl you in church shut yo mouth!" By the way, I'm still asking God to forgive me for keeping the $50.00 although he did say that it was for me.

The fundraiser was ending, and although I had expected more people to show up, the other members were excited about the outcome and wanted to do it again. I assisted with putting the church back in order for church service the following day. My Pastor stated that it was good and he admired my efforts. Overall, I was excited and felt good about us pulling it off. I was also excited about having another opportunity to speak with Spin.

I was leaving church that evening and my phone rang. The person on the other end said, "Hello young lady, your roses are beautiful!" I said, "Really what roses?" The voice seemed rather in person so I turned around noticing Spin had a beautiful bouquet of long stem roses in his arms to give me. I was impressed with his style of doing things. I told Spin that they were absolutely beautiful. He asked me was I in a rush to go home, because he would like to enjoy the gorgeous evening with me outdoors. I thought that was a wonderful idea and accepted his invitation.

Spin had started off the evening great. When I walked towards his truck, he opened the door and shut it once I was comfortably inside. I was so glad to have sat down because my Hip and my entire right leg were hurting me. But then I thought this is truly a gentleman because so far, he had been doing all the right things. He knew that I wasn't hungry because I had just left the church with all sorts of food as he had also enjoyed. To my surprise, he had first taken me around friends to a gathering inside of a center. He introduced me, we sat at a table, drank a soda, laughed a little and then he stood up, reached his hand out for me and we left. I thought Wow that was cute.

Spin and I had a great evening. We talked about so many things that kept us both intrigued with one another. He told me that he spent 15 years in prison because he had killed his mother's boyfriend due to him beating on her. He said that he had gone to visit his mother and she had been bruised up really bad. He noticed his mother frightened beyond control but insisted that she was okay. Then, he said while holding his mother the boyfriend walked out of the bedroom shirtless and the next thing he knew he had started fighting him and the boyfriend fell and hit his head on the table and died.

He asked me my feelings about him doing time for murder, and I said that I didn't feel a ways due to the reason. I have been in a few situations myself and I know that I'm not a bad person because of it. He was pleased with my response and then showed me the article regarding the incident that had confirmed it. It seemed as if he wanted to see if I would still be willing to talk to him without the article being shown. Spin had stressed sincerely to me that that wasn't his intention to kill him. He just wanted to beat the hell out of him like he had been doing to his mother. So when the guy hit his head, Spin said he called the Police.

He said he had been home from prison for six years and that he has a six year old son. He expressed how he had wished he could have stayed with his son's mother but somehow they couldn't get along and he thought it best to separate. Even at that moment, Spin was reassuring me that the relationship between his son's mother and him was completely over and that they had no future together. However, for his son's sake they agreed to remain very cordial towards one another.

I figured since he was decent enough to tell me that he had been in prison I can tell him that I had not too long ago come out of the hospital. And that I occasionally walk with a limp because my right Hip and entire leg often pain me. We talked about me writing and how I will be a famous Playwright someday. I told him that I'm currently in rehearsal for an upcoming play in a few months. I shared some of my past experiences with him and told him that I used to be a Lesbian. I had also told him that my life had changed since I accepted Jesus Christ. Spin and I were really truly enjoying one another's company that entire evening up until he had taken me home.

From that moment on, Spin and I too became inseparable. He had just started his Security business, and he needed an Assistant so I started working for him out of his house. I would set up the interviews that were being held in his basement. I would prepare documents and anything that came along with his business. We enjoyed each other's company. He had given me a key to come and go as I chose, and then it happened. I came into the house late that evening, and Spin spoke to me in a way that I didn't appreciate.

Spin – "Can you please go upstairs and clean the mess you left up there!"

# HANDLE IT

Oh no he didn't just talk to me like that besides, I know I didn't leave a mess when I left this morning, because I'm always conscious of cleaning up after myself.

Joy – "Spin, I didn't leave any mess upstairs!"

Spin – "Yes you did, and you need to clean it up! Check the bathroom and the bedroom."

Joy – "Let me see what the hell you're talking about."

Joy –"Oh my! Oh my! Oh baby!"

I saw purple Rose Petals in the tub with lit candles around the bathroom, and a hint of Estee Lauder perfume that enhanced the scene. The bedroom had White Rose Petals on a jet black silky sheet set. Champaign with two glasses was waiting to be poured. For the rest of the evening, Spin and I made love from the tub to the bedroom. Before I knew it, it was breakfast time which he served me in bed Pancakes, Eggs, Sausage and OJ. Afterwards we continued making love from the shower to the bed again. And that went on every night for two months.

This man was making the kind of love to me that when I walk down the street my body would shift because I would feel him. I would be talking to someone and start smiling because I had a Spin feel. My body felt so relaxed that I needed to sit down sometimes because I would always feel him. I had craved Spin like a drug. His company and our conversations were awesome because we would bounce ideas off of one another. I had learned so much from him. He just made me feel the way I only dreamed of feeling in a relationship with a man. I thought to myself that this is the kind of man a woman will do anything for.

Spin had a love for playing Pool. I guess that was why he had a Pool Table in his living room. I also enjoyed Pool from when I was a youth growing up hanging out in the Pool Hall with my mother and stepfather. Therefore, I had some skills as I continued playing over the years. At least twice a week Spin and I would play a few games. I must admit he was good, but so was I. Those games would turn into more fun, and then the fun would turn into new experiences. New experiences would turn into more fun and our sex life had gone to another level of bliss and I couldn't see myself without that man.

Turn with me to the book of 2 Corinthians 6:14-18 and if I shall choose a topic for today it will be "No Fine Print." And it reads, "Don't team up with those who are unbelievers. How can righteousness be a partner with wickedness? How can light live with darkness? What harmony can there be between Christ and the devil? How can a believer be a partner with an unbeliever? And what union can there be between God's temple and idols? for we are the temple of the living God; as God said. I will live in them and walk among them. I will be their God, and they will be my people. Therefore, come out from among unbelievers, and separate your selves from them, says the Lord. Don't touch their filthy things, and I will welcome you. And I will be your Father, and you will be my sons and daughters, says the Lord Almighty."

I heard a saying once when somebody said, "Why buy the cow if I could get the milk for free." Are you the cow that's giving the free milk? Or are you a child of the most High God? AMEN! AMEN! Let's give God the praise!!!!

You gotta be kidding me! I stopped being a Lesbian because of what I read, and from what I understood, being a Lesbian was wrong and immoral. I've read several scriptures that said that a woman should not lie with another woman and a man should not lie with another man. I got that! Now, I'm hearing, and reading, seeing with my own eyes, that I can't have that man who's been making me feel absolutely wonderful for the past couple of months. Ummm ummm, this isn't happening. I'm simply going to ask him to come to church with me. That's all at least it's a start! Then maybe we can grow in this together. I can't leave this man. As a matter of fact, I can't wait to see him because I miss him already. Is what I said to myself after church service.

After church I had met with Spin up the block for a Meet & Greet that we had set up for the new hires. When I walked in everything was set up just the way Spin and I had planned it. The Caterers had done their part well, and everything seemed to have all been in place. When Spin spotted me he looked at me as if he had seen an angel. He immediately walked over to me with a smile and then he kissed me on the cheek and complimented me on what I was wearing. I had made my rounds saying hello to everyone whom we had hired for the Security Team. Everything was going really well. Spin had made a joke saying while I was in church shouting, he was there holding it down. Then he gave me a hug saying that he couldn't have done it without me.

After the Meet & Greet, Spin and I went to his house which had become like home to me as well. I headed straight upstairs because my body and mind was exhausted. Upstairs was a bathroom, and two bedrooms one being the room that he slept in and the other he used as a walk in closet. Spin said to me as I was walking upstairs that he'll be up shortly. As I was taking my clothes off to go into the shower, my mind kept playing back on the message at church. The words "come out from unbelievers." I was so deep in thought about the message I seemed to have laid back on the bed and fallen asleep.

When I woke up he was lifting me to get into the bed properly so that we can go to sleep. I positioned myself to sleep in his arms. I kept saying to myself that I was falling in love with this man. I had loved everything about him and he was quite the gentleman.

During the week, Spin and I both had other obligations. For him, not only did he have his own Security Company he had also a Private Security gig for a rich Caucasian man who he had driven around Monday through Friday from 9 am to 5 pm. And I would have my rehearsals throughout the week and link up with Jean in whatever we had planned. Often times on Fridays Jean would have what she called her "short day." Jean would use that day to look for items being objects or clothes that she had been looking for, for a while. Jean would say, "Wooka, Babe is on a mission!" and I knew that we had to look for something.

The play was two weeks away, and I needed to find something really nice to wear. Jean had a fundraiser that she invited me to and she wanted a pin-striped blue pantsuit. Jean and I had been looking for this suit for quite some time but now it has come down to the wire. The fundraising event was two weeks away on Friday and the play was the following day. Therefore, we both were on a mission.

For some reason when Jean would want a specific item it was always a task. Sometimes after several tries we would find it and sometimes we would stumble across it at a later time when we weren't even looking for it. Like at a street fair. Still, while we would look for whatever we would look for, Jean and I would have a good time doing it. So I had looked forward to going on the hunt for the blue pin-striped pantsuit with my Babe.

We had no luck in finding the pantsuit. One of the stores that Jean and I both thought would have it had gone out of business. Time was near so she decided to order it from one of her favorite stores, and have them deliver it express. Before dropping me off at my rehearsal, Jean and I both decided that pizza was going to be our dinner due to time. She had a 7 pm ACORN meeting and I had a 6 pm rehearsal and it was already a little after 5 pm. She reminded me that after her meeting she was going away for the weekend and that she would see me on Sunday.

While sitting in the car eating our pizza Jean and I were laughing at some of the day's events. We commented on how people did or said certain things that would normally get a negative response from me. Jean said that she thought for sure I was going to say something to the lady who said to her, "We don't carry big sizes in this store!" She said it wasn't what the lady had said it was how she had said it that had pissed her off. But she was shocked I said nothing. I started laughing and said to Jean, "But you did!" Jean had said to the woman in return, "So do tell me where do you shop? On second thought that's not my style!" I told Jean she had already said enough!

Jean had witnessed many times when someone said or did something to either me her or T.J. She would hear how I would shut them down with words. Although I had out-grown the use of profanity during that time of my life my words would really hurt their feelings. Jean reminded me that before I started going to church when someone would piss me off in some way I would sarcastically let them have it. Then after going to church she said that I had turned soft. I shook my head and said that I wasn't that person any more. Still, often times Jean would remind me that she missed that Joy because she would get a kick out of what I would say because I would leave her and the person speechless.

It had become quite obvious God was doing something. I thought that if I wasn't going to take God seriously, then why bother because I would only be fooling myself. So Jean could understand why I was changing, I would actually read her what God said about it. I would do the same thing my Pastor had done whenever I would ask him a question. I went to the scripture. This way she wouldn't think that I made it up for myself.

# HANDLE IT

Proverbs 18:21 "Life and death are in the power of the tongue, and those who love it will eat its fruit." Proverbs 15:1 "A gentle answer turns away wrath, but a harsh word stirs up anger." Matthew 15:18, "But the things that come out of the person's mouth come from the heart that's what defiles you." Mark 21:31 "Love your neighbor as yourself. There is no commandment greater than these."

After rehearsal my Pastor asked if I needed a ride home because he didn't see Jean's car. He had known that after I had come out of the hospital that Jean would bring me to church, pick me up from church as well as bring me to and from rehearsal. I said no thank you and that I was fine. Being the person that Pastor is, he asked was I sure and looked around to see if someone was going to take me home. He was not leaving until he was sure that I had a ride. That's just the kind of person he is. So, I said Pastor my friend is here to take me home so I am fine, and that I would see him on Sunday. His response was, "God willing Sis. Joy, God's willing."

Its morning and I woke up lying on Spin's chest. He was sleeping so peacefully. All of a sudden, while I'm looking at him sleep, I heard all that the Pastor preached about being unequally yoked, and fornication, and not entering the Kingdom of God, and being disobedient. All the preaching that I heard regarding having sex with a woman, having sex with a man not being married, the woman who was caught in adultery, everything was flashing in my mind. I tried to ignore it saying to myself this man makes me feel good in every way, no way will I let him go. Then the strangest thing started happening, I started feeling guilty about all this good sex I'd been having with this man that I so much want to tell him that I love him. The guilt seemed to have been taking over and a tear fell from my eye onto his chest. I closed my eyes, hugged Spin real tight and fell back to sleep.

Spin – "Hey Love, do you want to go to work with me today?"

Joy – "I can't hear you I have soap in my ears."

Spin – "Would you like to go to work with me today?"

Joy – "I can't, I have my rehearsals today, and we have less than two weeks for show time."

Spin – "Are you excited?"

Joy – "This is actually my first real production outside of church, I'm so happy how it's all coming together."

Spin – "I'm proud of you Love, You're doing good things."

Joy – "Thank you, and so are you. You're doing all right for a brother who started his life all over again."

Spin – "I really think that we are a good match. Look at the time, I better put a move on it."

Joy – "You think maybe this Sunday you'll go to church with me?"

Spin – "That, I'm not doing! Besides, that's my haircut day. I don't do the church thing, so count me out on that, Love."

Joy – "Is that your final answer?"

Spin – "It's not happening! Lock up and have a good rehearsal!"

The Pastor's voice was ringing in my mind. I actually heard him saying, "ask an unbeliever that you're sleeping with to come to church, and listen to the excuses why they will not come to church." Well, Spin didn't give me an excuse, he basically said no! I felt like crap at that moment. I felt caught up. Caught up in something I didn't want to come out of. But this feeling inside me would not allow me to stay in this relationship comfortably. Caught up! Yeah, that's what I felt.

Romans 14v23 "you do anything you believe is not right, you are sinning." I laid across Spin's bed and cried like nothing before. It seemed as if I couldn't catch a break. But I know I can't stay in this relationship regardless of how much my flesh wanted that man. The Spirit in me will not allow me to stay, and I'm not in the habit of trying to change anyone. I looked up at the ceiling and decided to write Spin a letter saying why I couldn't see him anymore, and told him where to find his keys. Before leaving I walked slowly around the Pool Table, and looked around the house while standing in one spot and then I walked out in tears that would not stop falling.

# HANDLE IT

*Dear Spin,*

*I'm not sure of the real reason why I am writing you. I'm not even sure what is happening to me. What I am sure about is that a few years ago I started going to church, and ever since I started going to church some things have been happening to me that I can't explain. There are things that prior to me going to church I fully enjoyed doing. Afterwards, some desires vanished. Still, some I continue to struggle with.*

*I feel that I don't even know who I am. On one hand I'm learning who God is and on the other hand I'm becoming somebody else. It says in the Bible that when you give your life to Christ you are born again. Maybe part of being born again means that I will no longer be selfish in the things that I want. I also read in the Bible that when you give your life to Christ the Holy Spirit enters your body. Maybe it's the Holy Spirit that's allowing this change.*

*Spin, what I'm trying to say is that something is happening to me and I'm scared. I guess I couldn't tell you what I was feeling because I don't know what I'm doing. I don't even know how a man could make me feel as good as you do. Spin this letter is going to sound crazy because I feel crazy not knowing what is going on with me. It seems as if there is a particular way I am supposed to live. And if I don't live that way I'm going to hell.*

*It all sounds crazy right now, but I gotta figure this thing out somehow. Until then, I can't be with you. I crave you like when a woman is pregnant and she goes through her cravings. I think about you every second of my day. My body awakens when you touch me, and I don't want to live without you. But there is something going on inside of me that is way bigger than what I want that is telling me to stop! I hear voices of past sermons when I'm with you reminding me that I'm going against God. Sometimes my mind is in turmoil when I'm with you but I don't say a word. It's like I'm battling but I'm the only one I see.*

*I'll be honest with you, I really don't know what is happening but I don't want to go crazy either. I gotta walk away simply because of what I understand is right and wrong. And from what I understand, sleeping with somebody when you're not married is sinning. Sleeping with another woman is sinning. Sleeping with an unbeliever is sinning because then we are unequally yoked. It seems as if everything I'm used to doing is sinning and I just don't know what is happening to me right now.*

*Therefore, I need you to forgive me. I need you to understand that I cannot be with you right now. Also, you must believe that it was nothing that you did. You have been nothing but super wonderful to me. You are an amazing man. But there is something in me that will not allow me to stay with you and I can't fight it. I'm so sorry,*

*PS: I left the keys in the spot.*

When I had left Spin's house my tears continued to fall. I went to Jean's house and laid across the bed and continued crying. When Jean got home she looked at me and asked what was wrong. At that moment I sat up on the bed and told Jean how I had felt about that man. I told her how he had made me feel and how I had enjoyed him. I told her that it seemed like every time I would go to church the Pastor or whoever would preach on sexual sin. I told her how I was battling in my head about what was right and what was wrong. I said to Jean that I wanted to live right and do the right thing but it was starting to feel overwhelming. I started crying again and she opened her arms up and held me.

Jean didn't speak right away she just held me close. Finally, when she did speak she said, "That's why I don't go to church because preachers are always talking about somebody sinning and they be sinning themselves." Then she said, "As long as you know that you're a good person you don't have anything to worry about." I immediately wanted to say "get behind me Satin" but Jean would have thought that I was calling her Satin. But at that moment Satin was using her to try and discourage me and have me think that I wasn't doing anything wrong. So instead, I stopped crying and said Babe what you're saying is not true. I said one thing the Pastor always says is never look to him for truth but look to God. Then he would go to the scriptures. And Philippians 2:12 says, "Work out your own salvation with fear and trembling."

I also had to ask Jean what was her reason in always giving me a few dollars to tithe when I wasn't working, because some people really think that their good deeds will get them into Heaven. I picked up my Bible and read from Ephesians 2:8-9 "For by grace you have been saved through faith. And

# HANDLE IT

this is not your own doing; it is the gift of God, not a result of works, so that no one may boast." I explained briefly saying good deeds or being a good person alone will not get you into Heaven. At that moment I knew that although Jean was my friend, and that I loved her dearly, she was not the person that I needed to speak to. I needed to speak to Mother Love. I needed a Godly motherly conversation. I needed someone who can help me to understand what I was going through.

I can tell that Jean didn't like when I would go to the Bible when we would have certain discussions. I would even say to her that that was my way of explaining things sometimes because that's how I was learning. Yeah, before when I had to explain my actions or my issues, I went on my own head knowledge. And I thought I knew everything. But now I had been learning who God is and the only way I knew to explain anything about Him was to go to His book which is the Bible. Besides, if I wanted to know something about Dr. Martin Luther King I would have looked up his Autobiography. And of course, if there is anything that a person would like to know about me, they can simply read *"HANDLE IT."*

I realized that Jean wasn't the right person to help me so without making her feel bad, I told her that I'll be okay, and that I had to get my mind right. She started laughing and said that could take forever. I started laughing and asked how her day was and she started telling me about her crazy day at work that had us both laughing hard. Jean wanted to make sure that I was okay, and offered to go for a ride to get cream. We drove to Park Slope to our cream spot and sat outside and enjoyed our cream like two children.

I still couldn't get Spin out of my mind. I knew that during this final week before show time I would be busy working on the final preparations. I had to get in touch with my Tech guy, and make sure that everyone had submitted their bios and photos to go into the programs. There were a lot of loose ends that I had to tie up. With that said, I had less time to focus on Spin. Although when I walked I'd felt him.

The play was being put on at Boys and Girls High School in Brooklyn. I had an option to utilize the kitchen, as well. I decided to sell food during intermission to make extra money. The only person I thought to help me was T.J. Tony was at one of his conventions and couldn't make it. T.J. was excited about helping out so he asked his girlfriend to help out as well. Together the three of us would do our best. I could have used extra help, I just didn't know who else to ask.

There was so much to do. I was still selling tickets. I had to meet with people. I was still making phone calls to people for ticket pickups. I was spread out like an octopus and loving it. I was making it all come together.

Joy - "Hey you what's up?"

Layla –"Not much, not much at all."

Joy – "Wow, it's been a long time since I've seen you, you look good."

Layla – "Thank you! Thank you very much! You still look good yourself."

Joy – "Thank you! So you're coming to see my production tomorrow, that's good. I'm happy about that! So tell me how many tickets you need."

Layla – "I'm good for three."

Joy – "Cool! Three it is! $75.00 bucks please Thank you very much, and I will see you myana."

-----------------

Spin – "Congratulations! You look fantastic!! These are for you. And by the way I never said that I didn't believe in Jesus, I just said I don't do church!"

Joy – "Thank you, I'm glad you came."

Spin – "What, you thought I would miss it?"

Joy – "I don't know I'm just glad you came!"

Spin – "I wish you the best, Love. Now go and do your thing with the guests."

Joy – "I …"

Guest - "Hey lady, congratulations!"

When I turned around to face Spin, he was gone! Inside the bag that he had given me was a box of long stem roses, and a bottle of Veuve Clicquol

Champagne, and a card telling me congratulations. Instantly, a tear fell from my eyes. That was the last time that I had seen him.

The play was a hit! The actors were all amazing. But, I didn't get any footage from it because the Videographer had messed up somehow. He tried to explain that something had gone wrong. I was heated! And for some reason he thought that he should have still been paid. My old ways of talking had let him have it and he in turn went and spoke to the Pastor saying that it wasn't his fault that the footage was damaged and that I should still pay him. I didn't agree and I was still upset. But then the Pastor went scripture on me about Romans 13:8 "Owe no man anything, but to love one another: for he that love another has fulfilled the law." All I did at that moment was look at my Pastor, shake my head and walk away.

This guy kept showing up and my Pastor paid him some of the money. I didn't think that my Pastor should have given him the money so I returned the money back to my Pastor. At that moment my Pastor explained to me that an agreement was made and the service was provided, and although things didn't work out in its entirety, he was still entitled to some of the money. I said okay, but moving forward I would add additional agreements to all contracts.

I wanted to be with Spin and I wanted him bad. I started feeling like the reason why the footage didn't come out was because God didn't like my behavior, and that was His way of letting me know that I wasn't living right. I started thinking that was the consequence for me sinning. My mind started thinking crazy things about my church, the members, my life, the people who has come and gone in my life. How all that work that was put into the production will never be recognized, and I can never go back and enjoy it being the best production so far. I didn't even know what to say to the actors who were supposed to receive a video for their performance as payment. I just thought all that hard work was for nothing. Ticket sales didn't cover all of my expenses. I was glad that food was served because it had made up for funds needed to pay out. Everything that had taken place had become such a learning experience for future productions. I had to accept that I was out of any and all footage of my production and not to mention I was without Spin!

# UNSPOKEN

It was July 15, 2006, I had an awesome production put on the night before, and I woke up feeling like crap. In addition to my leg hurting, I knew something was wrong because I didn't feel like getting out of bed to go to church. Jean kept coming in the room to check on me because she knew I would have been up already. She knew that I needed time to make sure my dress was long enough, my hat was right if I was wearing one, and I looked appropriate. Yeah, preparation for me on Sundays was starting to be a bit overwhelming. But that wasn't it. I was thinking it was Spin, God, church, a bit of everything that was affecting my mood. For those reasons I had become depressed! Jean was asking me was I okay, and I said, "No!" But I couldn't say what was wrong. Besides, I didn't want to give her the wrong idea. So, I got myself together and Jean took me to church.

Let's give God the praise. Wow! Church was over, and the Benediction was being pronounced. I had no idea what church was about. It was like I blanked or zoned out or something. I thought that I better get out of there before someone look into my eyes and see my tears. Even so, they would have thought that I was so touched by the message that it had brought tears to my eyes. Mind you, I didn't even hear the message. I remember saying to myself that I had to get out of there. I had to go! I didn't think about staying for evening service. I had not a clue what was wrong with me, but I knew that I had to get the heck out of there! Or maybe, I should have stayed and prayed!

I had run out of the church and stopped dead in my tracks. I couldn't move. At that moment I said, I can't go home to my unsaved friend because she couldn't possibly understand what I was going through. I didn't feel like sitting with my church family right now because I started feeling a ways about them as well. I can't go and see Spin, because I broke it off with him. I felt so horrible about what I had done to him. I miss that man! And I still wanted him. But even though I felt that way about Spin, I wanted to grow as I went to church and part of growing was changing behaviors that were not pleasing to God. At that moment I started thinking that I…wanted to laugh! I wanted to cry! No, I want to laugh! Then I knew who to call.

Layla – "Hello"
Joy – "Hey u"
Layla – "Hey what's up, how you doin'"

Instead of me telling a lie, I decided to say

Joy – "I'm hungry"
Layla – "So what do you feel like eating?"
Joy – "What are you doing?"
Layla – "Nothing, you wanna go and get a morsel?"
Joy – "Where am I meeting you at?"

Layla – "Come in, it's open!"
Joy – "Hey you, this is nice. I like your place."
Layla – "Thank you, you look nice."
Joy – "Thank you! "
Layla – "Would you like me to fix you something to drink?"
Joy – "Sure, that'll be nice!"
Layla – "Here relax yourself put your feet up!"

Joy – "Thank you so much; I'm loving the treatment"
Layla – "Here you go it's my special Iced Tea."
Joy – "Thank you and it is good."
Layla – "So what do you have in mind to eat?"

Joy – "I can do some Island food. I think I'm kinda enjoying Island food more than American since that's what I've been eating at my church. Everybody is from Jamaica in my church except for me, and always on Sundays after service we go downstairs and eat. And girl, those sistas can cook. So yeah, I can do Island. What about you?"

Layla – "So what happened, why didn't you stay today?"

# HANDLE IT

Joy – "Because I had a lot on my mind and didn't want to stay. So do you know of a place?"

Layla –"I sure do, and I won't even drive. We can take a cab because it's rather close."

We pulled up to the restaurant, and we waited for seating for about five minutes. The restaurant was sort of small, yet cozy. When I looked at the menu, I was impressed with the dishes. The Waitress came by and asked what we wanted from the drink menu. Other than Champagne, I haven't had any other kind of drink since 2002 when I had gotten saved. So I didn't even bother to look at the drink menu.

Waitress – "Hi ladies, would you like to order your drinks now?"

Layla – "Yes, I'll have a Lechee Martini."
Waitress – "And you maam?"
Layla – "The Lechee Martini is really good!"
Joy – "Sure! I'll have the same."
Joy – "I must say their food is good. This was a great choice."
Layla- "I'm glad you liked my choice."
Waiter – "Ladies, would you like something else?"
Layla – "I'll have another" (Layla pointed to her drink).
Joy – "So will I."

Layla and I sat there for an additional 2 hours after we had eaten. We continued to talk, laugh, drink, and drink…

Joy – "Excuse me, I have to go to the little girls room which way is it?"

Layla –"It's right downstairs" (Layla pointed in the direction of the bathroom.)

To my surprise when I went to the bathroom my underwear were soaking wet! Not of urine, it was of the sensations that I was having while talking with her. I was enjoying this woman's company in more ways than I wanted to. Luckily, I always came prepared when going to church. I would carry an extra pair of stockings just in case of tearing. And I would also carry sanitary wipes just because I'm a woman. So, I took off my soaked panties threw them into the garbage, wiped myself clean, and put on the new stockings that were rolled up in my pocketbook. I looked in the mirror washed my hands, wet my face and returned to the woman who was making me enjoy her without a single touch!

Joy – "Sorry I took so long. My underwear was soaked!"
Layla – "Oh really!" (Layla signaled the waitress to bring us additional drinks.)

Before we knew it the place was empty and we were the only ones inside other than the staff. Layla and I were enjoying each other's company so much that neither of us wanted it to end. The waiter came by and asked if we would like to sit in the backyard, of course we said yes, and asked her to bring us another round. The lights were decorated beautifully which set the tone for us even more. Before we knew it, Layla and I had been in that restaurant for six hours laughing, talking, and drinking, drinking, and drinking until the place actually was closing. We got into a cab, and Layla gave the address to where we were going, and a new saga had started in my life.

Layla handed the cab driver the fare and then got out of the cab, leaving the door open for me to follow. And I did! As soon as we walked through her door we were passionately into one another. This behavior of ours continued for at least two years without ceasing. She and I were enjoying ourselves in every way possible. We communicated well with each other, we ate together, and often times we would pretend that we were at a club, while in her house and dance together, acting silly. We would role play while at our make-believe club. We would imagine our lives wishing it could be that way while allowing our minds to purposely stay together. Layla and I had gotten lost in each other. It was like we were in our own world, and nothing and no one mattered. It wasn't that we weren't thinking of anyone, it was simply because we were thinking about ourselves.

The hospital runs had really started to take a toll on the both of us. Jean was going to the hospital at least three times a week and being Intubated at least once per week and she hated it. She hated that tube being put down her throat. She hated the feeling while it was inside her throat and when they removed it because her throat would be extremely sore. She started saying that she'd rather die before having it done again.

I would beg Jean not to say that she'd rather die, and she should become more aware of what came out of her mouth. Proverbs 18:21 "The tongue has the power of life and death, and those who love it will eat its fruit." I would remind her of what I had said to my brother, and saying that I may not have any other children. There were other stories about the tongue I had shared with Jean that had proven that verse. For that reason I begged her not to ever say that and I would get furious with her when she did. I had learned how not to say anything hurtful to myself or others for that matter.

I understood her frustrations. I just wanted her not to add to them by saying the wrong things. We couldn't figure out why she was constantly going to the hospital. We would go to Specialist after Specialist, Doctor after Doctor, only to get more medicine without answers. At this time T.J. had been renting the apartment upstairs and he would often come downstairs to check on Jean as well because it had only been the both of us who had been taking care of her. If I wasn't home, he was. This way somebody would be around her just in case there was a hospital run. However, now I had become a phone call away, due to spending much time with Layla.

A few years had passed and I had returned to school to complete my BA at The College of New Rochelle on Fulton Street in Brooklyn, which was 10 to 15 minutes from the house. T.J. called and said that he was taking Jean to the hospital. When I had gotten out of school, I went up and relieved him. That night when I had reached home, T.J. was on a rampage. He and his father were working inside the room. The carpet was pulled up and the floor had needed a new covering. T.J. had thought that floor was a major contribution to Jean's breathing problems. T.J. and his dad had taken everything out of Jean's room. Tony had done the tile and most of the painting. T.J. was determined to get to the bottom of Jean's illness.

He didn't stop there! Jean was being kept in the hospital for a few days, and it was going to take a few days to get the room fixed up. T.J. had gone to Jean's mother's house around the corner and asked her if Jean could stay there for a few days. He explained to her what he was going to do and she agreed. She showed T.J. Jean's old room which was very clean, and T.J. set it up. He brought her medicine, her pajamas, and arranged it as best as he could so that she would have all that she needed while there for a short time.

When it was time for her to come home from the hospital, he went and picked her up, dropped her off and then went and got her prescriptions filled and brought them to her. Then, he explained what he was doing and why. At that moment, I think Jean realized that T.J. had loved her like another mother.

The day had come when Jean would come home. She appreciated her room make over. Tony had done a fantastic job. The carpet was gone. She had fresh wallpaper, fresh paint and a new floor. T.J. set her up and went upstairs. However, it didn't stop, the hospital visits continued. We just couldn't figure out what the real problem was behind her illness.

Layla didn't understand the connection between Jean and me and would sometimes feel a ways when I needed to stay with Jean after coming from the hospital. Honestly, I was having a hard time with the situation because I knew that I needed to be there for my friend because we were all we had. And I wanted to be there for Jean, because that was just how we were. But, I really wanted to be with Layla because our relationship was so intense from the moment it started. I would miss her if I was away for a second, let alone overnight. Still, explaining Jean and my relationship to Layla wasn't easily understood, however it was respected.

I was at my new job bored as hell. I was sitting in a classroom watching my one-on-one. Feeling pissed off because once again I was in a field of work that I didn't want to be in. I was working with the Mentally Disabled and I hated it. I had removed myself and went to the bathroom when my phone rang.

Joy – "Hey babe"

Jean – "Hey yourself, why you don't live here no more?"

Joy – "Of course I do, I just stay at Layla's house a lot because we communicate about church and planning things, stuff like that."

Jean – "Joy, are you and this girl screwing?"

Joy – "No! Why would you say that?"

Jean – "Yeah, all right!"

Joy – "Jean, I already told you that I am no longer in that lifestyle and I told you why. Yes, if it were up to me I would have stayed a Lesbian, but because

I know different today concerning it being wrong, I had to come out of it. Layla and I are just friends!"

Jean – "We gotta go and put another tenant out of mom's house. I picked up the court papers yesterday, and filled them out. All you have to do is serve this knucklehead the papers. Mom is a trip, I've been asking her for months was this man paying her rent and all she kept saying was, 'He's okay he's okay.' Yesterday she tells me that he hasn't' paid rent to her in six months. Girrrrl, Mom is funny!"

Joy – "You know your momma, but we gotta do what we gotta do, Babe."

Jean – "What she need to do is make some Fried Chicken, and some Potato Pie!"

Joy – "Yeah, how about we pick up the stuff that she needs to make it, so she won't have an excuse not to make it during the week."

Jean – "Yeah, let's try that! Woman you ain't cooked a meal in this house in a month, Babe want some of Wooka's Lasagna."

Joy – "While we're at the supermarket picking up what your momma needs, we can pick up the food that Wooka is gonna cook".

Jean – "When are you going to cook it Wooka?"

Joy –"Tomorrow Babe, I'll cook it tomorrow."

Jean – "How is the job going?"

Joy – "It's okay, but I can't stay there for long. It's just not my line of work. But for the moment, I'll do what I gotta do! And now I gotta get off this phone. Talk to ya later!"

Oh, Layla is calling me:

Joy – "Hey you, how is work?"

Layla – "Hi baby, it's good. I miss you! I can't wait to get out of here."

Joy – "I miss you too; you have about 20 more minutes to put in."

Layla – "Am I picking you up at Jean's house?"

Joy – "Nah, I'll meet you at home. Jean and I are going to the supermarket after work and I have to take care of some other things for her. I'll see you later on."

Layla – "Okay baby."

Joy – "Okay, love you!"

Layla –"I love you too, baby!"

-----------------

Turn with me to the Book of Proverbs. When you find Proverbs 26:11 say Amen! The topic for today is Don't Go Back. "As a dog returns to its vomit, so a fool repeats his foolishness." Let's read that again. "As a dog returns to its vomit, so a fool repeats his foolishness." Everybody read out loud. "As a dog returns to its vomit, so a fool repeats his foolishness."

Turn with me to the book of 2$^{nd}$ Peter 2:20-22. See my reason for bringing the message out of the Old and going into the New Testament is because some of you like to use as an excuse about what Testament you want to believe in. So here it is the same thing in two different books. Stop looking for excuses when God is talking to you! God speaks throughout the entire Bible. "And when people escape from the wickedness of the world by knowing our Lord and Savior Jesus Christ and then get tangled up and enslaved by sin again, they are worse off than before. It would be better if they had never known the way to righteousness than to know it and then reject the command they were given to live a holy life. They prove the truth of this proverb: 'A dog returns to its vomit.' And another says, 'A washed pig returns to the mud.'"

Again, these are never my words. You can never say the Pastor said, but say God said because these words are not my own. Remember what Jesus said to the woman who was caught in adultery in John 8:1, "Go and sin no more." Saints, whatever the Lord has delivered you from, or whatever you identified as sin in your life, don't stay comfortable in your mess. You don't have to go to the Priest, and you do not have to shed any blood. Repent, ask for forgiveness and allow God to help you along the way.

# HANDLE IT

He said in 2nd Chronicles 7: 14: "If my people, who are called by my name, will humble themselves and pray and seek my face and turn from their wicked ways, then I will hear from heaven, and I will forgive their sin and will heal their land." Let's stop playing church Saints. Amen! He said PRAY, SEEK and TURN and THEN He will HEAR, FORGIVE, and HEAL.

I felt like crap again! The Pastor gave it to us raw today. Or maybe because of the mess that I was in, I received it that way. I have been in this relationship with Layla secretly for a few years now, and we both knew that it must come to an end. Dang! The scripture said "as a dog returns to its vomit, so a fool repeats his foolishness." If I didn't see it for myself in the Bible, I wouldn't believe half of the stuff that my Pastor preaches.

At that moment I'd understood the hurt that I'd seen in Shynese's eyes the day she came to my house and broke it off with me. That hurt in her eyes said I love you, but I gotta let you go. At that moment she stopped allowing her flesh to dictate what she wanted to do. I understand that hurt that she was feeling, I'd felt the hurt because I didn't want to let this woman go. I enjoy her touch, her passion, the way she looked at me, when she talked to me, and how she loves me. She was more than everything in an aggressive woman that I wanted when I was an "out in the open" lesbian, because at that moment I was in the closet. I looked for a woman like her. I craved a woman like her. And now, I finally found her, I must let her go. DAMN!

Later that night I had met Layla at her house for dinner. I was in a lot of pain. My entire leg felt like it was on fire as usual. I also had a lot going on in my mind regarding the message Pastor had preached on. I had made certain that I didn't eat anything at church other than drink a cup of tea because I was looking forward to having dinner with Layla. Apparently Layla had something on her mind as well.

Layla – "Today the Pastor preached on Love."

Joy – "Really! My Pastor preached on returning to slop as a pig does."

Layla – "What are you talking about?"

Joy - "He preached from Proverbs 26:11 "As a dog returns to its vomit, so a fool repeats his foolishness." Look at it yourself after dinner. You know what, I never heard or read that before and it kind of cut me up a bit."

Layla – "Yeah I had a reality check myself. I know that I love the Lord, but yet I'm going against what He delivered me from years ago. Joy, I did something that I wasn't even aware of. I let you into my heart, girl. I really love you. It's killing me because I know I don't want to die living this life that I picked back up. You and I have been acting as if we were in a real relationship for a few years."

Joy – "This is crazy, we allowed ourselves to get deep in this thing. But I do know that through prayer and fasting we can come out of it. We have to Lay. We just have to!"

This has now become the beginning of Layla and I going back and forth with our behavior. It had become an emotional roller coaster. But we continued to love each other in spite of it all. Then again, did we love each other?

Joy – "Hey babe, I'm here."
Jean – "I'm coming down."
Joy – "Are you okay to drive or do you need me to?"
Jean – "You gotta drive."
Joy – "Is your Asthma acting up?"

Jean – "I'm having such a hard time breathing today. I took a treatment before I went to work because I felt bad when I woke up. But then I felt better and I went to work."

Joy – "Maybe you need another treatment. You are supposed to repeat the treatments a few times in between."

Jean – "How is my Wooka doing? Babe miss her Wooka."

Joy – "I'm okay. I just have a lot on my mind."

Jean – "Tell, babe."

Joy – "It's church stuff, and that's a topic that we don't agree on so…"

Jean – "Wooka hungry?"

Jean – "Always, but I want to get you home."

Joy – "Hello, can I have an ambulance at 1119 St. Marks Avenue. My friend is having an Asthma attack."

Joy – "Hey you, I'm starting to think you like this place. Excuse me Nurse can you tell me when will Ms. Wally have the Intubation Tube removed?"

Nurse – "I'll check for you mam."

Joy – "Thank you! The Nurse is checking for you."

Joy – "Babe, relax as best as you can. I know you don't like to be Intubated they should be coming to remove it soon. I brought some stuff to get you cleaned up and comb your hair."

Joy – "Don't cry babe. You're gonna be okay. Wooka gonna stay with you, okay?

When Babe's tear had fallen, only Jean and I knew how much my presence had meant. The sadness in my friend's eyes at that moment made me wish I could just wish her sorrows away. My friend was lying there having so many different emotions. Some of which I knew nothing of. However, I did see the pain and I wanted to turn it into happiness but had no powers, only a desire to do so. My love for Jean was natural, it was innocent, it was good, and it was real. And the only thing I thought at that moment to do was to make her feel as loved as possible.

I started to comb her hair and put corn braids in it going backwards so her hair wouldn't be all over her head. Then I bathed her and put powder and deodorant on her with some fresh PJs. Then I put fresh linen on the bed because I had gotten hair and water all over the sheets. Then I just sat there and talked to her about school, and matters of the heart.

It's been a week and Layla and I have not seen each other. It's been hard as hell. The only way it was somewhat easy was because we both had an extremely busy week. I wasn't going anywhere until I knew Jean was okay, and Layla had gone out of town for a few days, so that had helped. But then, neither of us could take it anymore. We were back in each other's arms. Enjoying one another like the first time we touched. The only difference this time was that when we finished we both cried, and cried and cried.

We tried planning how to stay apart. Instead, our relationship was just off and on for another year. And still in those moments we would just love each other as if it were the first time all over again. We would go out to eat and have drinks and it was on again and again. I started asking myself questions like "Would you want to go back to that lifestyle and stay there?" Then I'll say to myself, "Jesus did die for our sins so why not go back to being Gay, and stop torturing yourself, it's your life. God said that He loves me in His word. I can still go to church and be a Lesbian. They have Gay churches." Immediately, I was stopped in my thoughts! And the scripture in the book of Jude came to me.

"I say this because some ungodly people have wormed their way into your churches, saying that God's marvelous grace allows us to live immoral lives. The condemnation of such people was recorded long ago, for they have denied our only Master and Lord, Jesus Christ. So I want to remind you, though you already know these things, that Jesus first rescued the nation of Israel from Egypt, but later He destroyed those who did not remain faithful. And I remind you of the angels who did not stay within the limits of authority God gave them but left the place where they belonged. God has kept them securely chained in prisons of darkness, waiting for the great Day of Judgment."

"And don't forget Sodom and Gomorrah and their neighboring towns, which were filled with immorality and every kind of sexual perversion. Those cities were destroyed by fire and serve as a warning of the eternal fire of God's judgment." As my Pastor would say The Book of Jude, the 65th book in the Bible before Revelations 4-7. Dang! Dang! Dang! I can't stay in this place. The Holy Spirit won't allow me to stay. Now all of a sudden scriptures can pop up in my head. JEESH!

# I CAN DO THIS

I had gotten a call that a room had opened up for me at the YWCA, Young Woman's Christian Association on 3rd Avenue in Brooklyn. I had believed God said move so I did. I had figured if I focus on growing in the Lord, my writing and school, Layla and I would have no time. When I went to see the room, all I could do was Give God the glory because of where it was, and the people that would share my space.

Joy – "Who dat?"
Jean – "It's me Babe."
Joy – "Who dat?"
Jean – "It's me, Wooka, babe's home."
Joy – "Oh, Babe's home, hi Babe!"
Jean – "Wooka?"
Joy – "What?"
Jean – "Wooka?"
Joy – "What?"

Jean – "Let's get away this weekend. Call your time share and book us. I want to go to the Flea Market, and go Horseback Riding again. I need to get away."

Joy – "Okay Babe! Babe, I'm gonna get a room at the YWCA, I move in next month."

Jean – "Why are you moving again Joy? Every time you move you end up right back here. It's only me here. T.J. lives upstairs, we should just stay together in the house."

Joy – "I'm moving because I need my own bed, my own space, and I shouldn't be sleeping with Babe anyway. As well as me needing to get my own independence back. With the exception of asking my Cousin Dana for money from time to time, I depend on you for everything. I mean really everything. You keep a roof over my head, you feed me, clothe me, put money in my pocket, you literally take care of me. One minute I have a job, then I don't. I gotta get it together. I'm hoping that this new job with the Insurance Company will keep me for a while. I'm going to try my best and hold onto this job long enough until I can't take the pain in my leg anymore. Meanwhile, I gotta do this babe. I really believe that this is what God wants me to do."

Jean – "I help Wooka because you my Wooka and Wooka just needs help!"

Joy – "That's the thing, Wooka always needs help! It wasn't always like that with me. I've been standing on my own feet since I was a teenager. I have been fending for myself since I can remember. Then you came along and I got comfortable because you was that damn aggressive chick that wanted to take care of somebody. During that time in my life when I met you, I really wanted a break from everything, and you stepped right on in and gave me one."

Jean – "Well during that time, you were taking care of your Mom for a while, having major problems with your house, raising a male child by yourself, and you didn't have any direction, I wanted to take care of you in the midst of all my stuff."

Joy – "But, I can't allow you to continue to take care of me. It's like instead of me asking God I ask you and that's not the way a Christian should do things. In fact, none of us should be dependent on another person unless the person is ill and have no choice. Exodus 34:14 'You must worship no other gods, for the Lord, whose very name is jealous, is a God who is jealous about his relationship with you.' What God simply means is that I shouldn't put anything or anyone before Him. It's like you're my idol. An idol can be a car, like your Mercedes Benz. Girl you went crazy when they towed your car away by accident. An idol can be someone's house, jewelry, husband, child; you know how I am about my son. I have to get better at that too. Babe if I continue to come to you and depend on you then I am blocking my own blessings. I

# HANDLE IT

need to seek God in all things and build a relationship with Him. I hope you can understand what I'm saying. I know I have a weird way of explaining the things that I understand. But most importantly, I understand, and I know what has to be done. As I grow I'll get better at explaining. Meanwhile, let me make that call so we can get away!"

Jean – "Whatever Joy, you just better make sure you come and cook me some damn food around here. You know that woman been cooked the chicken we took over there for herself, and she didn't call me to say nothing."

Joy – "Hey you!"
Layla – "Hi Sweetie"
Joy – "What's up, what are you doing?"
Layla – "I cooked dinner."

I pray food don't be the death of me. For some people if you mention material things their eyes would light up. For me, mention food and I'm in. Especially when the person can cook, or it's a seafood restaurant. And Layla could cook! I figured when I show up to Layla's house that I wouldn't use my keys. I felt like doing a little role playing when I arrived.

Layla – "Who is it?"
Joy – "It's Amber."
Layla – "Hey, how you doing?"

Amber – "I'm doing very well. I followed the smell to your house. It smells so good! What are you cooking?"

Layla – "Well, I don't want to spoil it but I prepared a little ap-pe-ti-zzzer, then we have one of my sauteed favorites; following some de-zzzert that I'm sure you would like."

Amber - "So, when I met you at the club last week you never mentioned that you were such a great cook."

Layla – "Some things are left to share at a later time. And you are much prettier now than you were at the club."

Amber – "Thank you, so how long have you been living in this area?"

Layla – "All my life actually, I'm thinking about purchasing a Co-Op but I haven't decided where."

Amber – "They're building all over the place, so do you like the sky risers?"

Layla – "I sure do, I want to be high enough so I wouldn't need curtains. I like to walk around naked, and I wouldn't want anybody peeking at my sexy."

Joy – "Um, this food is delicious I might have to keep you!"

Layla – "Oh really!"

Moments like that would lead us into further enjoyment with one another. We would continue with going to a club that we had made up in her living room. We never moved any of the furniture around, we just pretended that it was a club setting. All we needed was us. We would dance and continue our role playing. It was fantastic because we would enjoy each other as if it were still the very first time. But then things started changing in the bedroom.

Joy - "I feel like every time I was about to have an orgasm, God said you will not enjoy this anymore. I kept hearing His voice. I kept hearing my Pastor's voice. Scriptures were going through my head."

Layla – "It was different for me this time as well. I am so afraid that I can't come out of this. I know that I have to, and I know I don't want to stay this way. I keep remembering the day that I gave my life to Christ and I was on fire for the Lord."

Joy – "We have to fast and pray. We have to be specific on what we need God to do for us. We know that God is a forgiving God…"

Layla – "So do we take Him for granted and keep asking for forgiveness for the same thing over and over again? That's not right either."

Joy – "It's not right but we have to ask Him anyway because we're still in this mess. Maybe we do have to separate. That's why I truly believe that God made it where my ex- girlfriend had to leave New York. I think she was only put in my life so that she could bring me to the Lord."

Layla – "We tried staying away from each other, but whenever we came back together we would pick it back up again. I cannot be around you without wanting you."

Joy – "Now I see why people who are in recovery have to stay away from their triggers. An alcoholic don't need to go to bars and be at parties that serve alcohol because they're going to be tempted. In the same way that you and I are temptresses to one another."

Layla - "Yeah but it's even bigger than that. When you are delivered from something what makes a person go back to the same thing?"

Joy – "Then I would say that we weren't delivered! I can say that He delivered me from smoking, because I have never picked up another cigarette since, nor do I have the desire to. I can say that I'm delivered from hurting people with words, because I truly stopped. And as much as I used to enjoy going to clubs, because I don't desire that any more other than when we're pretending, and have our role plays. And, I thought I was delivered from drinking but when I got with your butt…."

Layla – "So you don't think you were delivered from being Gay?"

Joy – "I'm lying in your bed, and you're a woman! No, I am not delivered! I thought that I was, but I'm not. Honestly, I think woman are beautiful. I think woman are passionate, sensual, nurturing, and I love being Gay. And there is a part of me that don't want to stop. Being Gay was where I found my place, my happiness, I felt safe. I came into myself when I became Gay. I keep it real with God about my feelings, He knows everything anyway. I would even come up with scriptures that could make my wrongs right by only reading part of a scripture."

Layla – "What are you talking about? There is nothing in the Bible that says what we are doing is right."

Joy – "For example when it says that Jesus died for our sins. I would try to…. notice, I said "try" I would try and make it up in my mind since the scripture already said that we were born in sin, I would put it with Jesus died for our sins. So in that case God already knew that we were sinners, and we are forgiven through Jesus. So because of that I figured I can stay in this sin."

Joy – "I know it sounds crazy, but that's how much I was trying to make sense of things since you and I started this. I was trying to rationalize things. I know that was the devil trying to make me think that I'm right in what I'm doing. But, because of the way that I was taught in my good old Pentecostal

Church, in order to understand the word of God fully we must read, and study as the word of God says in 2$^{nd}$ Timothy 2-15 'Study to show thyself approved unto God, a workman that need not be ashamed, rightly dividing the word of truth.' We have to read the Bible so that we can understand what God is saying."

Layla and I start having fun by talking in a West Indian dialect.

Layla –"Ya must turn to second Timotee verse tree, now reeeed!"

Joy – "Me not say tree me say toooo."

Layla – "Yo Joy, I don't think you understand how much I love you. But I also know we got to make it happen for us to get out of this. We gotta do what it takes. The Lord has brought me from a long way, and I don't want to be that person anymore, and my Salvation is important to me."

Joy – 'Okay, let's do what needs to be done. We gotta get strong in our weakness."

Layla – "Only the Lord can help us with that."

Joy – "This is true!"

# MOTHER LOVE

January 16, 2009 we had all gotten the news that Mother Love had passed. Everyone at church was saddened by the news. The Pastor announced that he will notify every one about the details and for all those that will be flying down, to let him know. I was speechless. I felt like I was swallowing frogs. Mother Love was the sweetest, most loving, kindest, caring, woman that I had ever known and now she was gone. I had already missed her daily and I knew that somehow I was going to make it to her funeral.

I wasn't sure of the exact day that I was going to Kansas City, but I knew that as long as I was there for the funeral I would be fine. I had to make Mother Love's funeral. I had to say goodbye. I had to see her beautiful face one last time.

I arrived at Kansas City Airport on Saturday, January 22, 2009. I had gotten a room at the Holiday Inn near the airport. I had called my Pastor who was already there and he had come and got me the day of the service, the following day. There she was beautiful as ever. Many people had come to pay their respects. My Pastor was the Master of Ceremony. The room was filled with tears. But without a doubt we all knew that Heaven was going to be her home. Goodbye Mother Love and I will see you again! January 23, 2009 was the last time I had seen her beautiful face.

# CONFESSION

T.J. had surprised me and started accepting my invitations and coming to church from time to time. This particular Sunday Sister Trudy preached. Sometimes Pastor would ask her to preach and this day she had accepted. "The Word" was the topic for the day. She said if God said it, then we can use it. If God said it, then we can believe it. Sis. Trudy preached passionately about the importance of God's words, and how we should always apply His words in and throughout our lives. She said that we must speak over our children lives. We should call out God's words by sending His words back to Him because He said it.

Proverbs 6:21 "Bind them always on your heart; fasten them around your neck." Deuteronomy 11:18 "Fix these words of mine in your hearts and minds; tie them as symbols on your hands and bind them on your foreheads." Proverbs 4:20-22 "My son, be attentive to my words; incline your ear to my sayings. Let them not escape from your sight; keep them within your heart. For they are life to those who find them, and healing to all their flesh." Sis. Trudy said basically what that means is we must learn what God says. Learn His words. We should change our language from cursing out one another and replace them with words to empower, strengthen, and encourage one another. If Jesus Himself had to use God's words for the Devil to flee then so should we. She said if we are fearful we can use 2 Timothy 1:7, "For God has not given us a spirit of fear and timidity, but of power, love, and self-discipline." If we are angry, James 1:19-20 says, "Understand this, my dear brothers and sisters: You must all be quick to listen, slow to speak, and slow to get angry. Human anger does not produce the righteousness God desires." If you need to forgive, Mark 11:25 says, "But when you are praying, first forgive anyone you are holding a grudge against, so that your Father in heaven will forgive your sins, too."

Instead of worrying, Philippians 4:6-7 says, "Don't worry about anything; instead, pray about everything. Tell God what you need, and thank Him for all He has done. Then you will experience God's peace, which exceeds anything we can understand. His peace will guard your hearts and minds as you live in Christ Jesus." For strength, Isaiah 40:31 says, "But those who trust in the Lord will find new strength. They will soar high on wings like eagles. They will run and not grow weary. They will walk and not faint." And for courage, Deuteronomy 31:6 says, "So be strong and courageous! Do not be afraid and do not panic before them. For the Lord your God will personally go ahead of you. He will never fail you nor abandon you."

Sister Trudy went on to say; "Those were just verses that I chose for the purpose of this message. What you need to know is you can choose whatever scriptural verse that works for you. What may work for my heart may not work for yours. But our God has something for every one of us. While the world says guns are the weapons of choice. God says life and death are in the power of the tongue. Use His words. He gave us the permission to do just that. God's words will help us in our time of need. If you just trust Him. He said if we have the faith of a mustard seed we can move mountains. Read God's words and listen to what He is saying to the church."

Before I knew it, altar call was called and T.J. went up and I watched as he accepted Jesus Christ as his Personal Lord and Savior. February 15, 2009 my son said yes! I was so happy I didn't know what to do other than look up and say "Thank you Lord! Thank you!" Moving forward, I will continue to trust God for T.J.'s life in every way. I will do my best in letting go my issues of concerns concerning him, and handing them over to God. Furthermore, I will continue with my daily prayers looking forward to the day that he not only accepts Christ into his life, but decides to live according to God's will. However, it is God's will and not mine. Therefore, T.J.'s relationship with God is between him and the Lord. Thus, while T.J.'s watching my life, I don't think that I'm giving him a good example of what a person who follows Christ life should look like. And watching me go to church simply isn't enough. Even though I know my changes are from the inside, and not yet visible.

# HANDLE IT

---

Joy – "Hey Babe, whatcha doing? Babe, are we asleep? Wake up, Wooka's home. Babe, you didn't hear me calling you, what's the matter? Stop picking your hand, I don't like when you do that!"

Jean - "Hi, Joy."

Joy – "Ahh hell, you're calling me Joy. What's wrong Babe, and why are you crying?"

Jean – "I'm tired Joy. I'm just so tired. I'm tired of my job passing me over for the Revocation Specialist position. They are still holding that incident that wasn't even an incident over my head. I'm tired of my brother calling every minute and I do my best to help him, but yet he's ungrateful. I'm tired of my Mom's bullshit. I'm her daughter why I don't have a key to her house, but yet I'm taking care of her. I'm tired of my wife always lying to me. I know she's not coming back. I'm always going to the hospital, and they can never figure out why. You're moving to the YWCA tomorrow. And then I'll be alone again. And I'm scared shitless that I will die in this house alone, because I don't have nobody. I know I have you and T.J., but you can't take care of this old lady all of your life. And I don't want T.J. to feel responsible for me."

Joy – "Babe, first of all you must know that no matter what, I'm going to always be in your life. I don't have to live here to be here for you. Even when I moved away I was here as if nothing changed. The only thing that changed was that we weren't sleeping together. But even that's not true because when I spend the night with you we still sleep together. We are Babe and Wooka and that will never change. As far as your job goes, you're going to get that promotion, because you keep passing the test and eventually somebody would have to do some explaining. Write a letter to who can look into it. Trust me, the position will be yours.

As far as your Mom goes, Babe look, she is not going to change! You already know how she is, who she is, and who she will always be. So try not to think about changing that 75 year old woman who gets around better than you and me. Your brother, you can never take a person who is on the narcotic serious! So either you stop what you're doing for him, or prepare to accept what he does to you. Babe, I don't mean to sound harsh to you, but

269

I love you so much, and I watch you get hurt. Sometimes we simply have to fall back and let people rock it out themselves for themselves.

I'm about to do something and please don't resist me, I'm going to pray for you, and if you are willing I would like to invite you to Christ. Is that okay?" When Jean shook her head yes I was more than glad.

Joy – "Our Father which art in heaven, hallowed be thy name, thy kingdom come. Thy will be done on earth, as it is in heaven. Give us this day our daily bread. And forgive us our debts, as we forgive our debtors. And lead us not into temptation, but deliver us from evil: For thine is the kingdom, and the power, and the glory, forever. Heavenly father I pray in your name Jesus that you enter Jean's heart and her mind. I pray that you free her of all wrong thinking, and develop a clean and renewed spirit in her. I pray that you have your way with her total being, and whatever is meant to be for her I pray and ask for your blessings in Jesus' name. AMEN! Repeat after me; 'I repent of my sins,"

Jean – "I repent of my sins."

Joy – "I accept Jesus Christ as my Lord and Savior."

Jean –"I accept Jesus Christ as my Lord and Savior."

Joy- "You are saved, Jean. And now of course you should go to church so that you can hear the Word of God and get clarity. But you can start by simply praying every day. Give me a hug Babe, you are Saved."

Jean – "Wooka, I'm not coming to your church because for one, I don't understand a damn thing they say. For two, I'm not wearing nobody's dress, and for three I don't like anything covering my head except for my work hat."

Joy - "That's fine with me, I understand them very well, and when I don't understand, I know how to find what I'm looking for. You just make sure you find a church that reads from the Holy Bible, and not only read the first clause of a scripture to suit themselves if you know what I mean Ms. I grew up in church!"

Jean – "Wooka, are you going to school tonight? You see what time it is?"

Joy – "Yes, but I have to make sure my Babe is all right first. Is Babe okay?"

Jean – "Babe needs work! I'll take you to school."

Joy – "Not with that hat you won't. I'm gonna get rid of that hat."

Jean – "What you talking about this my good work hat"

That evening on May 22, 2009, Jean had made peace with the Lord and had accepted Christ into her life. I'm not sure what she did or how was she doing in terms of having or building a relationship with the Lord, but I do know that she had accepted Him that night. I just thought that anyone who was hurting as bad as she was needed the peace of the Lord more than anything. Besides, I knew what the Lord's peace was doing for me and I loved her enough to want her to experience it too.

# IN ACTION

Now that I'm living at the YWCA, I am able to clear my head. It's not bad in here. The Lord blessed me with a decent-sized room. I can fit my Laptop and stand so I can do my homework, and continue to write plays. My TV and stereo fit well. I have a large closet. The kitchen is on my floor. I have a private bath. I'm in walking distance to the subway, buses and it's around the corner from Babe's job. And I am in between two protective and caring older women. Thank you Jesus, because I didn't know what to expect. All I knew was that HE said move and I did!

Heavenly Father I ask for forgiveness in anything that I have done that wasn't pleasing to you. Also I ask for wisdom, knowledge and understanding as I read your word. Let my heart be open so that your word may always be hidden there, and remove anything in my thoughts that is not pleasing to you and that you fill my mind with daily wisdom. I thank you in advance for this teaching that I'm about to receive. In Jesus' name, Amen!

"And we can be sure that we know him if we obey his commandments. If someone claims, 'I know God,' but doesn't obey God's commandments, that person is a liar and is not living in the truth. But those who obey God's word truly show how completely they love Him. That is how we know we are living in Him. Those who say they live in God should live their lives as Jesus did." John 2:3-6

"Dear children, don't let anyone deceive you about this: When people do what is right, it shows that they are righteous, even as Christ is righteous. But when people keep on sinning, it shows that they belong to the devil, who has been sinning since the beginning. But the Son of God came to destroy the works of the devil. Those who have been born into God's family do not make a practice of sinning, because God's life is in them." John 3:7-10

"Our Father which art in Heaven, Hallowed be thy name. Thy kingdom come, Thy will be done, on earth, as it is in Heaven. Give us this day our daily bread. And forgive us our debts, as we forgive our debtors. And lead us not into temptation, but deliver us from evil: For thine is the kingdom, the power, and the glory, forever. Amen." Mathew 6:9

Jesus, Jesus, Jesus! I'm crying out to you Lord. I know my help comes from above. Why am I still at this place Lord? Why am I still allowing my flesh to take over me? I need help in understanding who I am. Sometimes I feel confused, Lord. I'm confused in this body. I'm learning more about you every day and I know that what I have been doing is against what Christianity stands for. What I have been doing is even worse than that of a thief, a drunk, or a liar…the list goes on. That is because I am sinning against my own body, according to your word.

In 1 Corinthians 6:18 your word says, "Run from sexual sin! No other sin so clearly affects the body as this one does. For sexual immorality is a sin against your own body." Oh forgive me Father. I know there is something going on inside of me, and God I'm gonna keep on trying to do right because my Salvation is so important to me. Why I do what I do is not clear to me yet. My prayer is to please reveal whatever I need to understand so that I can move forward and not look back. I thank you in advance for what you have done and what you will do in Jesus' name Amen!

-----------------

I decided to get busy on another production while living at the Y. This time will be different because I wanted to work on two versions at the same time. I wanted to add and take away from the original play ***"Thank God for Jesus"*** and I wanted two different shows. I would work on a youth version and an adult version using the same script.

I didn't take much time getting started. I had located a church around the corner from the Y. I had met with the Pastor who was more than willing to allow me to utilize the space for rehearsals. I had worked it out so the youth would rehearse at the church around the corner and the adults would rehearse at my church on given nights. I was blessed that both my Pastor and this other Pastor were so willing to assist me with space. I held the auditions for the adults at my church and the auditions for the youth at the other. I felt very comfortable with the cast from both groups, as they all were very talented.

I had asked Captain Rece who worked with me at the Department of Corrections would she like to play the role of a Pastor. Rece had given her life to the Lord some time ago and was quite knowledgeable and passionate about the things of God. When I had asked her she was more than willing. It was during a rehearsal that her son would come to meet her and he too became a part of the production and did quite well. The woman loved him because he is a very handsome young man. My cousin Dana was also very willing and accepted the role for the second time of playing me. I was also honored to have three members from my church take part in the production and I was so grateful for them, and all of the others that would make this happen.

I thought that I would have no time for doing the wrong things when I was so tied up in doing the right things. Going to school and doing papers throughout the week. Holding rehearsals with two different cast. Mentoring, and attending church on Sunday mornings and evenings, in addition to Tuesday nights for Bible Study. I would say that my free time was to sleep and of course to eat.

# HELP!

Joy – "Hey you"
Layla – "Hey yourself, are you still at rehearsal?"
Joy – "No, I'm walking towards the Y, we just got finished."
Layla – "How was rehearsal tonight?"

Joy – "It was really good. I really have an amazing group with me. But one of the guys I think he's a playa with some of my girls. One of my lady bugs had a little talk with me today, so hopefully things will work out for the best."

Layla – "You want company?"
Joy – "Who, you? Of course! Where are you?"
Layla – "Behind you"

That night Layla and I talked about our day. We laughed and talked about the different situations that we had both experienced throughout the day. I decided to put some music on so we can listen to some of our favorite songs to sing and act silly. We vibed to Queen Latifa's album "***Simply Beautiful***" "***The Same Love that Made me Laugh.***" Then we listened to John Legend's "***Save Room for My Love***" "***Slow Dance***" "***PDA*** We ***Just Don't Care***" and then started kissing. Immediately after the kiss we both started to cry.

Joy – "Man here we go again! It's so hard because I love you so much! We can't do this,"

Layla – "I know Joy! I know! I'm so in love with you girl that it's driving me crazy. I can't even look at you without wanting you."

Joy – "You are everything that I wanted in a woman, but now is too late because that's not who we are anymore. It's the beginning of 2009 and we are still…"

Layla – "We keep on finding ourselves at this place. I don't think you really understand what happened to me that night when I first made love to you. That's the part of me that don't ever want to let you go. The rest of me know that I have to let you go."

Minister: Wiggins
Topic: Weeds that grow
Scripture: Romans 7:18-25

"We get saved, and look nice and all it takes is just one weed that will start to grow in a place where you never thought it would grow. Weeds are unwanted plants. It grows where it is not wanted. It lives on the source that it grows around. The weed will take from the source and stop the growth of the other plants. The other plants will lose their substance because the weed has taken what the plants need to grow. At times the weed will grow faster than your plant. It will come to a point where you will not recognize your plant, or recognize your harvest because the weed has completely taken dominance and overpowered the plant. These weeds can come like a stronghold, and they would wrap themselves around the tomatoes, the pumpkin tree, the potatoes, and they will strangle it, cut off the life.

This is why the tree don't bear the fruit because of the weeds' strangling power. Weeds could go unnoticed. Weeds can get to a place that if they grow in the house they could grow into the pipe and clog it up and eventually crack the pipe. There are many types of weeds. All weeds need is just a little dirt. We must pay attention to the weeds that grow in our lives. There are four different things that when it comes to us as human beings that we need to look at how things affect us as believers and as children of God. 1- the physical, meaning the flesh, 2- the soul, the part of you that God desires, 3-the emotional and mental part that we try to keep together so that we don't go crazy, 4- the finances are the part that will keep us from being envious or jealous of other people. At times we as believers are so caught up with the things of the world and we allow the devil just to come in, and while we are caught up we don't pay attention to what is being brought into ourselves.

That's why as children of God we have to be careful who we have as friends and who we associate with.

We can identify a weed that has been sitting in our lives, and has latched onto our spirits. A weed will cause you to do things that we normally would not do. A weed will allow you to be at a place that you don't want to be. Anybody and everybody can grow weeds. It's a matter of paying attention to what is going on inside of you. Physically we get caught up in the flesh and let things fester and grow. It is things we watch, or say out of our mouth, the people we hang around. There are situations we really don't want to be a part of but we entertain them and/or allow them to happen.

Paul said, 'Whenever I decide to do good, evil always presents itself. The things that are going on inside me, I'm wrestling night and day within my flesh, in my spirit. There is a war fare.' It is something that has gotten ahold of us, something that is keeping us back. It is something that is keeping us captive. The weapons of our warfare are not carnal, and we must ask ourselves how much do we want to remove ourselves from the situation? How much do we want God to get it out of us? How much do we want God to remove the lustful thoughts, the lying spirit, the envy and jealousy, and back-biting spirit?

As a tree by the water concentrates on being a tree, we as children of God must concentrate on being a believer of God. Meditate on His words to give us strength, courage, motivation, and boldness. They are God's words that would push us into worship, into prayer. God's words will make us want to love, and turn the other cheek. We need to get down on our knees and get to the place where we let God get to the root. Some of us need to trace our past and get to the source of the problem that continues to grow in our lives, and pull the weed out at its root."

I needed to go to the Y and meditate on that. I didn't even want to stay for evening service. That really gave me a reason to think about ALL the weeds that were growing in my life. Lord knows I had a lot of weeds that were choking the heck out of me. At that moment my phone rang and it was Layla. I was surprised I decided not to answer it.

Joy – "Hey Layla, I'm sorry for not answering the phone when you called, I was having some quiet time. But I'm calling to tell you that for the next few days I will be fasting so you will not be hearing from me. I really need to spend some quality time with the Lord, because I'm …"

Layla – "Me too Baby, I was calling you earlier to tell you that I'm going to be away for a few days. We both have to do what it takes. Pray for me, and I'll pray for you. I love you!"

Joy – "I'm always praying for you, talk to you soon, God willing. And I love you too."

-----------------

When I got the call that T.J. had taken Jean to the hospital, I stopped what I was doing and went to see her. Once again, Jean was Intubated. The next day when they removed it, Babe would not stop crying;

Jean – "You were at church, and I didn't want to bother you. I was in the basement changing Tuna's litter box, and when I came upstairs I had to sit down. Then T.J. came downstairs and asked me was I all right and did I need anything. I told him I think I need a treatment. He set me up with the treatment, and told me that he'll be right back down he needed to turn off the fire because he was cooking. When he came back downstairs, he took a look at me, and said he was taking me to the hospital. But I don't remember anything else except waking up being Intubated. T.J. saved my life Joy."

Jean – "What if he wasn't there? He always comes down and checks on me, he brings me dinner downstairs when he cooks on the days you don't come over to cook. I don't have family that call and check up on me other than my mother. What if T.J.…."

Joy – "Enough of the 'what ifs.' Just give God the glory and say thank you. Thank the Lord for placing us in your life in the same way I thank God for you being in ours. I know you're tired of being sick and coming to the hospital. I just wish we knew the real reason behind your illness."

Jean – "Don't you have mid-terms this week?"

Joy – "Yes I do, but I'm going to stay with you a couple of days, and go to school from your house."

# HANDLE IT

Jean – "Wooka, I don't want you to miss school, and work."

Joy –"I quit because the pain in my leg wouldn't allow me to continue. It's just getting worse. I guess I have to schedule the Hip Replacement soon because this pain gets unbearable at times. Therefore I'm staying with you, young lady, at the hospital. Besides, whatever I have to do, I'll go from your house until you feel better and return to work."

Once Jean came home she got comfortable and settled in. I had prepared dinner, and T.J. had come down for a while and ate with us. As the night went on, Jean wanted to lie across the bed and watch TV. I had sat up in the bed and decided to read the Bible. For some reason I turned to Proverbs 5:16-17, "Why spill the water of your springs in the streets, having sex with just anyone? You should reserve it for just yourselves. Never share it with strangers."

My understanding from that made me feel disgusting! I thought about my cousin raping me, his perversion entered me and then I too became perverted. I was perverted as a little girl, and continued in my perversion as an adult. My cousin is currently a Homosexual, and I am a Lesbian. I'm still so angry that he took my virginity. He was the one who broke my Hymen. He had no right to take my virginity, and not be punished for it. Was that the reason for my promiscuity, or is my promiscuity due to my mother not doing anything about it when I told her what he was doing to me? Was it then that I realized that my body meant nothing?

I thought why do I enjoy sex so much? I was violated by others at such a young age, but then he had to penetrate me. Why was it so easy for people to handle my body? Or is it because I never had a father figure in my life after I came to live with my mother? And since my body was already violated, and I didn't know any better, I just kept on giving my goods away. I wasn't taught anything about my body. Hell, I'm just learning how to buy the proper size bra so my breasts don't sag.

I can honestly say that I really didn't know any better. I feel like I missed being raised. I wish I was told as a little girl that my body was a Temple. I shore as heck don't believe it's a Temple now. I was never told that sex should only be with your husband. Or that my body is part of Christ. Therefore, since I didn't know, of course I couldn't teach these things to my son. And I couldn't blame my mother because she did the best she knew how. I needed to meditate on that for a while because once again God's words were penetrating my mind, and I had to get understanding.

I wanted to hear from God in a special way. I needed to get deeper into prayer for my child, Jean, Layla, my Christian walk, and my thoughts. I told Jean that I was fasting and she knew that I would be in constant prayer. She made her request that the day I came out of fasting for us to go and enjoy seafood because she was now craving it. Not to mention I welcomed it.

During my fasting period I would pray throughout the day and make it to Bible Study on Tuesday nights. I was still able to continue with going to school and having rehearsals. This day while at Jean's house, I decided to clean up and cook dinner. I thought although I was fasting it didn't mean that her and T.J. couldn't enjoy one of my meals that they both loved. The house wasn't dirty it just needed some of Joy's touch. Jean walked in the house and told me to read something that she had received. "Finally, I told you Babe you were going to get it. Congratulations Ms. Revocation Specialist. You are no longer a Parole Officer, I'm so happy for you."

Jean – "Girrrrrrrrl, I was getting tired of them passing me by. But I got it!"

Joy – "You need to be giving God all the glory honey, because He allowed that Jack! Count your blessings now while you still can and thank Him. Even through your stubbornness and your pride fullness, God blessed you. You better act like you got some sense, and give God the Glory. You'z saved now! And yes, God willin', tomorrow it is, and I am going to pig out to celebrate for you."

Jean – "Um that smells good. T.J. must be cooking upstairs because I don't see any pots on this stove. Either way, I know I'm gonna get some."

Joy – "How about, I take the Lasagna out of this oven, and you make sure T.J. comes down and gets something to eat how about that?"

Jean – "You made Lasagna?"

Joy – "Spinach lasagna, don't get cheesy happy. Everybody around here has High Cholesterol remember? Babe, are you good, because I need to run?

And by the way, there is something special for you inside the bedroom. And congratulations, God is able!"

Jean – "Bye Wooka and I'm gonna eat all the Lasagna I want."

Joy – "Yeah okay"

When Jean walked inside her room she was even more surprised I had gotten Babe loons in multiple colors as I had done in the past. The room was filled with them. All I can hear while I was locking the door was excitement from Jean from seeing all the loons in the bedroom. She shouted out, "Thanks Wooka!"

I was more than excited for Jean. I knew that she deserved that position. I knew that getting that position had meant a lot to her. And I had seen over the years how not getting the position had been affecting her. Not only did I know that Jean was a great Parole Officer, I knew that she had deserved a promotion, especially since she had been passing the test repeatedly. I wanted to get to the Y and give God some praises on her behalf. I don't know if she thanked Him, but I sure had to thank Him for answering prayers. After praying I went into reading more of God's words.

Romans 7:14-25 "So the trouble is not with the law, for it is spiritual and good. The trouble is with me, for I am all too human, a slave to sin. I don't really understand myself, for I want to do what is right, but I don't do it. Instead, I do what I hate. But if I know that what I am doing is wrong, this shows that I agree that the law is good. So I am not the one doing wrong; it is sin living in me that does it.

And I know that nothing good lives in me, that is, in my sinful nature. I want to do what is right, but I can't. I don't want to do what is wrong, but I do it anyway. But if I do what I don't want to do, I am not really the one doing wrong; it is sin living in me that does it.

I have discovered this principle of life that when I want to do what is right, I inevitably do what is wrong. I love God's law with all my heart. But there is another power within me that is at war with my mind. This power makes me a slave to the sin that is still within me. Oh, what a miserable person I am! Who will free me from this life that is dominated by sin and death? Thank God! The answer is in Jesus Christ our Lord. So you see how it is: In my mind I really want to obey God's law, but because of my sinful nature I am a slave to sin."

I felt at that moment excited. I had gotten excited because there was somebody in the Bible that I could relate to. I wasn't sure of what Paul was saying in its entirety, but for the most part I had understood that I continued to do what I didn't want to do and that it was the sin living in me. I knew that this scripture would take some further learning as I continued to grow in the Lord. Actually, I wanted to call someone to give me a little more insight on the scripture but I had to complete a paper for school and I knew that I was probably going to pull an all-nighter. So I closed up my Bible and started typing.

I had been communicating with Cozy towards the end of her sentence. She had been sent down from Bay-View Correctional Facility for good behavior. She was now at Metropolitan Correctional Center in Manhattan to be released soon. I was excited for her release and I would go and visit her and bring her daughter Rissa. Cozy had known that I had given my life to the Lord and was "supposedly" no longer in the Gay lifestyle. She respected it and would often talk about her relationship with God. I had said that when she came out I would like for her to come to church with me and she agreed. Later on in the mail I received the most beautiful picture ever that Cozy had drawn wishing me the best on my upcoming production. The roses were so beautifully drawn it looked as if they were real.

The following afternoon, I wanted to hear some gospel so I pressed play on my radio. My leg was hurting me really bad and it was almost unbearable. I normally dealt with the pain but this day I decided to take two Tylenols. I had a half a cup of juice in the fridge to wash it down. I stood there in the middle of my room in pain, and then it happened, I broke down and cried.

Hi Father, it's me again your daughter who you have been protecting since birth. Throughout this year I have been dealing with some things in my life all of which you are aware of. I can't work because of my Hip. I am always in constant pain. I applied for Disability, and they finally approved me but said that it can take up to a year before any payments. Jean is in and out of the hospital, and I'm worried about her. I have no food and nothing to drink. The one thing I have is a metro card which is the only thing I accept from my son every month. I know that I can go and get whatever I need from T.J. because he is doing quite well for himself. But I also know that I am not his responsibility and that my reasoning for moving to the Y, was to trust you and depend on you alone.

I no longer accept or ask Jean for money because I'm trusting in you to provide. What I am enjoying is church, rehearsals for the play, and school because I feel that I'm accomplishing something while I'm going through it. Father, I tell you something else, I keep saying to myself, I say "self" you know you cannot be with Layla in any kind of way. But God, I really wish that loving her was okay with you because I found love. I truly enjoy her company and how she makes me feel.

But I'm not a fool either! I know that being with another woman is totally wrong, and against your word. I have read with understanding too many scriptures, and heard too many messages regarding immorality. All I can do is trust you in everything that I'm going through. Lord it seems as if I am truly being born again. Being stripped of my old self, and coming into the new Joy during this Sanctification process. Yeah, I'm making mistakes. I'm making plenty of them, and this is my story. But Lord I'm trying! I'm trying! I'm going to keep on trying until my last day because I am learning what it truly is to love because you first love me, and for that reason alone, I desire to please you Lord.

It's funny though because in all honesty you want me to live a good life. I am the one who is making things complicated, and slowing down my progress to live a prosperous life. And that's because I want to please my flesh. Oh, and about my situation having no food, my finances, T.J., Jean, I'm casting everything over to you just like your word says in 1 Peter 5:7 "Casting all your care upon Him; for He cares for you." Yeah, I feel better every time I talk to you, now I'm going listen to you because it's not fair that I do all the talking…

----------------

Joy – "Hey baby girl, how are you today?"

Kasha - "Ms. Joy, we just got evicted, and I don't know what to do."

Joy – "I'm sorry to hear that! I'm not going to ask are you ok, because I can hear in your voice that you're not. But I am going to say based on what you had already talked to me about after rehearsals, you and your mom have no other place to go, am I correct?"

Kasha – "Yes Ms. Joy, you're correct!"

Joy – "Honestly, the best thing I can tell you is that you and your mom will have to go into the shelter system…."

Kasha – "Ms. Joy, I heard those places are horrible, we can't go there."

Joy – "Can I tell you, they are not as bad as you think; I have already told you girls some of my testimony but there is more to my story. So much more! I too used to live in a shelter with my son when I was about your age. While I was there, I went to Job Corps, and I applied for City jobs, and received my first apartment. We stayed at a decent place, but I knew it was only temporary. I didn't get involved with what others were doing I did what I had to do to move forward. You get what I'm saying to you?"

Kasha – "Yes Ms. Joy, I understand. But we don't even know how to go about none of that. Where do we get started? We don't have any place to stay Ms. Joy…"

Joy - "I know this is really hard for you right now, but you gotta know God has your back, girl. Where are you? I will meet you and your mom and show you what you need to do so that your journey will start today. It's going to be okay, meanwhile, while you're going through, you just continue to go to school and to church and let the adult, which is your mom and our Father handle the rest. Is that okay?"

Kasha – "Yes, that's okay Ms. Joy."

  Kasha was one of the 12 young ladies in the upcoming youth version of ***"Thank God for Jesus."*** It seemed that God had placed each one of those little angels in my life for a reason. It appeared that all that they were going through, I had already gone through or was currently going through. I had become all of their Mentors at the same time. I was amazed about how God was using me even while I was going through all my mess and my storms. Because in all honesty, I had a lot going on with me which had me cry out to the Lord many of times right inside my room at the Y. That's when I realized that God has a purpose and a plan for all lives. We just have to allow His presence to manifest itself within us.

Glory, Glory Jesus I thank you! Thank you Lord for allowing me to see another day. I thank you Jesus, you are worthy to be praised! You are worthy Lord, you are worthy. Our Father, which art in heaven, Hallowed be thy name, thy kingdom come. Thy will be done on earth, as it is in heaven. Give us this day our daily bread. And forgive us our trespasses, as we forgive those that trespass against us. And lead us not into temptation, but deliver us from evil. For thine is the kingdom, the power, and the glory, forever and ever.

Lord God Almighty I thank you for this day, for this is the day that the Lord has made and I will rejoice and be glad in it. I thank you for watching over my child Lord, you knew him by name even before he was formed in my womb. I thank you for your continual protection over his life. I pray that you keep him safe, protected and in good health. I pray that whoever is in his presence who wants to cause him harm is removed from him. I pray for his friends' Salvation and protection as well.

I thank you for keeping family and friends safe as I didn't hear a bad report in the night, so I thank you. Lord I pray for my Pastor and his family that you keep them safe and united and I pray for my church family's safety and wellbeing. Lord I pray for Shynese and her family and that you grant her the desires of her heart as your word says. Lord I pray that you put a smile on every elderly person's face. I pray that you bring something sweet to remember so their hearts can be filled with joy today. I pray for the helpless, the hungry, and the homeless. I pray for those that are in prison that they will come to know you as Lord and Savior. I pray for my friends today Lord, Jeanie, I pray for healing all over her body, and that she will spend time in building a relationship with you. I pray for Layla, that you answer her prayers and keep her focused on you.

I pray that you help Kasha and her mom in a special way during this time, and that you allow me to do what only you allow me to do. I ask for blessings for them Lord. I pray for every Gay friend that I have and that they come to know you as Lord. Father, I thank you for speaking to me through your word while I took time out to fast. I thank you! Father

God, I ask that you have your way with me today, and dress me with your complete body of armor, the helmet of Salvation. The breastplate of Righteousness, the shield of Faith, the sword of the Spirit, the belt of Truth, and Feet shod with Peace. I ask for favor from you Lord, bills have totaled $1,200. I need favor from you Father. Have your way with me today, and help me show love to others and be kind to everyone.

Thank you Lord, Lord I thank you. There is no one like you Jesus. I love you, Hallelujah! Hallelujah! Praise the Lord! Lord I praise you, I thank you Jesus! You are so worthy to be praised! Thank you, I thank you for yesterday, I thank you for today, I thank you for tomorrow! I just want to praise you and thank you for all you have done. I blow kisses to you, Hallelujah! Hallelujah! You're so worthy.

I thank you for feeding me your word as I turned down my plate to hear from you. Your word has truly been feeding me through this time of fasting. I pray for your strength in my weakness. I pray that I can be obedient to your word, and don't go back to my old ways of living but trust in you instead. I thank you for all that you have done in my life. I thank you for never leaving me nor forsaking me. Lord I thank you ahead of time for the food that I'm about to receive because you knowz I loves me some seafood, and I'm only able to eat it on few occasions. So I thank you for allowing me to come out of this fast and being able to dive into the food of my choice! Thank ya Lord, I thank ya! Lord I love you, and I give you the praise in Jesus' name. Amen!

I was on my way downstairs to meet Jean who was waiting out front to go and enjoy some seafood. I made a stop to check my mail and noticed there was an envelope that looked like a check was inside. I immediately opened it and to my surprise there was a check for $1,200.00. All I can do was stand there against the wall and cry. Then I started praising God as if I was the only one around. Lord, you are sooooooooo amazing! Thank you! Thank you! Thank you! God I love you! I adore you! You are an awesome God! Hallelujah! A woman walked past me and was looking at me as if I was crazy.

I said to the woman, "I'm giving God the glory because He is AMAZING! Do you know that God is AMAZING?"

# HANDLE IT

Woman – "Yes He is. Yes He is."

Joy – "Hey Babe, did I tell you how amazing God is? Well let me tell you how amazing He is. Today! Today! A few moments ago, I was praying to close out my fast. Afterwards, I prayed and told God an exact amount that I needed to pay my rent and some bills. Anyway, I came downstairs to meet you and stopped to check my mailbox and to my surprise there was a check in the amount of $1,200. It was the exact amount that I asked Him for. God is so Amazing Babe, you gotta get to know Him. Did you speak with Him today? Did you? Did you say anything to Him? You gotta talk with Him because He enjoys it when we talk to Him."

Jean – "What was the check for Wooka?"

Joy – "Oh, let me read the letter. I was so excited about the check I don't even know what it's for. Thank you Jesus! Oh my God. Oh okay, the letter say that it's overtime money that wasn't paid to me from my last job. Supposedly some people had filed a petition and they won the case and I was included. Wow! Ain't God good!"

Jean – "Why didn't you ask for more? Then you could have paid for dinner Wooka."

Joy – "He gave me what I asked for. Yeah, I better up my game. I had just asked Him for it. He knew what I needed. This is another amazing moment from God. He has proven Himself over and over and I keep messing up."

Jean – "Whatcha mean you keep messing up? Whatcha doin' Wooka? Whatcha doin'?"

Joy – "Forget about what I'm doing, I'll tell you what I'm fittin' to do. I'm about to eat me some Lobster fresh out of the tank is what I'm gonna do Babe! Babe there goes our song turn it up …"

Joy/Jean - "Y'all gon' make me lose my mind up in here, up in here."

Joy/Jean - "Y'all gon' make me go all out up in here, up in here."

Joy/Jean – "Y'all gon' make me act a fool up in here, up in here."

Joy/Jean – Y'all gon' make me lose my cool up in here up in here."

Jean and I always sang that part of the song when we heard it. We didn't sing the rest of the song because DMX gets vulgar with it. Still, we would always enjoy the lyrics in the chorus. I was a DMX fan and Jean was a Jay Z fan all the way.

---

Show time was coming up for the two productions of ***"Thank God for Jesus."*** April 25, 2009, was the adult version, and April 26, 2009 for the youth production. It was to be staged at George Wingate High School.

Today's topic is "Sanctify Yourself Today for Tomorrow Is on Its Way." Today's scripture reading will be taken from 1 Thessalonians 4:1-5. "Finally, dear brothers and sisters, we urge you in the name of the Lord Jesus to live in a way that pleases God, as we have taught you. You live this way already, and we encourage you to do so even more. For you remember what we taught you by the authority of the Lord Jesus. God's will is for you to be Holy, so stay away from all sexual sin. Then each of you will control his own body and live in holiness and honor not in lustful passion like the pagans who do not know God and His ways." AMEN!

In justification we are declared by Jesus Christ that we are righteous. Justification is what God does for us. Sanctification is what God does in us, and through us. It is how we build a relationship with God where we produce holiness, soundness, righteousness, which is God's character. When you are justified, you are in a right relationship. Or when you are sanctified, you begin to bear fruit. You are having fellowship, you begin to see the light, you begin to see holiness. The deity of Jesus must be seen in us. Your body is the temple of the living God. Sanctify the house of the living God and carry out the filth, the garbage, the sin, the things that are not pleasing to God. Get rid of them. Cut it loose. Sanctify yourself today, for tomorrow is on its way. Is what the Pastor preached.

---

It's April 25, 2009, and the auditorium at Wingate High School was not full but there was a very good crowd of people. Everyone put on a great performance. Many of my old co-workers from the Department of

Corrections were there, and some members from my church, along with other supporters. The following day April 26, 2009, I had my debut performance as a Pastor. There weren't that many attendees but the performance was awesome. T.J.'s response was the day that I become a Pastor he would definitely come to church on a regular basis I took that as if I too had done a great job. However, I'm not sure if me being a Pastor is in God's plan.

# BREATHE, JOY

T.J. had gone away to Miami but had returned a day early. He had called me and said that he thinks he had passed out because he had woken up on his kitchen floor. Jean and I were coming from downtown from her Doctor's appointment and she was still feeling bad, receiving no answers. I told T.J. that we will be there shortly. I told him to stay on the phone while I call the ambulance to meet us there. Well, when Jean and I got there, the ambulance hadn't arrived yet so Jean and I took him to Interfaith on Atlantic Avenue. When T.J. and I walked into the emergency room we both looked at each other and said, "Nah!"

We got back into the car and Jean drove to Methodist Hospital in Park Slope. I didn't want to have T.J. wait inside the waiting room because I wanted answers as soon as possible. So before I got out of the car I asked Jean for her badge. When Jean gave it to me T.J. and I went into the hospital. I held T.J. by his arm and very aggressively I spoke with the Security Guard letting him know that this young man had to see a Doctor immediately. The Security Guard let us pass and informed the Nurses' station. A Nurse came and assigned T.J. a bed to wait for the Doctor. Within five minutes a Doctor came over to us and began assessing T.J.'s medical situation.

T.J. had told them that he was away and came home early because he wasn't feeling well. He said that while he was away that he partied a lot. The Doctor wanted to ask personal questions so I walked away and used that time to go and return Jean's badge. I had also asked Jean did she want to see the Doctor because she still wasn't feeling well herself. She said that she was fine and just needed to lie down. I told her that I would keep her posted and to go home.

After a few hours the Doctor came out with the report. She said, "Young man you passed out because you were dehydrated. The Nurse is going to put an IV in so that you can get some fluids inside of you before you go home." She said, "But, we did see something else and it had nothing to do with you passing out. We saw a nodule next to your brain that would eventually need to be removed." She looked at me as if I had known that. T.J. and I both started asking the Doctor questions. I wanted to know how serious was it and can it be removed through his nose? She didn't have the answers because she wasn't a Neurosurgeon but she suggested that we see one.

I saw the concern in T.J's eyes. In the same way he saw the concern in mine. I told him not to worry because God is able. I told him that I would do some research on finding the best Neurosurgeon possible and that he was going to be just fine. All sorts of things were going through my mind. But then I started thanking God for bringing T.J. home from his trip safely. I really believed that God allowed the events to happen the way that they did. The reason they had given him a CT Scan was because T.J. had passed out. Had he not passed out there would not have been a reason for them to give him a CT Scan. Without having a CT Scan we would not have known what was growing. God wanted us to know that there was a problem in T.J's head that needed to be addressed and quick.

T.J. expressed his concerns to me, and I told him not to worry and just trust God. I told him that it was very important for him to trust God and to pray. I said read Philippians 4:6-7 "Don't worry about anything; instead pray about everything. Tell God what you need, and thank Him for all He has done. Then you will experience God's peace, which exceeds everything we can understand. His peace will guard your hearts and minds as you live in Christ Jesus." I asked T.J. if he believed that God brought him home from his trip early, and if he had a little bit of faith that God would heal him, then believe in His words and trust Him. I reminded T.J. that when he had gotten Saved the message that day was "The Word." Therefore, I told him to believe in God's word when he read the scripture. I asked T.J., will he trust God for his healing and he said yes.

I told Jean all about what happened. She seemed to have taken the news rather hard and started to cry. I told her that everything was going to be okay because we have faith. I told her not to worry about T.J. instead I wanted to know about her. I knew that I would begin researching for a Doctor the following day for T.J. But it was late and we all needed to get some rest. I had been with Jean at the Doctor for the first half of the day and with T.J. in the hospital for the other half of the night, and I was really tired and my brain was fried. And on top of that I had a major exam in class the following day. So at that moment, I showered and went to bed.

# MY FRIEND

Joy – "Hey Babe, what's up?"

Jean – "Joy, are you coming over the house from school?"

Joy – "I didn't plan on it, but do I need to?"

Jean – "I think so, Babe don't feel good."

Joy – "Did you take a treatment?"

Jean – "I don't need a treatment. I don't know what's wrong."

Joy – "I'm on my way."

Joy – "Hey T.J."

T.J. – "Hi ma, are you coming to the house soon, because I'm about to go out and I don't feel comfortable leaving Jean in the house? I just gave her something to drink and I asked her was she okay, she just said she was thirsty."

Joy- "I'm on my way. I'll be there in about 20 minutes. What is she doing right now?"

T.J. – "Sitting on her bed. Ma, what's wrong with her?"

Joy - "I don't know! I'm in route."

Joy – "Okay T.J., I'll take it from here. See you later."

T.J. – "See you later, but ma, call me if anything…"

Joy – "Hey Babe, how ya doing?"

Jean – "I'm having that strange feeling again the same as yesterday when we went to my Doctor and she said it was nothing. Joy, what is wrong with me?"

Joy – "I wish I knew! That is the million dollar question. I'm gonna go to the bathroom and Babe we're going to the hospital. Somebody is going to give us some answers."

Jean –"Joy!"

Joy – "What!"

Joy – "Jean you gotta wake up for me. Please Babe, don't do this. 'Hello my friend has passed out! 1119 St. Marks Avenue and it is a private house. Babe wake up for me please wake up! T.J., Jean passed out, I just called the ambulance. Okay, okay, okay, you're with me now, good! You scared me Babe. You gotta stay with me okay? The ambulance is on its way. Oh good T.J., you got here quick! Open the door for the ambulance so they can come right in."

EMS – "Ms. Wally, you gotta let me do this."

EMS is trying to intubate her on the bed, and Jean will not open her mouth. Then they brought her to the floor and she still wouldn't let them do it.

T.J. – "Jean, you gotta open your mouth, they are trying to help you."

Joy – "Jean, open your mouth."

T.J. – "Please Jean, open your mouth."

EMS – "Maam, we gotta do this, it's going to help you."

Jean – "Joy, you promise you gonna make them take it out before I wake up?"

Out of excitement and worry I shouted "yeah!"

T.J. – "Ma, calm down she's scared!"

Joy – "Please just let them do it, Jean please!"

I want to say that Jean wanted to open her mouth but by this time the muscles in her jaw were clenching and she was not able to at that point. We watched her mouth move like it was out of her control. EMS carried her out into the ambulance. And they continued to try and intubate her but were unsuccessful. I asked them which hospital that they were taking her to and

# HANDLE IT

they said Interfaith. I asked could we go to Methodist and they said that they had to get her to the nearest hospital which was Interfaith. Although I didn't want her there, we had no choice.

I called her Mom and her friends because Jean had told me the next time she goes in the hospital to notify them. So I did. During this time T.J., myself, and Ms. Wally, are at the hospital. After about 15 minutes they were able to intubate her. About an hour later we were told that we could see her. I waited for her mother to go inside and then when I came inside, Jean reached out to me and started crying.

"I know Babe! I know! Just relax as much as you can okay? You gotta get better. Remember we are supposed to ask the Doctor what's wrong with you, besides you gotta be with me when I become a famous Playwright. I held her hand and noticed she was starting to get excited so I went outside the room for a moment to get myself together. Jean's Mom stayed in for a few more minutes longer then she came out and sat with me.

Shortly after, my friend Barry and Jean's friend Ura showed up. Barry had wanted to be with me because he had seen the concern I had in my eyes when I had left school. He had asked that I call him, and let him know how Jean was doing. Ura went in to see her and then came out saying she thinks she's going to be fine. She said that she had to leave, but call her if anything happens. Within 20 minutes, Doctors were running to Jean's room. I attempt to go in but they wouldn't allow me. More Doctors and Nurses came running into her room. After 10 minutes they came out and a Doctor approached Ms. Wally and me.

Doctor – "She didn't make it!"

Joy – "No, no, no, no, no, no, no, no, no, no, no, no, no, no not Babe, no, no, no, not Babe! Please Ms. Wally let's have an Autopsy we wanted to know what was wrong. Please would you let them give her one?"

Ms. Wally – "No Joyce, I don't want that. She had the Asthma, that's what it is. It's the Asthma."

I called my sister Sherlene and Ura telling them that my Jeany had just died. I just couldn't get it together. My friend Barry took me into a room and I couldn't get it together. I could not stop crying. I couldn't breathe. I just couldn't believe it. My best friend who was like my mom, my big sister, my little sister, my buddy, my pal, and now she's gone! I couldn't believe it. I looked up and my sister Sherlene and nephew were there. For the remainder of the day I have no recollection of anything. I don't even remember getting from the hospital to home. Or who brought me. Half of me seemed gone.

Layla – "Joy, where is T.J.? "

Joy – "I don't know, when we found out, I don't know Layla. He's hurting real bad."

Layla – "I know, the both of you are hurting really bad. I'm so sorry! Is there anybody you need me to call from her family?"

Joy – "T.J., Tony and me were her family. Ms. Wally will notify whoever else."

Joy – "I can't do this."

Joy – "Oh my God, she is gone. My Jeanie is gone."

Layla – "You know you got to make the arrangements now right? Maybe her mother wants to be a part of it. And of course I'm here to do whatever I need to do."

Joy - "I'll call Ms. Wally, and ask her would she like for me to go on ahead with the arrangements, she might have a specific funeral parlor in mind. A long time ago Jean showed me the suit that she wanted to wear in the event of her death, and where the insurance policy is."

Immediately after members of Jean' family appeared, Ms. Wally and Jean's friend Uri, started treating me really bad. I mean really bad! Still, I had to do what I needed to do to have my friend buried the way she wanted me to, and so I did.

T.J., Tony and myself were hurting. I can't even explain that moment. I just had to get it together and prepare everything. I couldn't think about anything or anyone else. My mind seemed to have been blank other that focusing on getting Jean ready to look like I knew she wanted to look. I wanted to make sure that I did all she told me to do. I thank God for Layla, I don't think I could have pulled it off without her. She lifted me up when I was falling. She fed me so I wouldn't be weak. She prayed for me when I needed comfort. She listened when I spoke. She spoke for me when I couldn't speak. And she wiped my tears when they had fallen.

There were a lot of attendees at Jean's funeral, her co-workers throughout the years showed up. Many of my friends and family members had showed up. She really looked like herself. I'm glad that the Funeral Director went exactly according to the picture that I had given her, because Jean loved her curls. She had a head full of hair and she wore one style only as I had said before. Yeah, she looked good. T.J., and a young man who lived next door, put a really nice collage of pictures together. I had also got the young man and his sister to sing for the funeral. They sounded amazing! They sang *"**Swing Low, Sweet Chariot**"* and *"**His Eye is On the Sparrow.**"* Jean had watched those children grow up and they were honored to sing for her.

I had finally seen Jean's wife for the first time. I knew who she was the moment I laid eyes on her. I had seen a wedding picture on Ms. Wally's wall of their wedding. I introduced myself to her and I told her that Jean really loved her. I had surprised her when I had given her the matching gold bracelets that Jean used to wear. I had placed them in her hand and said, "I'm sure Jean wouldn't mind me giving these to you." She looked up at me with her watery eyes, and said, "Thank you!" I said, "You're beautiful," and hugged her and went my way.

At the burial I had given those in attendance balloons to let go into the air. "Wooka got Babe loons. I got loons Babe" July 2, 2009 my best friend left this earth. Still in 2015, I continue to grieve. Her birthday was coming up July 27th. She was going to be 58 years old. Yes, Jean was 15 years my senior, and she was my friend.

## My Friend

*True friendship is that unexplained heart connection between two people who enrich each other's life. They may not know exactly why they became friends, but they do know that their presence in each other's life is a gift.*

*True friendship is one of the most valuable treasures anyone could have. It is necessary nourishment to the heart and soul. It creates a feeling of unconditional acceptance between two people who allow each other to be themselves - just as they are.*

*True friends are sensitive to each other's own perceived flaws, insecurities, vanities, peculiarities, and opinions, but neither puts demands on the other to change. They just want the best for each other….always. This kind of relationship takes no effort and needs no rules.*

*This is our kind of friendship…the kind that exists between two people who understand each other and know how to communicate with each other often by not saying a word. Jean, thanks for giving me the gift of true friendship.*

*Friend Forever,*

*Love Joy/Wooka*

# HANDLE IT

July 7, 2009, my birthday. I'm sitting at the table staring at the wall. T.J. came in and gave me a hug and said, "Happy birthday Ma, I love you and so does she." He gave me a Hologram with a picture of Jean when she was a little girl sitting on her parents' sofa with her legs crossed. It was beautiful. All I can do was look at how the light just made it seem so real like she was smiling at me. It was so beautiful, and still is. I don't know how long I sat there, but when I looked up, Layla was wiping my face with a cool cloth.

Layla – "Have you eaten anything?"

Joy – "I'm not hungry."

Layla – "Joy, it's your birthday. I'm taking you to dinner."

Joy – "Isn't this beautiful, T.J. gave this to me for my birthday? Isn't it beautiful Layla? It's so beautiful."

Layla – "It is very beautiful, just like she was."

For a while, I would just cry. Layla and I would be out eating and I would cry. I would pass Jean's office building, I would cry. I would just cry because I was missing her. Layla was really there for me during that time. Sometimes she would see it coming and hand me tissues because she knew that I was about to cry. She didn't try and stop me or feel embarrassed, she just let me have my moments, and then we would continue with our day.

# RESEARCH

Dr. Theodore Schwartz and Dr. V. Jay Anand were listed as a dynamic neurosurgical team. It was posted with New York Super Doctors, 2008, Daily News on April 26, 2004, for Brain Treatment, New York Post, April 28, 2004, for Brain Tumor Removals. They were listed in the Institute for Invasive Skull Base and Pituitary Surgery as a Dynamic Surgical Team. New York's Best Doctors Special Double Issue - Theodore Schwartz for brain tumors, pituitary tumors, epilepsy, endoscopic surgery. Crain's New York Business. And The Daily News listed Dr. Theodore Schwartz in April 28, 2009 as leading the war on cancer. My spirit said yes, and now I had to set it up so that T.J. and I could meet the Doctors who would perform his surgery.

# NUGGIE

I decided to return to Jean's house and move out of the YWCA because I didn't want to leave the downstairs empty while T.J. still lived upstairs. Layla and Barry helped me move back to Jean's house. In that moment, Layla accepted Barry and my friendship because she knew we were colleagues, and she was aware of Barry being with me at the hospital when Jean had passed. But, even in that moment while they were helping me move I had noticed a pittance of concern from both of them. It seemed as if they both had silent thoughts about one another, showing facial emotions without them possibly realizing it. And once again, I said nothing.

Barry hung around me a lot and started helping me out around the house since he knew about the prior events regarding my friend's passing. I was enjoying our friendship because he made me laugh. Barry was a big guy about 6'2", 255 pounds, tan complexion, bald and attractive. He loved to joke around, sing, cook, and act. I liked that Barry was attentive to me, and that he also attended church. Barry would do things like carry my book bag as if we were in public school. He would cook for me and serve me, while I would type my papers.

Returning to school wasn't easy after Jean's death. Actually, I didn't want to continue. It was the end of the semester and it was mid-terms. I showed up but couldn't focus. I thank God for concerned colleagues. I was sitting at my desk in a daze with tears constantly falling from my eyes. I sat there without saying a word. I was encouraged to do what I had to do since I had come this far. A colleague walked up to me and said quitting wasn't an option. And the unthinkable happened. She had put all of her answers on my paper. The strange thing was I didn't even know this young lady. We had never spoken in class. However, I am forever thankful to her.

Barry would say things like I know you have some homework to do, just let me take care of you while you do what you have to do. He would say I'm just about done with school. Now you have to finish. I got you! While I would be typing a paper, he would be in my kitchen cutting up fruit and then he would bring it to me on a plate with a glass of wine. Barry had gotten accustomed to preparing dinner so that we would eat together. I don't know, maybe at that moment I needed that. I wanted to feel good. I enjoyed him. But there was a difference in this journey for me. And, the difference was enjoying the relationship without the benefits of having sex. Our friendship was strictly platonic.

Barry reminded me of Layla in ways that mattered. He was a great cook, and so was she. He gave the best massages, and so did she. He enjoyed singing to me and she tried singing to me. He would act like a clown with me and so did she. He was very attentive towards me and so was she. But, even with that I had some concerns while still enjoying every minute with him. Something had to be wrong. I was waiting for the truth to come out. The truth always comes out. Or was this a diversion away from Layla?

Barry – "Love, I found some information for you regarding your project. I made the copies and I emailed it to you. You might find it helpful."

Joy – "Thanks Huggie (Barry) we're having a concert at my church, would you like to sing?"

Barry – "How about you and I do a duet, would your Pastor allow it?"

Joy – "Sh sh sh! Would he allow it? Are you trying to get me kicked out of my church? Huggie, I can't sing."

Barrie – "Love, sure you can. You have the most sexiest voice ever. You probably just need to practice a little bit on breathing techniques."

Joy – "Oh, it's a whole lot more than breathing techniques for this voice. I'm telling you, I cannot sing."

Barry and I rehearsed and played with music and rehearsed. It was so much fun. He didn't laugh or judge my voice, he just allowed me to find a song that I can have fun with and then he would come in and do a switch. Church concert evening time, Pastor is excited because neither he nor anyone else in the church ever heard me sing, but now I signed up for a duet.

---

Pastor – "Bless them Jesus! Mike 'em up! Mike 'em up!"

*"Rough Side of the Mountain" by Rev. F.C. Barnes Chorus:*

Joy – "I'm com………in' up……………………………………..
On………………… the rough side…………………
Of……………….. the mountain…………………. I must……..
Hold…………………………. to God, ……………………………………..
His power…..ful hand………..

Barry - "We done came up on that mountain, now let's bring it up a little bit. Clap your hands. That's right, clap your hands everybody."

Then he went in singing, "I Can Do" by Nicole C. Mullen and everybody was enjoying it. They were on their feet clapping…even the children. I had enjoyed it so much. I had never had that much fun in church until that moment. I knew at that moment that it had taken a special kind of person to get me to do something like that. I had felt so comfortable with Barry.

Leaving church that night Barry serenaded ***"Reflections"*** by Luther Vandross to me. Then he grabs my hand, spins me around, and we continue walking. Then he sang, ***"Take you out Tonight."*** That night was absolutely amazing to me. I did something that I would not have ever had the courage to do with anyone. Not because I didn't want to but because I didn't have a singing voice. I always said that the good Lord knew not to give me a voice because I would be like Patti LaBelle mixed with Tina Turner and Mary J in another light. I would be DIVA LICIOUS on stage. Kicking my shoes off and working the stage. And I don't think I would have been singing gospel. But this night actually made it all right. And I was impressed with my friend Huggie for seeing that in me, and having a Pastor who allowed us to take the risk in front of his entire congregation. Not for nothing, my Pastor is a real cool person.

When Barry and I reached my house, although it was late, I wanted him to come inside. We stood in the kitchen enjoying a dance that he would sing to. I felt his presence poking me and I had gotten aroused as well. I visualized us making love to each other, and looked up at him and said we have to say good night. He said "I understand love! Get some rest." We said good night, and I said. "Thank God!"

# MOMMA B

I guess that saying is true regarding how death comes in threes. I had received a phone call that Momma B had gone to be with the Lord on November 11, 2009. Once again I was devastated because I had a love for Momma B after Mother Love had gone to be with the Lord in January. Somehow, I had taken to Mother B in such a way that I wanted to take care of her. Every Sunday she would ask me how T.J. was doing. By her always asking me about him, she was letting me know that she had been keeping him in her prayers with me. I had found myself oftentimes just going to her house to sit with her and to check on her. I enjoyed sitting next to her in church during any and all services. I simply loved her and now she was gone. Friday, November 13, 2009 Momma B was laid to rest.

---

T.J. and I had an appointment with Dr. Schwartz and Dr. Anand at New York Presbyterian Hospital. They explained all that needed to take place the day of surgery and they informed us what T.J. had to do for preparation before surgery. Both Doctors made T.J. and me feel very comfortable about the procedure that was going to take place. However, prayers were going to continue. The following Tuesday during Bible Study, I had let the congregation know of the date of T.J.'s surgery so that collectively prayers would go forth. And they did.

Joy – "Hey you!"

Layla – "Hey yourself, what are you doing?"

Joy – "Homework."

Layla – "I'm coming by to get you so we can get a bite to eat. Are you almost finished?"

Joy – "It's okay, it's not due till next week. I'm always ahead. I'll be ready."

-----------------

Joy – "I know you like that, right?"

Layla – "You are not the bomb in checkers. It's about time you can win a game!"

Joy – "You're joking right? You won one maybe two games since we've been playing, and you sum it up to thinking you're the best? Please get your calculations right young lady! You are not the champ!"

Layla – "Oh no, one more game."

Joy – "Your move, oh, that's my song. 'Sumthin' Sumthin' I got up from the table and started dancing.

Layla – "Don't think you're getting out of this game because I'm gonna show you a little somethin' somethin'

Layla started laughing then started dancing with me.

Joy – " That's what's up! They are jamming girl."

The Isley Brothers' **"Drifting on A Memory"** then **"Solid As a Rock"** by Ashford and Simpson came on. Layla and I started slow dancing. Next thing we were kissing passionately. My phone rang and I noticed that it was my Pastor. I looked at Layla and started smiling.

Joy – "Hi Pastor, how are you?"

Pastor – "I'm doing well Dear. How are you doing? You ran across my mind and I thought to give you a call."

Joy – "I'm fine, thank you for asking. I'm glad you called to check on me."

Pastor – "Okay, good. God willing, I'll see you tomorrow in church, right Sis?"

Joy – " God willing Pastor. Good night and God bless!"

# HANDLE IT

Pastor – "God bless you too Sis Joy, I love you and good night!"

Joy –"I love you also Pastor. Good night!"

Layla and I looked at each other and shook our heads laughing and said, "We better not!" Then I would say to Layla, "On that note, I'm going home. I had a great time, but I gotta run for my life." Layla smiled and said, "Yes, because you're trying to take my virginity!" For the next occasional attempts that Layla and I would be in those close situations, my Pastor would call right in the nick of time, and we would never go through with it. I must admit, my Pastor played a large role with interfering in Layla and my relationship. I thank God for him, and I will never stop praying for him.

I couldn't stop praising God throughout service this day. The worship service had brought tears to my eyes and the message was speaking directly to me. I had a trying week and I needed an extra dose of Jesus. Barry had come with me to church and he seemed to have been enjoying service as well. I couldn't hold back. I couldn't stop praising God. I had had some trying moments, and I almost allowed too much to happen. When I heard the topic for the message, I shouted Hallelujah and looked up to God.

Pastor Hattie- "Today's topic is "I Almost Did What I Didn't Do"

I know you're wondering what kind of topic that is but I come to let you know that I almost did What I Didn't Do. When I was a little girl I used to like going to the supermarkets because they would have these candy bars that look so good in the pack and I wanted them. I know y'all seen them big chocolate bars. I wanted them so bad I started to put one in my pocket but a lady came by me and gave me such a look that I didn't take it.

When I had gotten a little older, I looked under my mother's bed to get her shoes and I spotted a $1.00 bill. A dollar was a lot in the 70's for a 10 year old. I had gotten so excited. I already knew what I was going to buy. Then I heard my mother say "bring my money from under that bed. The broom swept it further when I was cleaning yesterday."

Then as I got few more years older, my friends were stealing coats, they were called "boosters," Today it's simply called stealing. I decided if they could get one, then I could get one too. As I was about to pop the alarm off, a little kid said very loudly, "Whatcha doin?" At that moment I realized

I didn't need the coat that bad so I said nothing to the boy. As the Security Guard was coming toward me, I was going toward the door.

Then when I got old enough to drink, I went to hang out at a club with some friends and I ordered me a drink. I turned my head a few times while my drink was on a table. When I was about to take a drink I mistakenly knocked it over. I was told that a certain individual was dropping mickeys in folks' drinks. I guess my mickey was tricky cause I didn't drinky. Praise God, Praise God!

Then later on in life, I read about a man named Joseph in Genesis 39:12, "She grabbed him by his outer garment, saying, 'Have sex with me!' But he left his outer garment in her hand and ran outside." Joseph fled, he didn't jog, he didn't hesitate. He ran! He said in no way am I committing adultery with this woman. I got to get out of here. Have you ever found yourself in a situation that you said to "Self" I gotta get out of here? And when you asked "yourself" did "self" listen before it became a situation? I Almost Did What I Didn't DO.

Saints, those are situations that we shouldn't be in. If you know that you were a drinker, then I don't need to tell you to stay away from the bars. In the same way I don't need to tell a diabetic to stay away from the candy and the bread. I hope y'all gettin' what I'm saying. Whatever your addiction is or whoever your addiction is towards, be careful! Be like Joseph and run. Our temptations can really take a hold on us and it becomes too much. Sometimes we must run for our lives. Then when you come to church, share the testimony with us by saying, what? *"I Almost Did What I Didn't Do."*

Pastor immediately started the congregation in singing, *"I'm running for my life."* The congregation got up to clap and sing. I really enjoyed my Pentecostal church because they would emulate running in the church while they were singing and praising God. I emulated it as well, I just did it all from my seat. Altar call came and I ran to the altar because I was convicted! These moments were part of what helped me with my struggle as I was going through my Sanctification process. Coming to church and hearing the word of God for understanding, and allowing the Holy Spirit to take control will sometimes have you "running for your life!"

# SURGERY

March 10, 2010, T.J. was admitted at New York Presbyterian Hospital Weill Cornell Medical Center at 5:55 am. The Endoscopic Surgery was scheduled for March 11, 2010. I took a seat inside the waiting room after T.J. went into surgery. Shortly after that, Tony had met me inside the waiting room. I had let Tony know that T.J. had already gone in for the surgery and then I sat in a chair and just read my Bible throughout the entire operation. I didn't say a word to anyone, I just prayed and read. Several hours later Dr. Schwartz and Dr. Anand came out to let Tony and me know that the surgery was a success. Tears rolled from my eyes as I thanked God, then thanked both Doctors. Dr. Schwartz said to give it 20 minutes before seeing T.J. in the recovery room. Tony had to leave for work a long time ago but stayed until T.J. was out of surgery. When we got the news Tony shouted out, "Thank God!" and said to give T.J. his love because he had to leave.

When I walked in to see my baby, his nose was bandaged. I kissed him and told him the Doctors said everything went well, and that he will be just fine. I also reminded him of who God is and to give Him thanks while he recovers. Other than my love I gave him his chap stick because a mother knows. I didn't stay long because there were some things I needed to do in his apartment for when he came home. T.J. had given me a look with his eyes that it was okay for me to leave and that he was grateful for what God had done, because clearly T.J. was still in his right mind. When I was leaving, Sherlene and my oldest niece had come to the hospital to see him. I showed them where he was and they went in while I waited for them to give an update.

Abby and Layla had helped me out with moving some things around in T.J's apartment. T.J. was discharged on March 13, 2010. I decided to sleep upstairs in a chair that I had placed next to his bed to monitor him. It wasn't recommended, it was my choice. I wanted to make sure that my baby was going to be okay throughout his recovery. I read the Bible to him, and I prayed over him. Barry would often call to check up on us and I had asked him to come by and pick up a few groceries because I didn't want to leave T.J.'s side

The third day since T.J. had been home, he complained of a headache, and having a funny sense of smell. Something didn't seem right so I read up on his discharge papers after surgery again. It said that after having Endoscopic Surgery, if the patient has a strange sense of smell to return to the hospital immediately. I told T.J. that he needed to get dressed because we were going back to the hospital. At that moment Abby was calling me and I told her that I was about to take T.J. back to the hospital and told her why. She said that she would be by me in 20 minutes and to wait so she could bring us and we did. Upon our arrival at the hospital I had T.J. pretend that he was sicker than he appeared so that we could be seen immediately. The plan worked! Dr. Schwartz was notified, and amazingly he was at the hospital just completing surgery. He came in and examined T.J. and said that he needed a Blood Patch.

It was explained that the Doctor had to withdraw a small amount of blood from T.J's arm and then inject it into his Spine near his CSF leak. I had gotten rather nervous because I remembered when T.J. was a baby when the Doctor had mentioned that T.J. had needed a Spinal Tap, my mother took her grandchild and we went to another hospital only to find out that he had an Ear Infection. It was then when Becky had told me the dangers regarding Spinal Taps. Dr. Schwartz had noticed the concern on my face and reassured me that the procedure was simple and that it was only 30 minutes at best. Then I realized that I had obviously trusted him already and felt comfortable. I asked T.J. was he okay with what had to be done as it was explained, and by the look in T.J's eyes he had trusted God, me and his Doctor. Shortly after we went home, T.J's recovery sped up, and went well. To God be the Glory!

The next afternoon, my Pastor and his wife stopped by the house to check on T.J. He let them in, as I was on my way home from school due to taking a final exam. I had felt comfortable with leaving T.J., because he was recovering well after the Blood Patch. When I arrived, T.J. was entertaining them well in conversation. I joined in and before leaving, Pastor led us into prayer. T.J. and I thanked them for coming and we both had expressed our appreciation to each other for the Pastor and his wife taking the time out to come and visit.

# THAT'S WHAT'S UP / CHURCH LADY

After T.J's full recovery, I had returned downstairs and started moving forward with the next production. I had written two plays that I was very excited about. I couldn't decide which one I wanted to do first, so I decided to put them both on. The cast for *"Church Lady"* were basically co-workers from the Department of Corrections, and the cast from *"That's What's Up"* were real actors. I was really excited about this production even more so because T.J. had accepted a role playing the son in *"That's What's Up,"* and my God Daughter Kentaya was performing in both.

I had utilized the backyard in every way for rehearsals and having BBQ's to feed everyone before. It was agreed that providing food and a copy of the production would be their compensation. The rehearsals were great and we all were having a good time. I must admit, it was a lot of work while still attending undergrad but I was enjoying every minute of it.

---

Joy – "That is not four that was three."

Barry – "My mistake, my mistake! See I don't have to cheat you to win. I just win!"

Joy- "Yeah whatever, I got my eye on you."

Barry – "Which one the eye over here, or over there cause you know ya cross-eyed right?"

Joy – "Am I really, Huggie? Because sometimes I think my eye be going somewhere else for real."

Barry – "Love, you are not cross-eyed. I was joking. Even if you were I would still love you. I would love you if you had your back in your front and your front in your back. Now come here and give Huggie some sugga before I start singing to ya."

Joy – "You know you don't need a reason to sing to me. Where do you want me to kiss you at over here, over here, over here, or over here?"

Barry – "Ooh love you better watch it, Pockie might wanna poke somethin'."

Joy - "Yeah, I better. No forni!"

Barry – "Let's go for a walk and walk it off. Is your Hip okay?"

Joy – "Never, but I can handle it."

-----------------

Barry – "Can I have my books hip lady?"

Joy – "Certainly! How was work today?"

Barry – "Oh I got fired, I didn't tell you?"

Joy – "Ah no, when did you get fired Barry?"

Barry – "Two days ago. They were having cutbacks."

Joy – "Huggie they just hired you two weeks ago. If they were having cutbacks this soon they wouldn't have hired you. Actually, a friend of mine who works for the agency called me and already told me that you had gotten fired, and it had nothing to do with cutbacks. You were sleeping. Damn! Why you had to lie to me? Why couldn't you be honest? And why did you wait to tell me Huggie really?"

Barry – "What friend of yours"

Joy – "Your Supervisor is a dear friend of mine! I'm getting tired of the lies, Barry the stories with you and your daughters, you being evicted again. Your annulment is at a halt because you have to pay for it, and you never filed. You seem not to be able to keep a job. What's going on? Don't you think that you should be getting to the bottom of your reoccurring problems? They don't just disappear. And from the looks of things you're not fixing anything."

Barry – "What are you saying Love? I know I have some things that I need to take care of. It's not like I'm not trying. But it seems like every time I make one step I go three steps back. The only good thing is next week I'll finally have a Bachelor's Degree."

Joy – "That's a wonderful thing! And I pray that you use that for your advantage. But Huggie, you and I got to chill because honestly, you got a lot going on in your life that you have to fix. And I have a lot going on in my life that I have to fix as well. To be quite frank we both need to spend some time alone to work it all out. Together, I would frustrate the hell out of myself trying to figure both you and myself out and I can't do it!"

Barry – "So you're breaking up with me?"

Joy – "Handle your business as a man. You have too much to take care of. I can't be there with you. Me moving forward is not going backwards with somebody else. I just can't do it. I would have loved to grow with you from what I see at face value, but your deep-rooted issues do not require my help. I'm not even mentally prepared to be with you. I'm sorry! I am truly sorry! I don't even mean to be harsh or cold, but I can't! However, being friends is an option which you can choose."

I had decided to discontinue the relationship between Barry and me due to some inconsistencies that had been affecting our relationship and my trust in him. Although he and I got along extremely well, and I enjoyed him tremendously, I understood that a relationship with Barry would have caused a major setback towards my developmental future. However, in my thoughts and often in my daily prayers, Barry is thought about in ways that matter. Overall he was a wonderful individual who just needed to find his way as I did…

I went to Barry's graduation and I was very excited for him. We kept in touch periodically until Barry and I totally faded out. How nice it was to have known him. I have truly accepted the idea of people coming and going in my life. Some are there for only a season, and even in that there is always a reason. He was there during a time that I needed friends and a friend he was. He was the diversion that separated Layla and me purposely.

# SNAKES

We had been rehearsing at a Black Box Theater in Harlem two weeks before our show dates. I had made an agreement with the owners of the theater to perform for five days, putting on both productions. The owners agreed to videotape the productions so that we can have the best footage out of five. I felt comfortable with the owners and was assured that all was well. I kept asking to get our agreement in black and white so that I can sign for it, but I was continuously told not to worry because they wanted to work with me. I was so busy on the productions that I didn't focus on the agreement any longer. I just felt comfortable with their word.

Both productions were going to utilize the five days. I had divided them up so that each production had equal runs. August 11th -15th, of 2010. One hour before the first performance the owners wanted all of their money. They were demanding it in such a way as if we had never spoken, and as if I had stolen something from them. I wasn't sure what was going on with them but the devil had showed himself through both men. I was told that we were not to perform until they were paid in full. I had only half of what they wanted in cash and asked could I write out a check for the rest and was told no. I was actually going to cancel the entire production because I had gotten so angry and I didn't have the money at that moment to give them.

I thank God for my friends Rece and Evie. Rece had performed in one of my other performances and was now in **"Church Lady."** Between the two of them they were able to get the money from their invited guest that were paying at the door. The money that I had already and the money Rece and Evie had given me was enough to pay those two characters in full.

We performed the two productions but I was stressed out because I was noticing some other underhanded behavior by the two characters that were really getting at me. However, instead of showing it, I tried my best to keep my cool after Rece had prayed. The performances by everyone were absolutely awesome! I had two amazing cast, but I had no footage. The owners had decided that they wanted more money for the videotapes. Thus, that wasn't the problem. The problem was, they wouldn't allow me to see what I would be paying for.

Everyone was really upset about what was going on because we all wanted a videotape and I did promise that they would have all gotten one. But I had nothing. After a while, I continued to work on getting the footage. When something was finally given to me, I had understood why they would not show it to me. The copies were horrible with very little footage. Therefore, I still ended up with nothing. Once again, I had two more spectacular performances that I had nothing to show for it.

# HIT THE ROAD JACK!

Well it turned out that Jean's niece is going to take over things in the house. When I met Jean she did say to me that she had only one niece and that would be the person she would leave her house to if anything ever happened to her. As time went on, 13 years later Jean had said to me that T.J. was like a son to her and she would be leaving her house to him. However, when Jean had passed the Will stated that the house would go to her wife. Well the wife decided that she didn't want anything to do with the house and turned everything over to the niece. In any event T.J. and I had to hit the road. The niece and mother wanted us out and I had nothing to say. So T.J. and I packed our things and moved one year later after Jean's passing.

Their decision was kind of hard for me and T.J. because we had loved Jean. We all had been a family for more than 13 years. It had always been Jean, T.J., Tony, myself and either Frenchie or Tuna Fish. Frenchie was Jeans' dog that had died during our fourth year. Then I brought Tuna home and that cat had been part of the family till the end. Actually we had given him the name Tuna Fish H. Wally. We were fine about having to leave we just wished that it wasn't done the way that it was. T.J. and I will never argue over something that was not or is not ours. Hell, I didn't even fight for my own house. We just wished that it didn't happen the way that it did.

There was a part of me that had gotten angry with Jean for not taking care of things differently. She would say that she would take care of the paperwork but she never did. Then I thought about it further as anal as Jean was, if she wanted to change any documents at all regarding her house or anything else for that matter she would have. So instead, my anger turned into acceptance because the Word of God says, "Dear brothers and sisters, when troubles come your way, consider it an opportunity for great joy. For you know that when your faith is tested, your endurance has a chance to grow. So let it grow, for when your endurance is fully developed, you will be perfect and complete, needing nothing." James 1:2-4

I had enjoyed that scripture so much I had found another one that would relax my spirit. "Put no trust in a neighbor; have no confidence in a friend; guard the doors of your mouth from her who lies in your arms; for the son treats the father with contempt, the daughter rises up against her mother, the daughter-in-law against her mother-in-law; a man's enemies are the men of his own house." Micah 7:5-6 I've learned how to trust God and God alone. In doing so, people are simply understood.

# ENUFF

T.J. had gotten an apartment with his dad. I was asked to come along because there were more than enough bedrooms. I was glad that Tony had found a place just in time for T.J. to transition, but I opted out and asked Layla instead. I had asked her if I could stay with her for three months until I completed my undergrad and got an apartment. Although we were not where we used to be, Layla and I would feel very comfortable lying in the bed together to watch TV, especially on those rainy days when I would lay on her stomach across the bed. We would be fine enjoying a movie laughing and making comments until a love scene would come on and it would be intense. That damn scene had aroused the heck out of Layla and me and at that moment when we would position ourselves to kiss, my phone would ring. This was how one phone call played out:

Joy – 'Hi Pastor, how are you doing?"

Pastor- "Oh Sister Joy H. you know I thought I was calling the other Sis Joy, but how you doin' Dear?"

Joy – "I'm, I'm, I'm doing just fine Pastor. You better go on ahead and call the other Sis Joy."

Pastor – "Okay Sis be blessed"

Joy – "You too Pastor, good night."

Layla and I looked at each other and started laughing, shouting "Thank You Jesus!" And we turned the channel. I don't know who had fallen asleep first, but we were fine. I remember falling to sleep thinking about my Pastor and why I had gotten upset with him and my entire church. I had really wanted my Pastor to see ***"Church Lady"*** be performed. I had written that play thinking about him. I had wanted him to see how things can happen within a church and I didn't want that to ever happen to him. But neither he nor anyone else from my church showed up.

All of a sudden Layla and I would argue over the silliest things. She would get upset if I was on the phone. I would get upset if she was on the phone. We would just argue and argue. It was crazy. I would ignore her and that would make her furious. She would ignore me and I would get furious. We were just two miserable people who probably wanted to have sex but wouldn't do it.

Joy – "Hey Cozy, what's up?"

Cozy – "Not much! I wanted to know if you wanted to come by Cres' house for the weekend. Were gonna have some food, play some games, just chill. You remember how we did it before?"

Joy – "Cozy, this is on time, because I need to get away for a minute. Does Cre still live at the same place?"

Cozy – "No, I'll text you the address. I'll see you tomorrow."

Joy – "Okay, later!"

I was excited because I needed to have something to do other than stay in the house and argue with Layla. When Layla found out who I was talking to, she had gotten even more upset. She had known the entire story behind Cozie and me, and she knew that Cozie was my first being in a Gay relationship. Still, I was moving around the house happy gathering my things for my weekend get-a-way.

Layla – "Can I ask you a question?"

Joy – "Yes!"

Layla – "Are you packing clothes to go to Cozie's house?"

Joy – "Yes, I'm going away for the weekend. I'll be back on Sunday to go to church."

Layla – "How you think that makes me feel, knowing that you are going away to be with her?"

Joy – "Honestly, it's not even about how it makes you feel. What I do know is that you and I need a break from each other. And for me, that's my only choice right now. You come and go and do your thing every day. I go to school and I'm right back in this house. I need to get out of here for a few days."

Layla - "So why you have to go over Cozie's house, why does it have to be with her, Joy?"

-----------------

The set up was like old times again. Cre, her girlfriend and I were sitting at the table laughing, talking, eating and drinking. Cozie was preparing to blend some more drinks, but still joining in the conversation.

Cre – "I don't know what had happened that night. All I know is that Cozie, you had got mad at China, and China said, 'go ahead, keep drinking and watch what happens.' And you paid her no mind. China was always like a quiet storm. You just didn't know how she was going to deal with you."

Cozie is laughing.

Cozie - "Right before I was getting in the bed, I said, 'I feel like I gotta throw up!'"

China is laughing (Joy).

China – "And I said, make sure you make it to the bathroom, when you do!"

Cozie is laughing.

Cozie – "And I did, I made it to the bathroom sink, and I let it all out. Then I took my drunk behind to bed."

China is laughing

China - "For some reason Cozie must have thought that I was going to clean that mess up for her."

Cozie – "When I got up that afternoon, I went to the bathroom. The sink was stopped up with all my vomit. I looked on the mirror she had a note saying 'I told you to stop drinking!' All I could do was laugh and start to cleaning!"

China – "She knew she was a one-drink-wonder. Instead she wanted to hang with the big dogs that night."

We all started laughing hysterically.

Cre – "China, when Cozie called me and told me what you did, we couldn't believe it. But you did say 'watch what happens.' You guys were too funny."

China – "And now she's over there trying to be a mixologist. You want some help, Cozie?"

Cre's girlfriend Sam – "I want to switch partners for the next game. My baby made us lose."

Cre – "I told y'all, I haven't played spades in years."

Cozie – "That's all we played in jail. I was killin' them for their commissary. I'm nice in spades."

China – "I know you don't think our win was based on your prison skills honey, because I am a force to reckon with when it comes to spades. Ms. Bidding eight when you know you only had three freekin' books."

Cre – "Yeah, what was up with that last play? Luckily China picked that up."

Sam – "Hey, what's up with the drinks? I needed a refill 10 minutes ago."

Cozie – "Well, if ya wait another minute, ya might just get one!"

-----------------

Cozie – "You know how I felt that night when you and I had gotten back together, I felt like I had a chance at life again. I felt I could finally breathe again. But what hurt me most was when you came to work and worked in the housing area that I was in. I thought my entire insides were going to fall out of me, and my breath had left my body."

China - "I couldn't deal with seeing you in there. I thought that I was going to have a nervous breakdown on my post. That felt like one of the hardest things that I had to deal with in a relationship. That day when you had left my house after we had gotten back together, I couldn't wait to see you again. I just didn't think that the next time I would see you would be inside jail."

Cozie – "China, we never broke up!"

China – "I know!"

Cozie – "Hey, why are your eyes so watery? You don't even have to answer that, I already know. So tell me what has been going on with you. Seems like you've been going through it these last few months."

China - "I just have to get my own again! I can't even understand why I'm even in this situation. I know I did it to myself, and now I just have to fix it, that's all."

Cozie – "Well you know I have the spare bedroom, if you want to stay with me you are more than welcome."

China – "I appreciate the offer. But, when I get out of this situation, I will never allow myself to be in anything like this ever again. It's too much! And on top of that I'm still grieving my best friend's death. I'm just not at a good place right now, and I'm so miserable."

Cozie – "China knowing you, you are going to bounce right back on top! You have only a week or so before you finish school. You're going to be fine. God is not going to give you more than you can handle, and you know that."

China – "I know. It's just a lot right now."

At that moment Cozie started massaging me to help me relax. It felt so good. Although Cre and Sam were in the other room the house was entirely quiet as if Cozie and I were there alone.

China – "You still know how to make me feel good. I need more of you rite now!"

Cozie – "You know I still love you right?"

China – "I know, I know! I don't think I'll ever stop loving you."

Cozie grabs me and kisses my neck and I appeared weak and hung my head allowing Cozie to do whatever she wanted to do.

China – "I'm going in the shower."

Cozie – "You know I still love your scent ?"

China – "I don't!"

Cozy – "You never did!"

China – "You know I can't stay at this place right?"

Cozy – "I know China, because of church you can't be with me."

China- "No Cozie, it's not because of church, anybody can go to church. It's because of what I know today about God Himself being against this lifestyle. It's not about what anyone said or made up. I can read for myself. In the same way I have to read from "books" to study from as I work towards my degree. I'm still trying to get it right Cozie because I want to. I'm not forced or anything. It's just that I truly love God. I have to trust Him to deliver me from this lifestyle and I'll trust Him till the day that I die. And, I'm still trusting God for you as well although deep down inside I already know that you know the truth because of some of our conversations."

Cozie and I continued talking while I was getting ready to leave. We had even cried because in our hearts we knew what we had felt but I couldn't stay. I felt like I had cheated on Layla. I had felt like I had no self-control. But then at that moment, I had realized that Cozie and I had needed closure. It didn't have to be closure in that way but closure was what we had needed. I had definitely enjoyed every moment while I was with her, and I'll admit that it was extremely hard for me to leave. The way Cozie and I had made love it was the same as if it were the very first time once again. It was a hard moment but I couldn't stay.

We said our goodbyes and we both knew that it wasn't wise for us to see much of each other for a while. As time went on, Cozie and I grew to have a respectful relationship without any slip-ups. I appreciated how she had respected me enough to keep our friendship healthy. And I truly love her for that even more because I know I need all the help I can get. Over the years Cozie and I would grow into a deeper friendship that allowed us to be there for one another in ways that mattered. She's the truth! The real deal when it comes to true friendship. So today, it's nothing for me to crash at her house because after all, Cozie is my friend.

Turn to the Book of Jude. Today's topic is "Listen! Listen! Listen!" "Jude, the servant of Jesus Christ, and brother of James, to them that are sanctified by God the Father, and preserved in Jesus Christ, and called: I am writing to all who have been called by God the Father, who loves you and keeps you safe in the care of Jesus Christ. May God give you more and more mercy, peace, and love. Dear friends, I had been eagerly planning to write to you about the salvation we all share. But now I find that I must write about something else, urging you to defend the faith that God has entrusted once for all time to his holy people. I say this because some ungodly people have wormed their way into your churches, saying that God's marvelous grace allows us to live immoral lives. The condemnation of such people was recorded long ago, for they have denied our only Master and Lord, Jesus Christ.

So I want to remind you, though you already know these things, that Jesus first rescued the nation of Israel from Egypt, but later he destroyed those who did not remain faithful. And I remind you of the angels who did not stay within the limits of authority God gave them but left the place where they belonged. God has kept them securely chained in prisons of darkness, waiting for the great Day of Judgment. And don't forget Sodom and Gomorrah and their neighboring towns, which were filled with immorality and every kind of sexual perversion. Those cities were destroyed by fire and serve as a warning of the eternal fire of God's judgment.

In the same way, these people who claim authority from their dreams live immoral lives, defy authority, and scoff at supernatural beings. But even Michael, one of the mightiest of the angels, did not dare accuse the devil of blasphemy, but simply said, 'The Lord rebuke you!' But these people scoff at things they do not understand. Like unthinking animals, they do whatever their instincts tell them, and so they bring about their own destruction. What sorrow awaits them! For they follow in the footsteps of Cain, who killed his brother. Like Balaam, they deceive people for money. And like Korah, they perish in their rebellion.

When these people eat with you in your fellowship meals commemorating the Lord's love, they are like dangerous reefs that can shipwreck you. They are like shameless shepherds who care only for themselves. They are like clouds blowing over the land without giving any rain. They are like trees in autumn that are doubly dead, for they bear no fruit and have been pulled up by the roots. They are like wild waves of the sea, churning up the foam of their shameful deeds. They are like wandering stars, doomed forever to blackest darkness.

Enoch, who lived in the seventh generation after Adam, prophesied about these people. He said, Listen! The Lord is coming with countless thousands of his holy ones to execute judgment on the people of the world. He will convict every person of all the ungodly things they have done and for all the insults that ungodly sinners have spoken against him. These people are grumblers and complainers, living only to satisfy their desires. They brag loudly about themselves, and they flatter others to get what they want. But you, my dear friends, must remember what the apostles of our Lord Jesus Christ said. They told you that in the last times there would be scoffers whose purpose in life is to satisfy their ungodly desires. These people are the ones who are creating divisions among you. They follow their natural instincts because they do not have God's Spirit in them.

But you, dear friends, must build each other up in your most holy faith, pray in the power of the Holy Spirit, and await the mercy of our Lord Jesus Christ, who will bring you eternal life. In this way, you will keep yourselves safe in God's love. And you must show mercy to those whose faith is wavering. Rescue others by snatching them from the flames of judgment. Show mercy to still others, but do so with great caution, hating the sins that contaminate their lives. Now all glory to God, who is able to keep you from falling away and will bring you with great joy into his glorious presence without a single fault. All glory to him who alone is God, our Savior through Jesus Christ our Lord. All glory, majesty, power, and authority are his before all time, and in the present, and beyond all time. Amen."

Again, these are not my words but they are the words of our God. The topic was Listen! Listen! Listen! But you can all go home and Read! Read! Read! All through school we read all types of books that we learned from and became educated. We never questioned who wrote the books. But today we hear people all over the world saying "I don't believe in the Bible because it was written by man." Well can an elephant write? Can a cow write? Or maybe if we pulled some fish out of the sea you think they could write? In 2 Timothy 3:16 it says "All scripture is given by inspiration of God, and is profitable for doctrine, for reproof, for correction, for instruction in righteousness."

I don't know what type of feelings I was having after service. I was thinking about the message. I was thinking about Cozie. I was thinking about my living situation. I had even remembered a similar message Pastor had preached some time ago and how convicted I had felt then but yet, I still found myself at the same place. I was thinking about writing a 35-page paper for school. And knowing that my paper had to be extremely great, due to my GPA dropping from 3.566 to 1.842 after Jean's passing. I had been working extremely hard for my last semester to raise my GPA, in the midst of Layla and I continually arguing. Not to mention Layla knowing what I had done.

God help me. Please help me Lord. You gotta help me because your word says ask anything in the name of Jesus and it shall be granted according to your will. God put my request in your will. I want help! I need help! I want you to do for me what I obviously can't stop doing myself. I enjoy having sex. It's like that's the only time I feel something of an emotion. It's seems as if that's the only time I give all of me. My womb constantly wants affection from the people that I desire. My body craves what is natural but in an unnatural way. I'm afraid, Lord! I'm afraid because I keep sinning against my very own body, and I desire to stop. I understand the messages that are preached on Sundays, and I understand what I have been reading for myself. What I don't understand is why can't I stop doing what I'm doing? Lord Jesus, the ball is in your hand. You are a miraculous God. You are my strength. You are my deliver. There is nothing too big for you. If I haven't said it before, Father, please forgive me. I have sinned against you over, and over and over again! And I fear you just as much as I love you. Please remove this sickness from me, and fix me so that someday I can be happy with myself. Maybe someday, I can even love myself. God, no one ever told me when I was a little girl that my body was a temple. No one ever told me that I shouldn't have sex until marriage. I guess no one told my cousin that this little girl was precious before he took what should have been precious to me! Show me how to love myself, like you love me! PLEASE!"

Layla – "Joy, so how was your weekend, did you enjoy yourself to much?"

Joy – "I enjoyed myself. How was your weekend?"

Layla – "Come here!"

Joy – "For what, I'm good right where I'm at."

Layla – "Okay, I'll come to you."

Layla – "Are you kiddin' me? Are you freekin' kiddin' me? Joy, you slept with her. You actually slept with her?"

At that moment I looked in Layla's eyes and through her eyes I had seen hurt and pain. I didn't want her to be hurting, nor did I want to mistakenly die that night. Despite the craziness in my behavior, and my bizarre way of showing love, I really did love Layla. I was in love with her and hurting deeply knowing that Layla and I would never be able to be in a relationship because of who we were. Hell we both were hurting because we knew that we couldn't be together. But once again without me thinking and acting without thought, I did what I do. Still, the way she looked at me at that moment, no way was I going to tell the truth. I had only one good leg and it would not have gotten me far. I knew that if I had told Layla the truth she probably would have tried to kill me in that house. Instead, I started rambling saying,

Joy – "We kissed! We only kissed! We kissed and that was it! It was like we had never broken up throughout those years. I can't really explain it. When I was with her it was like we were where we left off 12 years ago before she went to jail. I'm so sorry. I know that it shouldn't have happened but I…I…I can't explain my sexual appetite. I know I had no business there, but you and I kept arguing and arguing. I did what I always do. I ran, I ran, because I knew that I was going to laugh and have fun. So I ran to her. I am so sorry that I hurt you."

As best as I could I shared my feelings with Layla so that she could somehow understand what I was going through. Layla had admitted to me that she understood what it was like between a first love relationship, and she understood that Cozie and I had never had closure. Then she was honest enough to tell me that she understood how Cozie would still love me after all those years. Still, she expressed her heart was hurting because of what I had done, but Layla had forgiven me because she had loved me.

We had decided to get past it as best we could and move forward peacefully. I knew the love that Layla had for me, and Layla knew that I had loved her. But, because we knew that we couldn't be together, it was just something that we had to accept in our own way. It wasn't an easy process by far, but with the help of the Holy Spirit, prayers, and having my Pastor call me at the "right" time, I knew that we were going to be okay moving forward. We had to be! But still I needed to get out of her apartment and get my own.

Layla – "I know you are happy that tomorrow is your last day of school."

Joy – "You ain't never lied. I had a lot going on throughout my entire time attending college. There was really a lot going on with me. Now all I need is for that Landlord to call me and tell me that I got that apartment that we went to see yesterday."

Layla – "Yeah that apartment is cute. The kitchen is big, and the layout is nice. Don't worry, they will call you."

Joy – "I prayed about it, I have real strong feelings that it's gonna be a yes!"

Joy – "Hello!"

Cynthia – "Hello Joyce this is Cynthia, you came to see the apartment on Dekalb Avenue."

Joy – "Oh yes, hello how are you?"

Cynthia – "Hi, I was wondering were you still interested in the apartment"

Joy – "Yes, I am still interested. Thank you soooo much! Thank you!"

Cynthia – "When would you like to move in?"

Joy – "Since this month is almost out, how about next week on the 1st?"

Cynthia – "Great! I'll see you then."

Joy- "I got the apartment. I got the apartment! Thank you Jesus! Hallelujah! Praise the Lord, praise God! Thank you Jesus! You're so awesome! You're amazing! I love you Lord! Lord I thank you! There is none like you in all the earth! Hallelujah! Hallelujah! Hallelujah! Oh He's a great God! Whooo thank you! Thank you! Thank you!"

Layla – "I'm happy for you Joy. Look at that! You start a new job next week. A brand new apartment and you'll be getting your BA in a few days. Yep! Give God the praise. And to top it off, I'm cooking the master meal with dessert."

    Layla and I wished that we could have stayed in our secret lives, but because both of us were Christian woman, we knew that we couldn't. Although we attended separate churches, we received the exact teaching regarding same sex relationships. For this reason, we knew that our relationship had to stop! What was it inside of me? I felt like I was damaged being in and out of relationships moving from place to place, changing jobs constantly. I had become my mother. I guess just like she had her reasons for living such a life, so did I. But somehow, I had to brake this chain of bondage.

I realized that I had a serious problem. The Devil was running my life. I had a sickness inside of me that only the Great Physician Himself who is Jesus Christ could heal. I was invaded, violated, I felt infected so early in my life that I couldn't stop what had started. I was thirsty for something and nothing could quench it. Inside I was on fire, and I was running to put the flames out but couldn't.

-----------------

**Joyce Harriet**
**The Degree of**
**Bachelor of Arts**

Congratulations to me! Congratulations to me! Congratulations to me! Congratulations to me! It was time to graduate from The College of New Rochelle Brooklyn Campus. The Hooding Ceremony was Saturday, May 14, 2011, outside on the grounds of the college. The Campus Director himself had asked that I read a poem on that day and I felt honored. I had invited my Pastor and his wife to attend and trusting that it would have been announced after church service. Since the Hooding Ceremony was held outside, anyone was able to attend without tickets. The attendees that had come out to support me were T.J. and his young lady, my cousin Dana, my God Daughter Kentaya, Layla, my friend Evie, my dear friend Vida, her son and her fiance. I was so happy that they had all come out to support me. Then at City Island, I was blessed to see my good friend Tess who came and joined us for dinner.

The Commencement Exercises were held on Thursday May 26, 2011, at Jacob K. Javits Convention Center and it was another great moment for me. I was only given three tickets. I wanted to give my Pastor and his wife another shot at coming. I had given them the tickets and they said that they would try and make it. I knew that T.J. and Layla would be out of town, and would not be attending. My friend Evie was so excited for me and said that she would love to attend. My Pastor and his wife didn't show. I was absolutely crushed! Still, I gave God all the glory. I think at that moment my friend Evie and I had become closer as friends.

# STEPPING IT UP

January 27, 2011, I had completed undergrad school. My GPA had gone up to 3.135. February 1, 2011, I had moved into a new apartment on Dekalb Avenue in Brooklyn. And February 7, 2011, I had started working as a Case Manager in the very same woman's shelter that I had once stayed during one of my "I can't stay with Jean" moments!

The last few years I started to feel like something was missing from me within a church. I kept expressing my feelings to Evie and Avery who both attended Brooklyn Tabernacle Church in Downtown Brooklyn. I needed to do more. I wanted to do more. I didn't think that Christians should be behind the doors of the church **ALL** the time. I just felt that we should do more as Christians. Evie and Avery both would explain to me that within their church there were many ministries that supplied the needs of others.

Evie and I were really growing as Sisters in Christ and she understood that I needed more. She thought that I would be great with the Drama Department in her church so that I would be around like-minded people and get better at my craft. She also knew based on our many conversations that I was very passionate about the youth. Therefore, with what she had known she would bring me along with her when she would meet with young ladies at a homeless shelter where she ministered with others. I was overjoyed and excited every time we would go. But the amazing thing was I was able to speak with them. I didn't just sit there and look on. I was allowed to share testimonies after testimonies and speak and be a part of the ministry in every way. Oh my God, just to think of it brings tears to my eyes because I had loved it! Eventually, I had to stop coming because the rules had changed. The order had come down saying that only members of the church can participate in any and all ministries that are affiliated with BT. Well, I wasn't a member. Therefore, I was no longer able to participate.

Afterwards, I started to feel like a fish out of water. I wasn't ready to break ties with my church yet, but I wanted to minister to those girls. I wanted to do more with helping people outside of the church so I often ventured off to other churches. I had started attending my church less although still attending. I had started a ministry with a friend of mine that I went to public school with. During one of our conversations we had expressed our frustrations about the church. Apparently, she too had attended a small church and they all ministered to each other. We decided to pick a busy location in Brooklyn to hold an open ministry. We chose Broadway Junction Train Station where there were five train lines and the traffic of people flowed freely and constantly. We ministered inside and outside of the train station. We handed out tracts and shared our testimonies and the people gathered. I mean they were gathering. We never asked for any offering, we just offered ourselves. I loved it! Apparently my friend and her husband loved it as well because they had suddenly quit with me and started pastoring a church of their own. When that happened I had to stop as well because ministering alone wasn't an option.

I had fallen in love with the Brooklyn Tabernacle's Choir with their angelic voices that were constantly ministering to my heart. I would visit sometimes after my church let out or sometimes before. Services were at 9 a.m. 12 p.m. and 3 p.m. Sometimes as soon as my church service was over, I would travel quickly to make the 3 o'clock service if they had a concert or a guest speaker, which they had often. But mostly, I would make the 9 a.m. service then go to my church immediately after. I was getting the word in two different ways. Both Pastors spoke the truth, and they both stuck to the word of God.

I had finally submitted my resignation to my Pastor. I couldn't take the spiritual state of mind that I was in any longer. I had received so much and I wanted to be in an outside ministry to help others. I started to allow small things that were occurring in my church to affect me. Notice I said small things. Every time I would leave my church I would be depressed. I started feeling like I couldn't even talk to my Pastor without people raising suspicions that made me feel very uncomfortable. The looks that I was getting from a certain member had really started to affect me. I decided to talk to my Pastor only when others were around because I didn't want anyone to think the wrong thing. Throughout all of my testimonies because I did share many that others would have kept to themselves, I never said that I was after or desired anyone's husband. I simply enjoyed our conversations as we both would express the needs of others and what could be done. There were times that my Pastor had pissed me off, but he's human in the same way I'm sure that I may have pissed him off with my on again, off again, behaviors. Still, I would have done anything for him as a member of the church and as a Servant of Christ.

However, I do contribute my spiritual growth 100% to Ecclesia Deliverance Church of God in Brooklyn. I also recommend this church to EVERYONE. And I will always keep them in my prayers and visit as often as I can. It was there where I learned who God is. It was there where I learned who Jesus Christ is. It was there where I learned about the Holy Spirit. It was there where I learned how to study the Word of God for myself. It was there where I met a group of people that loved me. It was there where I met a Pastor who genuinely cares for people and who preaches the true Word of God. It was from the people of that church that has kept T.J. and I in their prayers. And it is there that my Love for the Lord began.

I started attending BT on a regular basis. I was undecided about becoming a member so I didn't. Although I had submitted my resignation to my Pastor, I couldn't quite let go. It was like I had come out of a relationship still being in love and couldn't move further. It's funny how relationships never had me that way, but yet I had that feeling when it came to my church. I have a love for not only my Pastor, but for the members. We were a family for over 12 years. And within those years I had learned so much. I often feel like I had made a mistake in leaving but I'm trusting in God as I continue in His word. Who knows maybe someday, God's ***will*** will bring me back to where I first saw the light. Maybe I'm just the Prodigal Daughter!

------------------

During the time I lived at the women's shelter, Ms. Johnson was the Director of the facility. Over time she had been promoted to the Executive

Director. I had admired her ever since I met her. The way she had spoken to the clients, including myself, was with respect and out of concern. Anyone could tell that she had loved her job because she loved people. She was in a field that she was obviously passionate about and was willing to bring all she had into it. I remembered what my experiences had been years ago when Tony, T.J. and I were going through those times. But Ms. Johnson was of a different spirit and I appreciated her for that. I had stayed in touch with her letting her know that I was completing my BA. She said when I completed undergrad to give her a call and I did. And Ms. Johnson was true to her word.

When I came aboard as a Case Manager, I said to Ms. Johnson that I wanted to learn everything that she knows. I told her that I will be sticking underneath her like glue. I had let her know that I admired her and I was grateful to work under her. She in turn said to me that she was thankful and also very willing to show me everything.

Working as a Case Manager for the homeless population was a blessing. I was helping individuals in ways without realizing it. I spent time listening to them. I enjoyed helping and being the best Case Manager that I could have possibly been. I had known many of their stories because I had known my own. I treated every client the same, but assisted them all differently. I would go above and beyond my job description to make sure that I had done my best for the day.

I enjoyed doing whatever was in my control to assist the clients. The clients sometimes would cry in my office letting me know how much they had appreciated my service. I had become their Case Manager, their Housing Specialist, their Advisor, their Job Developer, and that person who showed concern. I made certain that I didn't cross boundaries with them by becoming too personal. However, I was at a good place with the clients and they were at a good place with me.

While sitting at my desk at work, my instincts, (The Holy Spirit) said call your grandmother. Without thought I dialed her number. My grandmother has had the same number ever since I can remember. Her number to date is the only number other than my own that I know by heart. I hadn't seen my grandmother since 2003 when there was a Northeast Blackout. Jean and

I knew we had to check on her mother and my grandmother because they were elderly and living alone. It was a natural instinct on both of our parts. T.J. was away at college and said that all students were instructed to stay in-doors therefore I had no worries regarding him.

Jean and I always kept plenty of water and food in the house so we had taken water and food with us on our journey for them. It was rather scary driving, but we made it. At that moment, I had formed a deeper love for Jean, because I knew that Jean did not walk up more than one flight of stairs and that had to be because she didn't have a choice. But this day, as bad as her Asthma was, she didn't in any way sigh, murmur, or express anything negative about walking up five flights of stairs in a pitch black stairwell in the projects. Jean and I were a team, and we did what we had to do from the very beginning of our relationship. Without making the other person feel bad in any way.

Although I hadn't seen my grandmother since 2003, I would call from time to time simply to say hello. Still, it didn't take away from how I felt towards her. But, I always kept what my mother had said to me in my thoughts when she told me to forgive her because she had. And no matter what, I do have a good heart towards all people. And if I can help in any kind of way I would, with no ill intention, just pure sincerity.

My grandmother answered the phone and said, "Who dis?" I said, "Hello Ma, this is Joyce, how are you doing?" She said, "Oh, dis Joyce, hi baby, I fell in da kitchen tryin' ta fix ma coffee, and I couldn't get up. I finally made it to da couch but I think I hurt maself." I said, "Where is your Home Attendant?" She said, "Home Attendant? I hadn't had one of dem in a while." That's when I said, "I'll see you shortly, I'm on my way."

I notified my Supervisor and let her know that I had had an emergency and I had to leave at that very moment. When I reached my grandmother's house, it was very apparent that nobody had been there in a while. I sat with her to make sure that she was okay, and then walked into the kitchen to clean up the spilled coffee and fix her something to eat. While my grandmother was eating, I went into Joy cleaning mode and started from the kitchen. I threw away old food that was inside the fridge, and cleaned it out. Then I went into her cabinets and did the same. Surprisingly, my grandmother just sat there and didn't utter a word because my grandmother was the most independent and outspoken person you could meet and the most stubborn. You could not just go into her refrigerator or cabinets without permission or else you were prepared to get cursed out because my grandmother was also very vulgar.

Afterwards, Ma summoned me to sit down and take a break from cleaning. We sat and talked for a while. She said she didn't know why her Home Attendant wasn't coming but told me that she had all the papers on the table to read that she had gotten in the mail. Once I read through her mail, I understood that the reason behind her not having a Home Attendant was due to her not recertifying. There were certain documents that needed to be filled out within a certain time frame that was not done. I figured out what steps had to be taken to get her certified for another Home Attendant. I told her that first thing in the morning I would get started with phone calls starting with getting her an appointment with her Doctor as soon as possible. I couldn't leave my grandmother that day, so I stayed and slept in the recliner while she slept on her sofa. For her own reasons, she didn't want to sleep in her bedroom.

I, on the other hand, slept very well in the recliner. It was actually more comfortable than beds that I have slept in. The following day I had taken off work. Eventually, the right connects were made and all that had to be done was action on our part. The earliest appointment was that following Wednesday to get Ma to her Doctor. Unfortunately, Wednesdays were mandatory meetings all day at my job and I couldn't take off to bring her. I had called my Aunty Sylvia who lived in Brooklyn near me to update her on everything. Aunty Sylvia often went to my grandmother's house to help her out, but I think because of my grandmother's disrespect, Aunty Sylvia and others had finally gotten fed up and visited less often.

Sylvia, without hesitation, agreed to step in and take Ma to her appointment. Once that was takin care of, I had scheduled an appointment with The Visiting Nurse Services of New York, and the Social Services agency. Everything was in place for my grandmother to get the ball rolling so that she could get another Home Attendant.

# HANDLE IT

I had two weeks to play with before everything would be done. Meanwhile, I would come over every day after work and bring food or cook. Sometimes I would stay over and other times I felt comfortable leaving. Ma and I talked and laughed more than ever. She wanted to know more about me and I was excited to talk. It was during that time I would see my grandmother in a different view. I actually had started to love her. I invited my cousins Dana and Thomas over to celebrate Dana's birthday at Ma's house. We had a great time laughing, eating, taking pictures and simply enjoying ourselves. On some occasions my friend Evie would come by and spend time with us.

It wasn't until I began writing this book that I had to dig deep into myself realizing the damage that Thomas caused in my life. It didn't take therapy or counseling, it took me to allow God in, and let my hurt out. And when I did, the healing process began. It seemed to have been a blind spot in my life because I had blocked out all of my pain. I had never known that I was damaged and scorned. So regardless of how or what I was feeling, I made myself numb by not thinking about anything or anyone that had hurt me. In doing so, Thomas and I were very close in my numbness. He was the one that told Sherlene and me to take the Correction Officer's test. I have come to realize that I had to forgive him, and yes, I do love him. It's what he did to me is what I hate. In the same way God loves us totally. It's the sin in us that He despises.

During my visits Ma had some visitors who would come to check on her. There was this one young lady who I was reminded of her name later as T, who was obviously Gay. I could tell by the way of their conversation that she genuinely cared for Ma. She didn't stay long, but I can tell that my grandmother was happy to see her. A funny moment was when Ma asked me to get her phone book. She said, "Joyce han me ma phone book so I can call Scooter. He gets me ma cigarettes for cheap and I don't have no mo." Sure enough she finds his name in her phone book, and gives him a call and he came over within 10 minutes to supply her with her smokes. And yes, my grandmother still smoked.

My grandmother's phone had rung and it was my Aunty Rose from the South. She seemed very shocked that I was there with my grandmother, hell I was shocked my damn self. I decided to explain my purpose for being there because by the sound of her voice I needed to. I had also let her know what was being done moving forward. I had let her know that the last thing to be done would be in four days from that day on Tuesday Ma had an appointment at the Department of Social Services. I told her that Ma had a 9:30 a.m. appointment to bring in all of the documents that we had gathered. I said that everything else was done and that was the final step towards getting Ma her Home Attendant. She said that she would come up to New York by then and that we could go together. I said great!

I was glad that she was coming up. I already did what I had to do for my mother and it had taken no thought in doing it. The way I had looked at it, I was temporarily filling in until I was no longer needed. And I was fine with that.

My grandmother and I continued to enjoy one another on levels we had never before. She shared some memories regarding my mother and other childhood stories. The day before her last appointment I had gone home. I told her that I would call in the morning so that I can meet up with her and Auntie Rose. When I called that morning I felt like I was sucker punched in the face so hard without me seeing it coming.

Joy – "Hey Aunt Rose."

Rose – "We don't need you, I took care of it!"

And the phone slammed in my ear. I was furious! I called back and my grandmother answered the phone. I said "Ma, why did Aunt Rose talk to me like that and hang up on me?" She said, "I don't know baby, hold on." She tried to get my aunt on the phone but she wouldn't get on. Instead, my grandmother got back on the phone and said, "Don't pay she no mind I know God sent you to me, and Ma loves you, you hear me?" I told her that I loved her as well and hung up. After that conversation I was so angry, I was so hurt. I was repeating in my mind that I was doing her a favor. That was her mother. I was just trying to help! Then I called my Aunty Sylvia and she told me to not let it bother me, and she thanked me for stepping in. I then called my Aunty Beverly and she pretty much said the same thing. Still, I continued to let it bother me until I turned it over to God. He let me know that I had served His purpose, and I received from my grandmother what I needed to receive. My grandmother had told me that she loved me. WOW!

While at work I had to keep reminding myself that I was no longer going to Brownsville after work to my grandmother's house. I was actually missing spending time with her. A few days later my Aunty Sylvia had told me that all the work that was done was done in vane because my Aunt Rose was taking my grandmother back to the South with her. What can I say? I just mustered up the strength to make my way back over to my grandmother's house the day before she left to give her a hug and kiss her goodbye. The funny thing was when my Aunt Rose saw me, she thought I came to help pack and greeted me very politely. God give me strength, was all I could ask for. At that moment, I acted as if my aunt was invisible and sat next to my grandmother, hugged her, kissed her, and told her that I loved her and shortly after, I was on my way.

Although, I had enjoyed working with the clients, I hated being a Case Manager. There were other aspects of the job that I had to keep up with which I did. I can do any job I applied for. But in doing so, I had become stressed out. Every day it seemed that there was another form that needed to be added to our assignments, and it was mandatory to respond to all emails that were new every day. There were mandatory meetings, case file adjustments, quotas to keep up with, weekly reports to complete, audits to rush and prepare for and mandatory meetings with your caseload of 25. And the kicker, if you worked with an evil person and shared the same office space as I did, it just wasn't working.

At that moment, I had understood why people who often held those positions were evil, and disrespectful. They were stressed out. They had hated what they wanted to love. I also understood why client's needs weren't being met and so they would end up back in the same system. We are individuals. God created us as such. Therefore, to fix the problems that people often face can't be fixed with a one-size-fit all band aid. Individual needs must be addressed so that their quality of life can change. Instead, the goal for society is to build more homeless shelters, more Residential Treatment Facilities for adults and youth, and soon more prisons because of the plans before-hand. I can go on and on and tell you much about the "system" and how being oppressed is grouped for a purpose, and how it is never about the individual, but more about keeping up with quota of the oppressed. But I will not. Instead, I'll continue to share my own mess and not tap any further into the way of the world.

So yes, part of my stress would take on something new within my body. I would get these twitches in my eyes that were uncontrollable. I would go home feeling completely drained out. After five months of feeling like that I knew that that was not the career choice for me. I had been communicating with Sharon who was the Team Leader and she said to me without knowing anything about me other than admiring my work ethic, that it would be in my best interest to return to school for my Master's Degree. She had let me know about an accelerated program at Metropolitan College of New York for only one year, and how the program would be great for me, as she herself had recently completed it.

It was always a thought to return to school for a Master's Degree after having the privilege of being taught by Professor Durant D. Fuller in undergrad. Professor Fuller taught Oral Communication at The College of New Rochelle, and she would insist that her students continue to seek higher education. I had admired this woman with my heart, and she had captivated my mind. I admired this woman so much, I used to sit in the class and imagine what being her daughter would have been like. I'm certain that my life would have been different. The funny thing about her was that she often reminded me of myself, through her sarcasm. The difference was she was intellectually sarcastic and I was simply sarcastic.

Prof. Fuller heard when I called her that after she had made a valid point in class, followed by sarcasm. And me being the person that I am, I said "Intellectually sarcastic is who she is!" At that moment she had asked me to repeat what I had said and I did. She started laughing and said, "Ms. Harriet is that who I am?" I said, "You sure are!" Professor Fuller started laughing, then smiled and continued to teach the class. For the remainder of the semester she would remind students the name Ms. Harriet had given her with a smile. I would say that she concurred! Although many students opted not to take her class due to her reputation as one of the hardest, most challenging Professors in the college, I had felt blessed to have been under her as a student. She was the epitome of what a Professor/Teacher should be, not to mention that she loved the Lord. And by the way, her sarcasm only seemed to come out when students would think that they had gotten over on her. For that reason, I welcomed every bit of it, because I'm a no nonsense person as well.

# HANDLE IT

And now once again it's being mentioned by a mere stranger to return to school. So I thought that I can live off of my Disability to pay my rent, and simply trust God to carry me. My Disability would not have covered me entirely. However, I felt as long as my rent was paid, everything was going to be all right. Therefore, I prayed about it. It seemed right with God. So I put the plan into action and decided to return to school and not work for an entire year since I had to do an internship.

I decided to speak with Ms. Johnson and let her know my decision and why I had made it. At first with a humorous response she said, "Hey, I thought you were going to work underneath me and learn all that I can show you?" and then she smiled and asked if I would reconsider. Ms. Johnson had gone further in telling me that in the Social Service field it would be in my best interest to be a Case Manager for at least two years. But no way could I have possibly done that for two years. I had thanked her and I said to her that I will be returning to school for my Master's Degree so that I can have other options.

Ms. Johnson had wished me well and said to stay in touch with her. I knew that she was giving me great advice and I had received it. Don't get me wrong, I'm not saying that being a Case Manager is a bad job. Somebody has to do the job. What I'm saying is that being a Case Manager wasn't the job for me. However, I think I understand why I had to go through my injustices over the years with Case Managers that I had come across. I believe those experiences are what taught me how to be compassionate towards others.

---

Layla and I seemed to have faded away because we understood what we couldn't do, so moving on was expected. We communicated from time to time but remained focused on our own lives. It was good that I was building a relationship with Evie because she helped me out in ways that I will always be grateful for. The specialty of our friendship was partly growing spiritually together. I had even come aboard to be a part of a ministry with her and others. She didn't like the fact that I still didn't have a church home although I attended hers frequently. She would tell me the importance regarding belonging to a church for a covering. Thus, she had also understood that I hadn't quite let go of Ecclesia.

I went and applied to Metropolitan College of New York. I was signed up to begin Tuesday August 9, 2011. And the date of completion was said to be August 23, 2012. My scheduled days were evening classes on Tuesdays, Wednesdays, and Thursdays. In addition to applying for an internship that was a requirement.

It was a very challenging school year however without complaining to anyone I stayed focused as best as I could, given the situation. Here is my truth. As I think about that time, tears fall down my face. No one! I mean no one really knew what I had endured during that time. But I thank God for the people that He had purposely placed in my path, because together they all helped me in their own way.

I was receiving my Disability check each month for $ 1,647.00. My rent was $950.00. Cable and cell $300.00. Light whenever I could pay $60.00. Personals/bills $180.00, and Metro card $130.00 of which T.J. started supplying. I may have been left with probably $50. 00 for the month, not to mention I needed to buy food. I had really stepped out on faith when I had made the decision to continue my education at that moment in my life. It was my decision and I had to live with it.

There were days that I didn't know what I was going to eat. I know I could have picked up the phone and given T.J. a call, but it was my life and I knew that I would eventually be okay. Besides, I never wanted T.J. to worry about me because he had his own concerns with life. I knew that the Lord was with me. However, T.J's spontaneous offerings helped me out tremendously.

"Who shall separate us from the love of Christ? Shall tribulation, or distress, or persecution, or famine, or nakedness, or danger, or sword? As it is written, "For your sake we are being killed all the day long; we are regarded as sheep to be slaughtered. No, in all these things we are more than conquerors through him who loved us. For I am sure that neither death nor life, nor angels nor rulers, nor things present nor things to come, nor powers, nor height nor depth, nor anything else in all creation, will be able to separate us from the love of God in Christ Jesus our Lord." Romans 8:35-39

I was blessed to have my Heavenly Father, and having the gift of a son who cares for his mother. Still, I would often tell him that I was okay although I wasn't. I didn't ever want to become dependent upon anyone but God ever again. I did however allow him to do my laundry when he insisted. Whenever he would do his laundry, T.J. would come and pick mine up and drop it off. He had known that my leg was always in pain, and he didn't want me to walk up and down my three flights of stairs with laundry. Therefore, he had taken care of it, and I give God all the glory.

My cousin Dana who is still like a sister to me would always loan me money when I'd ask. She is like a sister/cousin at best. Without hesitation she was always willing. And I always thank God for her willing heart. Evie was a gem, and she had opened her family up to me as well. Almost every Sunday I would have dinner with her and her family and I was grateful.

And then there was an addition to my heart and her name is Tanya. This young lady not only helped me by volunteering to bring me home every evening from class, she demanded it. I didn't want her to because she lived all the way in Long Island. I would often tell her that I was fine with taking the train but she wouldn't have it any other way. Tanya and I connected instantly at grad school. If it weren't for her, I sometimes wonder how I would have gotten past our computer class because the Professor was going too fast for me. That's all I'm saying! So I knew the Lord had placed her in my path. And trust me I'm still thanking Him for her.

Tanya and I were going through our own struggles in grad school. But we stood by each other through them all. And let me not forget my brother. It was amazing to me how my brother Anthony would call me out of the blue and say, "Hey Joyce how you doing? Do you need a couple of dollars?" I would look up and thank God, because only God could have had my brother call to offer me help during times when I needed it most. I would shout out to my brother and say, "I sure do!" and he would come and bring it right over to my house. Ironically, my brother also needs a Total Hip Replacement. Maybe we both fell in the same place at the same time. Who knows!

"For I have learned how to be content with whatever I have. I know how to live on almost nothing or with everything. I have learned the secret of living in every situation, whether it is with a full stomach or empty, with plenty or little. For I can do everything through Christ who gives me strength." Philippians 4:11-13

Well, I had started my internship in Queens at the Saratoga Family Inn. Yes, my internship was at the exact shelter that T.J., Tony and I once lived in 28 years ago. When I heard that was one of the places on the list to intern, I was overjoyed and more than willing to accept it. I was under great leadership. Tinnycua Williams, the Education Programs Coordinator, was my Supervisor. I had come in with a plan from A -Z for my internship. I had already known what days and hours that I could work, and I already knew what the expected outcome was going to be.

I explained to Ms. Williams that my ideal plan was to have the opportunity to oversee an innovative project which centered on empowering homeless youth and adults in crisis through the forum of creative arts. I said that I was very passionate about helping disenfranchised and minority youth develop skills to rise out of their circumstances. I said that I believed in creative expression through stage work, and personal sharing would be my medium of choice to help youth. For this reason, I would develop a series of creative expression workshops that would result in a biographical play about the youth.

I was passionate, short and to the point. Ms. Williams looked ok at me and she said, "Go ahead Ms. Harriet, let me know what you need to succeed." She let me know the days and times that we would have Supervision, and reminded me that during Supervisions would be the time for us to discuss progress, issues and concerns. I thanked Ms. Williams for allowing me such an opportunity to come in and have total freedom to work with the clients.

My project was a total success, and my learning experience throughout the entire time was God driven and awesome. As I moved forward I realize it was meant for me to be there and to be able to do what I had done. It was a blessing to work with Ms. Williams as she and I both remain friends.

I had to step out into the deep, and got a part time job as a Child Care Worker working in Upper Manhattan on the overnights. The shift worked out well because if I was called into work on a school night I would go straight from class. I worked in a way that didn't conflict with my internship or school. However my Hip pain showed no mercy. I was only going to be working in Manhattan part-time until the new facility opened in Brooklyn. Then the job would turn into full time.

We had formed a little sorority with a group of five: Tanya, Sha, Tee, and Omar. Together, we did the damn thing, and it was all good! Whenever anyone of us would say "T.FI.T," we knew that it was food, libations and laughter. Sometimes it would be planned but then there would be those spontaneous moments when we needed to hang out, no matter what. I must admit, I truly love those guys. Although Omar was the only guy, he fit in like a missing link. The funny thing was before we had allowed Omar to be a part of T.FI.T he had to go through a series of things. Obviously he made it in. Still today he is like my brother from another mother.

T.FI.T was so together and on point our Professor had even invited us to his home. But I'll never forget the night on our last day of class, T.FI.T and our Professor went and hung out. We had great food, and great fun. We sang karaoke that night and had a blast!

Tanya and I had planned a cruise following our last day of school. We had tried to get everyone aboard but everyone had their own plan and that was fine. In addition to the cruise I had set up to go to my Time Share in the Poconos immediately following the cruise. The cruise was from August 24th - 30th. Then I had to be in the Poconos from August 30th - September 3rd, that was usually the time of year that my Pastor and others would make themselves available to get away utilizing my Time Share. And immediately after that I was scheduled for my Hip Replacement.

With all of the events that were about to take place I was prepared to submit my resignation at my Brooklyn job where I had been working full time for five months. I had to resign because I had decided to have my surgery and I wouldn't be able to work for a while. Therefore, my only option was to resign since I wasn't there long enough to accumulate sick time and I wasn't sure how long it was going to take me to walk again. For that reason, my last day was August 21, 2012.

The following morning after we had all hung out, Tanya, myself and another friend went on a cruise to the Islands. Evie planned to go with us, but unfortunately when we arrived to the ship, Evie realized that she had forgotten her Passport and her Birth Certificate. REALLY!

We cried, and we tried everything for her to get her Birth Certificate. Tanya was even allowed to work the computer to see if she could go into Documents. Nothing seemed to work. But the ship was not leaving without us so we said bon voyage to Evie. The three of us had a great time. It was a vacation well needed and well deserved. I was glad that I had planned to have my Hip surgery very soon because I had to stay inside the cabin for an entire day because I could not walk at all. Tanya was so worried about me. I told her that I would be okay and that I had just needed that day but to go on ahead and enjoy the day.

Upon our return Tanya was unable to go to the Poconos with us because she had other business to take care of. Evie had met me at the Airport and we went to get my little cousin and her godson. We had experienced some car trouble but were blessed with another car and then we were on our way. We had a great time away in the woods with the children and my Pastor and other members. Yes, he will always be my Pastor. Whenever I would check in with my Pastor and his friends and family they all said that they too were enjoying themselves, and that made me happy.

Evie had wanted us to do a make-up trip since she had missed the cruise. So with the help of her Mom, and Auntie Von allowing us to utilize their Time Share, we were all able to go to the Dominican Republic from December 7-14th. Evie's Mom and Aunty Von were sisters and also the very best of friends. This trip was extra special for me because T.J. was also with us along with his young lady. We really did have a great time in DR. And immediately following our vacation I was going to finally have my Hip Replacement on December 20, 2012 at New York Methodist Hospital. "O Lord my God, I cried out to you. And you healed me." Psalms 30:2.

My Hip Replacement was a total success. I stayed in the hospital for three days then I agreed to go to a rehabilitation center where Aunty Von was. At first it was kind of rough for me not being able to fend for myself. However, the Nurses were really good to me as well as very accommodating. However, what had made my stay really special was that I had spent it with Aunty Von. It still amazed me that she and I had to have a Total Right Hip Replacement. We unknowingly had the same Surgeon. Her surgery was November 20, 2012 and mine was held on December 20, 2012. I don't think that it was a coincidence. I truly believe that it was all God. During that time Aunty

Von and I had grown even closer than we had already been. We had so much in common and I simply loved her and I'm certain that the feelings were mutual.

T.J. didn't stay long during his visits, but he had visited me often. For the most part he just wanted to make sure that I had all that I needed and to make sure that his Mom was okay. He would go and check on Aunty Von as well because she was two rooms down from me. I thank God for friends because almost every one of them had come to see me. Everybody seemed to have chosen their own day and in doing so they would spend the entire day with me. It was also nice to see my sister Sherlene. She had gone to the hospital first thinking I was still there, and still she had pressed her way to make it to the Rehabilitation Center.

I was still there on New Year's Eve and I had looked up and to my surprise Tanya walked in excited. She said, "Now did you think I was gonna let my friend spend New Year's Eve by herself?" Tanya had brought her overnight bag to stay the night with me. I actually cried because I thought that was the sweetest thing ever for a friend to do. Then, about an hour later, Evie and her sister Vee had come to bring in the New Year with Aunty Von and me. We all had gone into the lounge area and celebrated with prayer and laughter bringing in 2013.

The funniest moment was when one of my friends from Corrections came to visit me. I was sitting in the lounge area when a Security Guard said, "Ah, maam! Is your name Joyce Harriet?" I said, "Yes it is. Is everything okay?" He had looked kind of scared for me or something. Then he said "Ah, there's somebody here to see you maam in your room." I said "Okay, thank you sir." When I walked inside my room, Brigg was in her full Class A Uniform. She was on a detail assignment nearby. Brigg and I had met during the beginning of our careers as a Correction Officer. She had also accepted the invitation to be casted in two of my plays that I had written. And to hear her sing is priceless.

Well the Security Guard must have been afraid for me thinking that I was in some kind of trouble or something. So he stood by waiting, I guess for me to come out in cuffs. Instead, Brigg and I just sat and chatted for a while until she had to leave. Her visit had really meant a lot to me. When

I came out of the room with Brigg laughing while walking to the elevator, I smiled at the Security Guard so he could relax from whatever thoughts he was having about my visit.

I had pushed myself during my recovery. I made sure I did whatever was asked of me by my Physical Therapist. My Physical Therapist was persistent and I had appreciated him very much. I was walking with a cane in three days. Finally on January 9, 2013, I was ready to go home. I didn't want to leave Aunty Von there, but she was leaving right behind me, and I knew that I would see her soon. T.J. made certain that he had made all the arrangements for me to come home. He had called his Dad to help set up my apartment and I was on my way to the next chapter of my life.

# INSIDE OUT

I had taken my recovery very serious. And I had been praising God throughout the entire time. I thought it was amazing that God would have man create an object that is now inside of me that had taken away all of my pain. I felt honored and even more blessed to be pain free after six years of being in constant turmoil. I had felt a need to go on a major fast because I wanted to come through my recovery with direction from God. I didn't want to move forward on my own ever again. I had come to realize my plans had never worked. I wanted to hear from God, and I needed to hear from Him. And I knew that fasting was a very important part of a Christian's walk as I had learned that early on. "It is written, 'Man shall not live by bread alone, but by every word that comes from the mouth of God.'" Matthew 4:4

I began my fast on March 8, 2013 for 21 days. I would not eat anything for the first seven days. I would just drink water. I wasn't on any type of medication other than Cholesterol pills, which I opted not to take. However, I do not advise anyone to stop taking medications. I chose to do it because my Cholesterol had been controlled. I had a plan after my prayer to read certain books of the Bible. As I was reading the Book of Job, I felt led by the Spirit to go to the beginning of the Bible and read.

I did exactly what I had felt instructed to do without hesitation. I started reading the Bible beginning with Genesis. While I was reading, I came to the part in Genesis 6:14. God began to give Noah specific instructions on how to build an Ark because He wanted to destroy the earth. What struck me was how specific God was. I meditated on that story for an entire day realizing that I never waited for any instructions. I had never waited on God. But at that very moment, I had come to realize how important it was to do things the way God wants things done.

I kept reading the Bible realizing that I was enjoying God's words more and more. I had come across Genesis 9:13 "I have placed my rainbow in the clouds. It is the sign of my covenant with you and all the earth." Pausing for a moment thinking how foolish I was to affiliate the rainbow with being Gay. I had gone along with something without knowing the real meaning behind the rainbow. I kept reading and reading. But then I stopped when I was led to begin writing from the beginning. Then I saw a vision of three stacks of papers to be placed on the floor next to the window that I faced. I was completely amazed.

I had understood that I had to write about my life starting from the beginning as I knew it to be. I had understood that the writing would become a book, a play and a screenplay. And it had to be placed specifically in the spot that was shown in the vision.

In addition to my writing, every day and every night I would do my leg exercises. I was challenging myself going up and down the stairs. Evie would come and get me and we would go to church if I had decided to attend her church that Sunday. She would bring me to Mom's house, or out to dinner or to the ministry that we were in together along with others. Aunt Von and I would often sit and talk and discuss our recovery process. If we felt something or thought something wasn't normal Aunt Von and I would talk about it. I had a great recovery. I think it was part of the team of people that I believe God purposefully placed in my life. To God be the glory!

Two weeks into my recovery I said goodbye to the cane. Now I was feeling secure in my walk. I was thinking about what type of shoes I would wear for my upcoming graduation. I decided that I was going to wear some kitten heels. I had it all figured out because I wanted to look really good.

It's graduation time 6 months later since I actually completed my MPA. I was excited, proud and amazed all in one. I was thanking God because I was at a place in my life that I hadn't even thought about. Even in my daydreaming moments I didn't think of obtaining a Master's Degree. But here I was Joyce Harriet MPA, Graduate of 2012. I was glad that T.J., Evie, her Mom and a young lady that I was Mentoring at the time were a part of the attendees. I was so glad that they were there to support me. I mean really, I was glad. Without people supporting you it can lessen a person's will to move ahead. On the other hand, like in my case, it makes me strive. Before leaving, we all enjoyed some photo shots with Tanya and her family, then it was off to dinner. I was blessed by Evie and her Mom to have taken me out to dinner, and to my surprise Evie's sister Vee had joined us. Vee and Evie have the best sister relationship ever, and often times I admired that. May God continue to bless and keep them forever close.

Congratulations to me! Congratulations to me! Congratulations to me! Congratulations to me!

## Joyce Harriet
### Master of Public Administration
### Public Affairs and Administration

I was sitting at my computer writing in my book on July 31, 2013. My phone rang and it was my Aunt Sylvia. She told me that Ma had died, and that the funeral was going to be in North Carolina. I couldn't speak. I couldn't even ask her how she was doing. At that moment all I was able to do was think about those few weeks that I was able to spend with her, and how we had bonded. It was during that time that I allowed myself to love my grandmother. It was during that time that I had decided to forever be proud to have been the only one to share the name Harriet. Aunt Sylvia snapped me out of my thoughts when she called out my name.

T.J. had given me money that would cover airfare going, my hotel stay, pocket money and a Greyhound bus ticket for my return. T.J. wasn't able to make it to the funeral because he was already booked to be in LA within that same time. My Aunt Rose's house was where we all would gather. I had already forgiven her through my prayers regarding the way she had treated me. I stayed at a hotel nearby during my stay, and pitched in wherever I could while others were doing the planning and preparations. It was good to see so much family come together all the way to North Carolina. However, I just wish that it wasn't under those conditions.

On the day of the funeral, I asked my Aunt Rose about a young lady who I knew was a good friend of Ma's. I had asked was she notified of Ma's passing. Immediately my aunt knew who I was talking about and said that Tee was on her way and should be arriving shortly. While we were all at the church everybody was taking photos before the service. During the service I had an opportunity to speak about the few weeks that I had spent with Ma. I shared that it was during that time I was able to love my grandmother, and that I had appreciated the time that we had spent together. I was at a good place and I felt really good that I was able to honor Becky's wish to forgive.

After service, Tee was crying. I had put my arms around her and thanked her for coming all the way to North Carolina to say goodbye to my grandmother. I didn't even bother to ask her if she was okay because it was rather obvious that she wasn't. Tee said that she had driven all the way to North Carolina from Brooklyn by herself. I said to her that she must have really loved my grandmother to have done that. And I thanked her again. Well Tee looked right in my face, tears and all, and said, "Don't thank me! I loved your grandmother. She was my friend, and like a mother to me." By the way she spoke about Ma, I was amazed. I wondered how was it possible that the Ma she was talking about was my grandmother. In any event I had come to understand throughout further conversations that the love that Tee had for her, was a deeper kind of love.

Tee was a Gay aggressive young lady, and she and I were vibing really well. Our vibe was so good that I didn't take Greyhound back, I rode back with her. I had listened to many of her stories regarding my grandmother and I really wanted to hear more. I enjoyed how Tee would go into certain characters and dialects and I would laugh. I had told her that I believed her calling was acting. But then I would come to realize that she was multitalented because she had the most beautiful voice ever.

I experienced a sadness come over me during a conversation that Tee shared with me regarding Ma. She told me how they would sit, talk and laugh and how Ma would call Tee her baby. I wasn't jealous but at that moment I wish I had that with my grandmother growing up. In my mind I had asked myself why didn't my grandmother ever show that kind of affection; why was she always hateful towards me? I had never gotten anything from my grandmother but here it was Tee said that Ma would even hug and kiss her often.

During these moments, I was enjoying my grandmother all over again through Tee's relationship with her. I know that it sounds crazy, but when you have gone through what I had gone through, you kind of appreciate hearing that a person wasn't all bad and there was someone who had really seen beauty in my grandmother. Yeah, I know that Ma had her favorites, but even they can't share or express the love that Tee was expressing. Tee had seen NO wrong in my grandmother. NONE!

Soon after, without warning and without any fault of my own, I had received a notice from my Landlord to move by March 1, 2014. I was absolutely devastated. I didn't know what I was going to do about another apartment. The Landlord was in her rights to the apartment because I wasn't given a Lease. At the time during my need, I didn't think about not having one. I thought as long as I paid my rent and on time I would be fine. Still, that wasn't the case. She and her wife had rights and I had none. I did know that I had no money saved. I was living on Disability. And my credit was jacked up. I knew that nobody would rent to me under those circumstances so why would I waste time searching for an apartment? However, I knew that I was given an assignment from God. God had given me the vision and the location of where the stacks of my completed work had to go. I thought to myself that I was far from completing what He told me to do, but I better do what He said. I had been slacking in my writing because of other activities and thinking that I had time because I wasn't given a deadline until now.

During that time I was taking a class at the Brooklyn Tabernacle Church titled "To Be Transformed." I had been trying to get into this class for a few years but I was unable. It was strongly recommended that if anyone was attending school of any sort to wait until it was over so that they can be more focused on completing the work that was given. And now that I had completed grad school I had signed up and was already in week four having four more classes to go. The eight week course was every Thursday evening and it was just what I had expected it to be. I was being transformed in ways that mattered. I had a great Facilitator and awesome peers as we studied God's words.

There was homework every night of the week. There was reading and meditation that needed to be done. And there was my writing that I was instructed to complete. Not to mention, I had a little less than one month to move. I had inquired about a few places and put the word out regarding an apartment. T.J. had told me if I were to find something that he would put up the money for me. He had given me the $5,000 to hold on to just in case. I thought that was great, but Landlords wanted to see a steady income, which was double the amount of what I was receiving monthly. I had stopped focusing on an apartment and put all my time and energy in completing what God wanted and completing "To Be Transformed."

One day in class it seemed as if we all were facing some life challenges. And still we tried to be there for one another as best as we could. It was amazing that we all were still hanging in there. I had one more week to go before leaving my apartment. T.J. had expressed his desire to help me in whatever way but I wasn't sure about anything. So I encouraged him to go on to Atlanta and that I would be all right. I reminded him that I was trusting in God to do something. I know that he wanted to help me move my things, but I had nowhere to move them. Besides, I still needed to utilize what was inside the apartment for another week. I had given him the okay to leave and letting him know that I didn't have the answers at that moment but God promised to never leave me nor forsake me. And I trusted Him. Evie didn't seem to understand what I was doing because I didn't seem bothered. All she knew was that I was always writing, I was still attending the class and my time was up.

I had to put a rush on my work. It was the day I was supposed to leave but I decided to give myself another day. I still had not completed everything. I finished up what I could. It was a book and a play/screenplay. There were two stacks. I had figured that the way I had written the play, I would be able to eventually develop the screenplay. I had gotten it all printed out, and made the stacks. I had gathered my things together inside my apartment and I had taken some things to the church up the street. I had admired how almost every day they would sell things very cheap to the needy. Since they didn't take furniture I had taken it outside and placed it in front of my door near the curb placing a note on it saying "FREE God loves you!" Then I watched from my windows as tears fell from my eyes as people scurried down the block with it.

The only thing that was left inside my apartment was my brand new bed, a dresser and the clothes that I would take with me when I would go to my final class the following evening and wherever I landed for shelter. I opened a bottle of *Jeunesse* my favorite red wine poured me a glass, and sat on the floor facing my window looking at the darkness in the sky. I sat there talking to God, while tears fell from my eyes. I saw my Landlord and her wife pull up. I knew that it would be a matter of minutes before they would knock on my door to ask why I was still there. And I was prepared to tell them.

I hear the knock on my door. I got up from the floor holding my glass of wine and walked to the door. The Landlord said, "Joyce you were supposed to have left today but instead you're still here." I took a sip of my wine, looked at them both in their eyes and said "I sure was! And I will be gone tomorrow evening. And don't worry about the apartment being clean I have already cleaned it up very nice for you in the same way that you rented it to me." I then let them know that I had a gentleman coming tomorrow afternoon to pick up the bed and the dresser. I ended the conversation by saying, "I thank you both for allowing me to rent the apartment. You said yes when I needed it most. I was blessed to have been able to accomplish going to grad school, having my surgery, writing a book, and finding myself within the time that I lived here. I appreciate you both for that." I reminded them that I will be leaving at 6:30 p.m. the following day because I had a final class that I had to attend. I ended our conversation by saying, "And on that note, I thank you once again and good night." I tipped my glass up to them and closed my door. Then I resumed my position sitting on the floor talking to my Father.

We did it we did it! I have completed the eight week course "To Be Transformed." I had my knapsack and a rolling cart with my belongings. I didn't know where I was going. I had over $5,000 in my pocket and I had not a clue where I was going to lay my head. Tears rolled down my face and I wiped them before anyone would notice as I listened to everyone talking about going home. I kept speaking to God in my head asking Him to lead me as to where to go. I didn't want to make the wrong call. But the only name that kept popping in my head was Cozie. I said Lord I pray this is in your will. Cozie answered the phone and immediately told me to come to her job and get the keys. She told me that I can stay in the spare bedroom. I did just that and went to her house in Staten Island. When I walked inside the house, I felt a relief. I had been given my own room and it was peaceful.

I prayed that night and I asked God to speak to me so that I can know the direction to go as far as employment. I had asked God to only give me a yes to the job that He wants me to have. In the past I had been able to get any job that I applied for. This time I decided to only work when God said yes. A few days later I had gone to see Evie, her mom and the rest of her family letting them know where I was staying and that I was looking for work. Evie's mom had said to me that I may end up taking a job that will not pay me what I'm expecting but placed where God wants me to be. I had totally understood that considering the way that my life was shifting.

I was at total peace at Cozies' house. I was able to pray and read my word in peace. I was eating healthy being able to juice. Cozie respected me as we understood from our last episode. I had noticed a church directly on the side of the house and so I googled what type of church it was and whatever else I could find out about it. To my surprise, it was a Baptist church and I decided to pay them a visit on that Sunday morning. This is nobody but God. I thought to myself. The topic for the entire month was "To Be Transformed!" It is now the third Sunday and I get to enjoy God's words with a new set of Brothers and Sisters in the Lord. It was totally in line with what I had just learned through my eight-week course. The congregation was very nice towards me, and it felt good to be there. As a matter of fact, I couldn't wait to close out the last week of "To Be Transformed" with them.

As always I try to stay on top of my health. I was sitting at my Doctor's office waiting to be called and out of nowhere I decided to call a number that I had forgotten about. I had originally called the number wanting to know more about the position since there wasn't any information on it when I saw the listing. I left a message and didn't think any more about it. Ironically, I had put the number in my notes in my phone and that was how I was able to go right to it. Well, when I had called, I was told to hold on. The supervisor had picked up and she and I talked for a while. The conversation went so well, I was practically hired over the phone. I couldn't believe what I had just heard.

I traveled to New Jersey and was interviewed by the same woman that I had spoken to over the phone. The position as a House Mother was explained in detail. I would live in a house with another House Mother and up to three Moms. The Moms were young women who were either pregnant or had their babies. These young women came to the shelter because they were in threat of having an abortion and being homeless. The agency itself was Pro-Life. My position was to assist these Moms with whatever they needed assistance in. Thus transporting them to and from appointments was the bulk of the job. I was amazed at how much God loved me. He had provided me with free room and board, and a job that I had wanted for years, being able to work with young girls and help them develop into young responsible adults. Not to mention that it was a Catholic organization. And I would be able to assist them with the Word of God openly.

The job pays $23,000 a year, is what she said. Then she said it again. I was speechless. Even in my younger years, I made more than $23,000 a year. Then immediately the voice of Mom (Evies' mom) popped into my head when she told me that I may end up with a job that does not pay what I want, but instead where God wants me to be. Then I thought about the love that I already had for every Mom that I would meet. I was just excited to get started. I thought to myself, being God's hand extended doesn't have anything to do with a Master's Degree. I accepted the position and was excited to be used by God in every way that He wanted me.

My start date was April 14, 2014. I had let Cozie know that I was moving out and I had thanked her for allowing me to stay at her home. I was assigned a house out of the three and later on, after a road test, I was assigned a van. I had met the Moms coming and going. Some of the Moms had taken to me instantly while others didn't. I was learning a lot from the Founder as she had just come out with her very own book and was doing book signings based on the movie that had come out prior. I was enjoying every bit of what I was doing. Every so often I would think about the salary, but then I would say "Lord I trust you!" and forget about it.

Three months into working for the agency I noticed that the agency was more of a disadvantage because the Moms were not being helped in the way they needed. They needed parenting skills, some skill-building techniques. They needed to be prepared for the next step. They couldn't live there forever so where were they going? They didn't have a home to go to. What were they learning? I decided to speak with my Supervisor to see if we can implement goals and strategy planning. I asked her if we can start case conferences so that we can know how we can assist each of them individually. She loved the idea that I had pitched and I began putting it all together.

I had been going to Evies' house whenever I didn't want to stay in New Jersey on my days off. But one day I cried out to the Lord and said, "Lord, PLEASE help me get a place of my own." I kept praying this day because I had really wanted to be in my own space. The following week I had received a phone call asking me did I still want the apartment in New York City Housing best known as the projects. In a way I thought that I was dreaming because I didn't remember filling out the application for New York City Housing. However, I do remember a year ago when they notified me, telling me that I was on a waiting list. I had forgotten about it. Actually, I never thought that I would go backwards. But, it was an apartment and I was going to see it the following day.

Yes, I'll take it. I thank you Lord for answering my prayers and keeping your promise. John 14:14 "Yes, ask me for anything in my name, and I will do it." Also Psalm 84:11 "The Lord will withhold no good thing from those who do what is right."

Now I had a place that I could call home. Yes it was in the PJ's but I had my own keys and was happy about it. I figured that I had a fresh new start. Besides, it couldn't be the loft that I wanted making only $23,000 a year which was exactly $740.00 every two weeks. Yep, that was a salary for the PJ's.

There were some things that I didn't agree with but I tolerated it because I knew the God I served. I would talk to the Moms and House Moms about the things of God. They would often come to me for answers. I would hold Bible Study with the House Mom that I worked with. I was being used in ways that mattered. I would roll up my sleeves and clean as if I was cleaning my house. I would stay up sometimes until 3 in the morning helping a Mom get over her pain. I would assist in helping them with their babies. There was nothing that I wouldn't do because I wanted to be all that I could be for those girls.

Catholics have a way of utilizing statues in a way that Christians simply turn to Jesus. While at a meeting one day with all the staff, the Founder joined us and placed a statue on the table so that we all can see it. She shared with us the importance of having peace. During this time there was a lot of craziness going on with the Moms and House Moms. The program itself was dysfunctional due to it having no structure, no proper guidance, and no leadership. The Supervisor was causing chaos between the Moms and House Moms. Therefore, the Moms felt like they can do what they wanted to do. And I was so against the wrong thing that I came out at the end. My tolerance for behaviors that they all would overlook made it appear that I was part of the problem. In a nut shell, I guess I wasn't a good fit and here's part of why.

The Founder asked everyone at the meeting what did the statue mean to us. I was dumbfounded when I had heard what everyone had to say. They all clearly stated that the statue gave them peace and how they felt protected when they looked at it and they welcomed it. Then it was my turn and the Founder specifically said, "Joyce, what does it mean to you?" At that moment, I'd known that I was in trouble because I was going against the grain. Ask me a question, and I'll tell you the truth in whatever I know the truth to be. Ever since I had been working there, I had been avoiding making certain comments on things because it didn't affect me. I would even excuse myself before it was my turn to answer certain questions because I didn't want to offend anyone. I had answered by saying, "Unfortunately, it's not the statue that gives me peace. The peace that I receive is the peace that Jesus left me with. My peace comes from above and I thank Him for the peace that passes all understanding!"

Oh my, ever since that day, the Founder hated me. She wouldn't even look at me. She never even uttered another word to me. Well before you knew it, I was fired five months before my six month probationary period had ended. All I can remember is the Founder shouting out to me during my termination was; "You're not a team player, Joyce!" And she repeated that over and over letting me know the real reason why they were letting me go.

I was beyond crushed. I was hurt! I wanted to be there. I wanted to help those girls. But, I had to go and so I did. Even though I had gotten fired from the organization, I think that it is great that the organization exists. There are many young women that will become pregnant and having no place to go. And for that reason that organization will help many from unfortunate situations while saving the life of an unborn child. I myself had said and thought often times, that I wish I'd known about the organization during my early years. Therefore, it is great that it exist. However, my prayers are more for the Founder. "You shall not make for yourself a carved image, or any likeness of anything that is in heaven above, or that is in the earth beneath, or that is in the water under the earth. You shall not bow to them or serve them, for I the Lord your God am a jealous God, visiting the iniquity of the fathers on the children to the third and the fourth generation of those who love me and keep my commandments." Exodus 20:4-6.

I thank God I had an apartment to go to. I have a Lease, keys and guess what? I'm still praising God. He had obviously knew what my response was going to be, because He knows me!

# A DIFFERENT PLACE

I'm not certain as to how the rest of my life will go as none of us do. But I do know that I am Blessed and Highly Favored. I know that although I never knew my biological father, I do have a Heavenly Father that loves me unconditionally. From the beginning without me even knowing anything about God, He was there protecting me. And for that reason, I know that God has a purpose for my life. I talk to my Father about everything because I know that He listens. I cry to Him often because He wipes my tears away. I pray to Him all the time because He answers prayers. And I praise Him throughout the day because I have reasons to praise Him. I am totally aware that God is the only judge over me therefore I have no worry of others. I'm not saying that I will not make any more mistakes because I'll be lying. The Word of God says that there is only one that is perfect and that was Jesus Himself. However, I will say when I fall again in any way, I will look to the Heavens from where my help comes. And I will continue to trust God for my total deliverance during my Sanctification process.

If you want to know if I am delivered from wanting to be with woman, the answer is NO! However, I am not ignorant of God's words. His words are in black and white and I am not color blind and I do know how to read for myself. I also understand that God allows us to make our own choices because He is such a gentleman that He will not force Himself on us. Therefore, my choice to please God is totally voluntary because I'm learning how to truly love Him in return.

However, I am no longer struggling regarding my thoughts of another woman. As I move forward in this life as I trust in my Lord, I will no longer struggle with anything. Instead, I will receive my learning experiences smile at my storms put on my big girl panties and trust God throughout the remainder of this earthly body. I understand that I am no longer a slave to sin because I understand the purpose of the cross. I am freed from the thoughts that were inside of my head that kept me in bondage. And being in bondage I was allowing myself to self-destruct. I was destroying myself by not letting go of all of my past hurts and pains that I had not dealt with. I was destroying my body thinking that I was already destroyed by what my cousin and others had done to me.

I am also free from people pressure when preaching, and being under the assumption that I had the ability to deliver myself. Today, instead of beating myself up mentally, thinking that I "should" be delivered from wanting to be with woman, I place it all in God's hands. However, because of the love and the fear that I have for God, as well as the understanding of His love for me, I have a desire to want to please God. Love is an action word. It takes sacrifice. Jesus died for us on the cross and He is alive. For this reason and for many other reasons I too am willing to die to this sin and eventually I'll be completely delivered because I am willing for God to deliver me.

Also, I realized while I was writing this book, that forgiveness comes through understanding and then love. I forgave my grandmother. I thank God for allowing me to hear her voice that afternoon at work which made me go to her house. Then, allowing me to spend quality time with her, for both of us to get to know one another. Not forgetting that Momma Beck asked me to. I can finally forgive my cousin because I truly believe that perversion entered him first before he was able to pervert me. I can forgive my mother because I know that she was the best Mom that she knew how to be. She dealt with the situation regarding what I told her the way that clearly her mother must have not said anything when it happened to her. In my grandmother's era, people kept quiet when their daughters were raped and molested. The quiet voices started when white men used to rape colored girls and nothing was ever done. In my understanding, they had to simply "*Handle It*!"

# FREE

PRAISE THE LORD

PRAISE THE LORD

AS I LIFT MY VOICE

I SAY PRAISE THE LORD

AS I STAND HERE

WITHOUT FEAR

WELL ASSURED THAT JESUS IS NEAR

AS I PREPARE

YESTERDAY IS GONE

---------AND-----------

TOMORROW IS NEAR

A SHOUT OUT TO JESUS

FOR WIPING MY TEARS

I WAS A -------SLAVE

A-----------SLAVE

A SLAVE IN BONDAGE

I CAME TO THE LORD

BROKENHEARTED

DISGUSTED--------BUSTED

YES! YOU GUESSED IT

I COULD NOT BE TRUSTED

I WAS SEPARATED FROM THE LIGHT

MY LIFE JUST WASN'T RIGHT

IN MY EYES

I WAS ONE OF THE GOOD GUYS

UNTIL I REALIZED

THAT I WAS HEADED FOR ONE BIG SURPRISE

SMOKING, DRINKING, ORGIES, PARTYING

LOVING THE LADIES

ALL--------NIGHT----------LONG

MONEY FLOWIN

I WAS GOIN

I WAS LIVIN

I-------WAS-------SIN----KING

YOU SEE

ALTHOUGH I SMOKED

I WAS NEVER ADDICTED

NOR AFFLICTED

ALTHOUGH I DRANK

I WAS NEVER AN ALCOHOLIC

ALTHOUGH I WAS OUT THERE

I AM HEALTHY

I GIVE THANKS TO THE LORD

BECAUSE IT IS HE

# HANDLE IT

WHO SAVED ME

I SHARE THIS POETIC TRUTH OF PRAYER

IN THE HOPES THAT SOMEONE WOULD CARE

A SLAVE COMES IN ALL COLORS

ALL SHAPES AND SIZES

THANK YOU LORD

FOR USING PASTORS, AND TEACHERS

MOST OF ALL

I THANK GOD FOR JESUS

SOME ARE SLAVES TO THE PEOPLE WE LOVE

TO THE DRUGS WE CHOOSE

TO THE ALCOHOL

WE CALL BOOZE

TO OUR JOBS WHICH WE DESPISE

TO OUR FAMILES WHOM WE LIE

TO THE CREDIT CARDS

THAT KEEP US

FLY-----EYE

OR THE LENDERS ON WHOM WE RELY

FOR THE THINGS WE DON'T NEED

BUT-------- WE BUY

TO OUR HOMES

TO OUR CARS

TO THE CIGARETTES AND CIGARS

TO EDUCATION

TO FORNICATION

TO OUR VERY OWN STIMULATIONS

TO NAME-BRAND SHOES

TO FINE JEWELS

TO THE SINFUL FLESH

LIKE THE WOMEN

I ONCE CARESSED

WE BECOME SLAVES IN OUR MINDS

WRAPPED UP IN TIME

A TIME THAT'S NEITHER YOURS NOR MINE

THE LORD SAYS

FOLLOW HIS COMMANDMENTS

LOVE THY NEIGHBOR

AS THY SELF

DO NOT COMMIT ADULTERY

FORNICATION, MURDER, LIE

CHEAT OR STEAL

MAN WITH WOMEN

WOMEN WITH MAN

I FINALLY REALIZED

I MUST TAKE A STAND

SO STEP BACK

STAY ON TRACK

LET'S TAKE BACK WHAT THE DEVIL HAS STOLEN

RECOGNIZE THAT WE WERE CHOSEN

SO LIFT UP YOUR HEADS

HOLD THEM UP HIGH

# HANDLE IT

SALVATION IS HERE FOR YOU AND I

WE ARE FREE

WE ARE FREE

WE ARE FREE

NEVERTHELESS

ALLOW GOD TO DO THE REST

Now I understand the scripture when it says do not forsake the assembly. I needed to go to church to be among other Christians so I can hear and understand what God is saying through His words. I needed a Pastor, I needed the church which are the members because He says iron sharpens iron. Of course I was dealing with certain people in my life who would say things like, "you could be Gay and go to church." When I would hear statements like that, I would smile and shake my head lightly because no one ever said that "Gay" people shouldn't go to church. Jesus died on the cross for the Homosexual, the Lesbian, the Prostitute, the rapist, the thief the list goes on and on. However, He did not die for us to continue in the behavior.

Christianity may be metaphorically compared to a race. A race to reach the finish line (Heaven) is our ultimate goal, but how we run the race is important. We pause to help others along the way (benevolence, and bringing others to Christ), and sometimes stumble on obstacles in the way. Christianity isn't an easy path. It may be easy to 'run the first lap', but the race becomes more difficult as we mature in our faith. Never forget to ask Jesus' help, because we are not alone in the 'race'. Faith is what kept me going; the Holy Spirit is what kept me at Peace; the Word of God is what directs me. God's love is what is keeping me today. And because of Gods' love I am FREE!

And then He (Jesus) told them "Go into all the world and preach the Good news to everyone. Anyone who believes and is baptized will be saved. But anyone who refuses to believe will be condemned."

Mathew 16v15

# ABOUT THE AUTHOR

Joyce "Joy" Harriet is a mother, a sister, a friend, a Poet, Playwright, a Producer, Director, and now she's a first time Author. And most importantly Joy is a Child of The Living God. Her passions are; writing, producing stage plays, encouraging the youth, and productive conversations. She enjoys inspiring the youth to realize their most inner strengths, and often volunteering to assist the elderly. Joy has been a Playwright since 2002, and in 2013 she received her MPA in Public Administration & Affairs.

In 1992, Joy made a decision to live an "Alternative Lifestyle" which ultimately led her to God. Because of Jesus' sacrifice and His love, she chose to live in the Will of God. Joy enjoys conversations about God and being Gods' hands to serve in any capacity without limitations. Today she loves the Lord with her whole heart and continues to grow in His grace.

Joy admits as much as she enjoy the "Alternative Lifestyle" she trust God will totally deliver her from it. Joy realizes that deliverance is a process and she is standing on the Word of God. Approaching life with a No-Nonsense, "leave the drama for the stage" type attitude, she remains a loving and compassionate woman who never minds giving of herself. Joy is a humble woman whose loyalty is to God first, to family, and friends…And with all sincerity, Joy loves you!!!!

joyhandleit@gmail.com